Value-Based Business Creation

**Strategic Business and Capital Planning
for
Entrepreneurs in the New Economy**

Nils Randrup, Torben Moller, Dan Hoeyer

Edited by Laura J. Spurrier

Published by Management Publishing Company

Value-Based Business Creation: Strategic Business and Capital Planning for Entrepreneurs in the New
Economy

© 2002 by Nils Randrup, Torben Moller, Dan Hoeyer. All rights reserved.
This book has been submitted for registration in the U.S. Copyright Office.
Published by: Management Publishing Company (info@management-publishing.com)
Distributed by: Samfundslitteratur (http://www.samfundslitteratur.dk)

Cover Design and Drawings by: Christian Winther
Illustrations and Layout by: Steen Nielsen

Printed in Denmark by: Clichéfa Tryk, 2002
1st edition, 1st printing

Suggested Library of Congress cataloging in publication:
Randrup, Nils, 1964-
    Value-based business creation : strategic business and capital planning for entrepreneurs in the new econ-
omy / Nils Randrup, Torben Moller, Dan Hoeyer ; edited by Laura J. Spurrier.
        p. : illus. ;   cm.

    Includes bibliographical references.
    ISBN 87-91251-00-1

    1. New business enterprises. 2. Electronic commerce. 3. New business enterprises – Finance. I.
Moller, Torben, 1949- . II. Hoeyer, Dan, 1971- III. Title.
HD62.5
LCCN
60.1
CIP

Management Publishing Company ApS
Vesterbrogade 40
DK-1620 Copenhagen V
info@management-publishing.com

Table of Contents

List of Figures

Preface

This book is aimed at entrepreneurs — business people, garage innovators, people with a mission, *etc.* – indeed, all who are striving to become successful entrepreneurs leveraging the opportunities of the "new" economy. If you either want to start a new company or, if you have already started one, want inspiration to further strengthen the strategic platform on which your company is built, then this book is for you. It is also intended for use in advanced business courses in M.B.A. and similar-level management programs.

Our goal for this book is ambitious: we want to redefine how a company in the new economy should be started in order to become a commercial success. The result of this redefinition should be a concept of strategic entrepreneurship that is more up-to-date and more relevant to the situation of today's entrepreneurs.

Specifically, we argue that the most critical issue for entrepreneurs starting a company today is not how to get rich fast, but how to find and nurture a good idea through the first years to create value. Equally important is how to spot the mediocre but tempting idea before too much is at stake and too much money and energy have been used.

The last few years have been full of small "e-s," "e-" this and "e-" that — business models that were surefire successes one day and discredited the next; start-up companies, the market value of which overshadowed successful multi-generational companies; "new" economy companies; "old" economy companies; and, lately, "new new" economy companies — all in all, a sure sign of opportunity. We have just gone through a technological revolution so the perspective is, not surprisingly, a little confused.

The driving force behind this book is a wish to give something back to current and future entrepreneurs in the form of key strategic insights and advice on how best to exploit the opportunities brought about by recent technological changes. We describe the insights we have acquired over the last five years of working with both traditional and dot.com companies and their e-Business initiatives, as well as insights generalized from new theories and models that we have seen pay off in practice. We also give advice on how to avoid the pitfalls which a number of both large and small new-economy companies have stumbled into over the last year or two. Our focus is on strategic, timely advice.

Acknowledgments

Nils Randrup:

I dedicate this book to my son Marcus Randrup — for reminding me that
family should be the no. 1 priority in life — and to my most feared critic, my
wife Annika Randrup – for her support and encouragement.

My special thanks goes to Paula Doyle for sharing comments and thoughtful
insights, and for her long close friendship from our schooldays at Kellogg in
Evanston.

A big thanks goes to my "inspirators" and special friends in the industry from
and with whom I have gained invaluable insights, inspiration and experience:
David King, CEO of J. Walter Thompson EMEA (Digital@JWT), e-Business
Director Kjetil Undhjem of Kraft Jacob Suchard Europe, Marketing Director
Alex Carrel of Nestlé, Christian Pedersen of MediaMix Advertainment, Max
Sejbæk, Managing Director of ProActive, and Arne Åhlander, Strategic
Business Development Director of AU-System.

Torben Moller:

I would like to acknowledge all my customers, past and present; I have learnt
a lot from them. I would also like to thank the anthropologists in my life who
have helped me with the qualitative part of things. Finally, I would like to
thank my wife, Laura Spurrier, M.A., M.L.S., who not only edited the book
but could always be counted on for a considered opinion, often of the "now
why didn't I think of that?" variety.

Dan Hoeyer:

In memory of Erling Høyer – Thank you for **always** believing in me!
I would like to thank all the people inspiring and assisting in making this
book possible. The names are listed alphabetically by first name: Allan
Nylander, Anders Uttrup, Anita Søgaard, Ewa Monika Høyer, Kristian Groth,
Lee E. Hargrave, Jr., Mark Augustenborg Ødum, Pia Chartell Abildsø, Torben
Aagaard, and Zindy Laursen.

Also a special thanks to the Aston Group for all the help with this book, the
University of California, Berkeley - Haas School of Business for our fruitful
cooperation, and all my business partners throughout the years. And last but
not least to my family and friends!

Introduction

We're probably 10 years further along than we otherwise would have been ....
Within a very compressed period, we got a tremendous amount of experimen-
tation. Not all has been lost.
— Jim Koch, Director of the Center for Science, Technology and Society at
    Santa Clara University[1]

The "e"-Revolution is over! It started sometime in 1999, peaked in March
2000, and is really over now. Everybody went home except the insolvency
administrators, the forensic accountants, and the janitors. Everybody? Well,
not completely. The business executives and entrepreneurs who thrive on
change are busy looking at what changed and how to benefit from it.

This book is intended to help you be successful through sharing our experiences and academic advice on how to go from business idea to success. We
shall look at starting a company in the so-called "new economy," how to coin
a business idea, how to make your first strategic business plan, how to secure
needed capital, how to hire your first people, and how to outline an operational business plan.

But before we do that, let us define a term or two:

To "e" or Not to "e"

Had Strunk and White[2] been alive through the e-Revolution, we would have
gotten a rather stern lecture on capitalization and on gratuitous creation of
new words. Everything had a small "e" prefix, *e.g.*, e-Commerce, e-Business,
e-CRM, *etc.*, and many participants acted as if they were in a transition so
unique that if you did not "get it" immediately, you were hopelessly out-of-
date. Time for a reality check.

The second definition of the word "revolution" in Merriam Webster is:

2 a : a sudden, radical, or complete change b : a fundamental change in poli-
tical organization; especially : the overthrow or renunciation of one govern-
ment or ruler and the substitution of another by the governed c : activity or
movement designed to effect fundamental changes in the socioeconomic situa-
tion d : a fundamental change in the way of thinking about or visualizing
something : a change of paradigm <the Copernican revolution> e : a
changeover in use or preference especially in technology <the computer revo-
lution> <the foreign car revolution>

Using the definition "a fundamental change in the way of thinking about or visualizing something," there is no question that the period from approximately 1999 to 2001 qualifies as a revolutionary period. Our perspective on connectivity, access, and reach changed fundamentally.

However, revolutions – whether technological or societal – are nothing new. Think of the steam engine, the telegraph, the Personal Computer, *etc.*, as examples of technological revolutions, and of the growth of the middle class in the Western world and of the French Revolution as examples of societal revolutions. We do not know when the next one will happen, but we know it will.

Whether a revolution succeeds or not, it changes the normal environment. And, while it is almost a truism that a business idea developed by an entrepreneur must take advantage of the current environment – both business and technology – and must take advantage of, and plan for, the future environment, it is particularly importance at a time such as this — when the changes forced by the latest revolution have not yet settled in and become commonplace – that we look carefully at what changed and how it effects what used to be the norm.

So, were we to re-define the term "e-Business" in a few years, it might be as: *a term coined at the end of the second millenium meaning "conducting business using Internet technology." The term had a heavy technological slant based on the then rapid evolution of the Web, and is now obsolete due to the universality of the Web.*

This book will use a few "e"s where they make sense, but the thrust of the book is on **how to create value in a business in the new economy**: an economy fashioned by incorporating what was "e" into universal requirements for business and an economy ready for the next change, whether societal or technological. We intend no technological slant. Technology facilitates new or changed business models, but technology in and of itself rarely creates a viable business model.

We recommend that while you read this book you spend some time thinking about what the next revolution might be, when it might happen, and how it might influence your business idea. Some pundits claim that it will be in the mobile communication area: 3G – third generation mobile phones, *etc.*; others claim it will be in the societal area, based on the recent recession and the anti-globalism movement.

What Changed?

As mentioned above, the changes brought about by the e-Revolution can be stated in shorthand as changes in connectivity, access, and reach. Put differently — and we shall expand on this in Chapter 1 — the material changes are:

- The introduction of true global markets and competition
- The emergence of hybrid business models
- Lower cost of entry
- Shrinking of the time-to-market window

These changes have a fundamental impact on determining viable business models: what you can sell, how you sell, how your customers view you, how you treat your customers, and how long you have to adapt your business model to changes in the business climate.

So What is the "New" Economy?

The change in viable business models brought about by the e-Revolution effects change in the economy, if in no other way, through changes in the valuation of companies. The "new" economy is a work in progress, as are changes in business models, but certain characteristics are becoming clearer:

- The economy is becoming global
- The new and the old work best together
- Most everything can be a product
- Transaction costs can be lower in new business models
- The rate of change is faster
- The response time is shorter
- The market still values "new" economy companies based on off-balance-sheet items

Business Strategy

The term "strategy" is a bit like "new" economy – a common buzzword very hard to define in a uniform way — because the term is used for a myriad of different business approaches and actions. We like to think of strategy as **what you plan to do in order to achieve an objective**. The objective can be very important to a company's survival, *e.g.*, the goal of becoming the most profitable company within the industry. In such a case "strategy" means the business's overall plan for deploying resources to create a competitive advantage. Or the objective can be to finish a report in three hours, in which case "strategy" is the plan for how to use time effectively. The concept of strategy is, in essence, thinking before doing, with a specific objective in mind.

The most fundamental strategy is the basic company positioning strategy, by some called the competitive or overall business strategy. There are strategies that deal with how to optimize the use of resources and money to be efficient, and there are operational strategies of how best to do different tasks in practice. These are all strategies, ways of achieving specific objectives that are thought out and planned ahead of time. When discussing strategy, make sure that everyone knows what kind you are discussing.

It can be helpful to view strategy as a planning hierarchy: in a company, the overall corporate business strategy includes and impacts the individual business units. On the basis of the overall corporate strategy, an individual business unit develops its unit strategy involving the different departments, and so on.

We shall deal with strategy at length below when we talk about the Strategic Business Plan.

Starting a Company

There are many ways to go about starting a "new economy" company. We have outlined creating a company as a process with certain key milestones. But it could just as well be looked upon as a series of projects, a to-do list, or a checklist of activities that need to be done. This book is a business handbook because it's a compilation of building blocks that can be read separately or sequentially. The order is based on our experience of the smartest way to proceed so that resources and time are used as effectively as possible. When companies have been set up in a different order, the results have often been major problems and large inefficiencies later in the process.
The stages of starting a company can be graphically presented as shown in Figure 1.

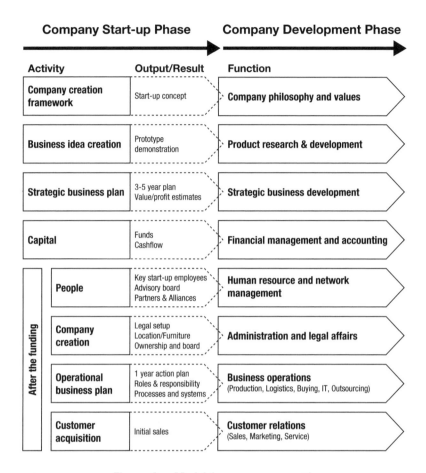

Figure 1   **Model for company creation**

The first milestone has two parts: to achieve a good understanding of the context, background and platform for starting a company and to identify explicitly the reasons and potentials behind the decision to start — Chapter 1 (Company Creation Framework). The next challenge is to actually coin the business or company idea — Chapter 2 (Business Idea Creation). The third milestone is to validate the idea by creating a Strategic Business Plan in which all the issues of bringing the business idea to life — the costs and benefits, the business potential and risk — are thought through, evaluated and quantified — Chapter 3 (Strategic Business Plan).

The next big milestone is to plan and secure financing for the company. If external financing such as venture capital is needed, it's necessary to market the business plan in a persuasive manner in order to secure the capital —

Chapter 4 (Capital). Once the capital is found, a formal foundation for the company is needed, *i.e.*, incorporation with a board of directors, advisory board, *etc.*, and recruitment of the right people and competencies must begin. Along with all the practical aspects, the final milestone is development of an Operational Plan in order to get rolling — Chapter 5 (After the Funding).

Chapter 1

A Framework for Creating a Value-Based Company

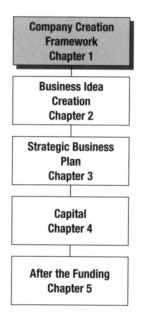

As this chapter is being written, Western Europe and the U.S.A. are both in a recession. Why, you may ask, does one talk about creating a company in the middle of a recession? First of all, companies are founded all the time and, secondly, because the underlying advice to, and characteristics of, a company which creates true value, a visionary company, is the same whether you are in a recession, in a growth spurt, or in a business revolution or catastrophe.[3]

And, yes, "e" was a revolution; nothing prepared the business world to evolve into the chaotic behavior of 1999 and 2000. This particular revolution is now over[4] – the idea of "permanent revolution" having been somewhat discredited – but as with any revolution it changed what is normal. For example:

- A number of Web sites started with great fanfare to support on-line shopping in some industries have now morphed into information/marketing sites for "brick and mortar" companies,[5] proving – even for the laggards – that the Web is an important part of a company's strategy, and

- Every General Electric company has targets of using e-Auctions for 60 to 70% of total expenditures,[6] proving – by way of the early adopters – that there is a lot more to the Web than Infomercials.

The rest of this chapter will be spent looking at what creation of a company means after the e-Revolution. We shall look at how the "normal" business environment has changed, how new business models have emerged, and how to adapt to this new reality. Lastly, we shall look at the concept of company value.

Let us begin by getting some advice from 40+ senior executives in large European corporations.

1.1
Entrepreneurial Advice

We gathered and analyzed advice to new entrepreneurs from more than forty experienced super entrepreneurs in regards to what a new entrepreneur should focus on during a recession. All interviewed entrepreneurs lead or have led large corporations in Europe, such as Volvo, STC, Tetrapak, Ecolean, Brindfors Advertising, Turnit, Sonet.[7] Many of them have been through more than one economic crisis period. The methodology was simple: we asked each to select the three most important pieces of advice they could give to new entrepreneurs facing their first recessions/crisis situations. Here are the top ten:

1. Understand your product fully and work closely with product development.
2. Understand your customers better than anyone else. They feed you and your company. Form personal relationships, follow their developments and interests, test ideas with them, and in some cases hire them. Don't let your key focus be on the financial market or investors.
3. Think long term, even though it is tricky. Thinking short term is lethal and will kill your business.

4. Be realistic, not just "visionary," especially about turnover/profit expectations. Remember to tighten all costs, including salaries, to match reality.
5. You cannot be friends with everyone. When you need to cut costs by reducing manpower or salaries, you will face a lot of angry people with a lot of criticism directly aimed at you as a person and in public. Do what you must.
6. Make money. Don't over invest and don't grow at any price.
7. Take responsibility; don't blame clients, employees or suppliers because they did not do what they were supposed to do. And don't leave major decisions to someone else.
8. Don't make the same mistake twice. Analyze failures completely, not just product problems but also loss of customers, loss of employees and loss of competitive advantages.
9. Supplement the top management with people who can deal with structural problems and who can implement a reconstruction. Sometimes a reconstruction means that all the bricks must be torn down first before a new and better house can be built and some of the materials must be new.
10. Learn company law, so you do not risk being personally responsible for a bankruptcy. Make sure your company can take a dive without losing everything.

You will see as we go through the chapter that this advice is universal; it is good whether in a recession or not.

1.2
Creating a Value-Based Company

Companies are started to create some kind of value. Even though this does not absolutely need to be monetary or the equivalent, we shall ignore other forms of value – it can be ego — in this discussion and use the first definition from Merriam Webster for "value": *a fair return or equivalent in goods, services, or money for something exchanged.*

Value in a normal purchase transaction is straightforward: if you buy steak knives on a late night television show, you expect to get a product which will perform according to what was advertised, *viz.,* help you cut steaks. Not receiving value in a purchase transaction is also straightforward: it is very likely that we have all bought something advertised to do a task that it did not do at all.

Value in the case of a corporation is slightly different. Not only is there more than one group which can be recipients of value from the corporation — customers, employees, and shareholders come to mind, as does society (at least as a taxing authority) — but there is also the time horizon.

Take a look at the graph below:

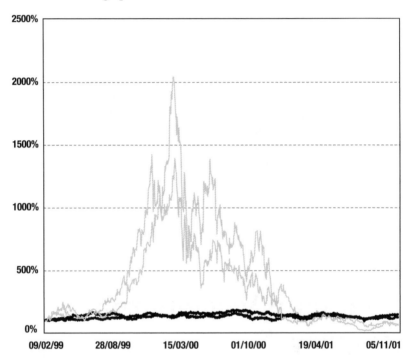

The graph shows stock price over time as a percentage of the stock price on February 9th, 1999. Four companies are listed, two very "e" and two not. Which of these companies has created value? If you had bought stock in one of the high flyers before August of 1999, say, and sold before March 15, 2000, you could have multiplied your investment roughly fifteen or twenty times. If you had bought stock in the same companies on March 14th, 2000 and held on to it, you would have decreased your investment to one fifteenth or one twentieth of the original value. If you had invested in one of the two companies represented by the lower curves at the beginning of the graph and held on to the end, you would have, respectively, 122% or 156% of your money, not counting dividends which both these companies pay. By the way, the two lower companies are General Electric and IBM!

The point is that the time horizon is very important when one talks about company value. Both of the "e" companies in the graph above are respected companies in their field and, although their executives probably believed their valuation just prior to March 15th, 2000 as little as they believed their valuation on December 28th, 2001 (the last day of the graph), much money was made on stock in these two companies in the market during the interim. And certainly, GE and IBM have created much wealth. We shall meet both in the section on visionary companies below.

It is your choice as the company founder to decide – to the degree the market and your investors will allow — what you set out to do: a fast start in a hot niche for a quick sale or an IPO (Initial Public Offering), or creation of a visionary company for lasting value. There is no "wrong" way in that sense, and either can create substantial value.

There are clearly "wrong" ways to start and run a company, ways that are unethical, immoral or illegal. This is not a textbook in forensic accounting so we shall not spend a lot of time on this, but the "e" world has seen its share: from setting unreasonable expectations of amount of time spent at work without compensation, through selling of stock by insiders with questionable timing, lending employees money to buy stock to create a bull market, to tying employee retirement funds excessively into company stock.

A good example of practices that create serious questions about executive behavior is the World Online debacle in Holland. The stock went public at €43 a share in March of 2000, shortly after which it became public knowledge that the chairperson of the company had sold her stake three months earlier for €6 a share![8]

Another example of questionable behavior, this time not only on the part of executives but also including the auditors, and the board, is the current Enron scandal in the U.S. It is way too early to make any final comments, but you are well advised to follow what happens.

1.3
Creating a Visionary Company

For value-generating companies there is a basic decision to make: do you want to run a visionary company, or are you satisfied to "just" run a competitive operation?

Collins and Porras[9] define a "visionary" company by six criteria:
- *premier institution in its industry*
- *widely admired by knowledgeable business people*
- *has made an indelible imprint on the world in which we live*
- *has had multiple generations of chief executives*
- *has been through multiple product – or service – life cycles*
- *over 50 years old,*

using a peer process to select for the qualitative characteristics. Their companies include GE and IBM.

Many entrepreneurs we have met are idealists and want to start a visionary company like Nokia, IBM, Motorola, Sony, or Wal-Mart, which have shown themselves as some of the most visionary companies in the world, especially over the last ten years. It's interesting to compare these visionary companies, which are partly active in the "new" economy, to high-profile dot.com companies like Amazon, AOL, Stepstone, or Yahoo, which are more purely "new economy" companies and recent start-ups.

Some of these dot.com companies seem to have the potential to become "visionary" if they can prove over time that they can thrive on development and change, still to be seen, and if they can deliver outstanding ROI (return on investment) in the long run. Of course, we shall have to wait thirty to forty years to find out.

Most dot.com companies, however, more often resemble second or third rank players which have lost the battle of superiority, like the BUNCH – Burroughs, Univac, NCR, CDC, and Honeywell — (collectively to IBM), Zenith (to Motorola), Kenwood (to Sony) and Kmart (to Wal-Mart). They are good companies but not the best. They are not entirely un-visionary, perform better in terms of cumulative stock ROI than the general stock index, and have had some successes. The visionary companies, in contrast, are more than just successful, the best of the best, role models and icons for the practice of management around the world.

Interestingly, Collins and Porras debunk a number of myths related to the success of companies. We have listed them below, not as the myths, but as the realities:

1. It does not take a great idea to start a great company. A visionary company often stands out by being built around a corporate idea and people, not a single specific product idea. Regardless of the founding concept, visionary companies are significantly less likely to have had extraordinary early entrepreneurial success than others. Start-ups should focus on creating a company concept rather than just a product. Waiting for "the great idea" might be a bad idea.

2. A charismatic, high-profile visionary leader is absolutely not required. Leaders in visionary companies concentrate more on architecting enduring institutions than on being perceived as great individual leaders. Think of HP, their founders, and the "HP way".[10] Start-ups, therefore, do not need to recruit brilliant, extrovert, very charismatic CEOs or chairmen of the board who can take a company to the stars.

3. Visionary companies pursue a cluster of objectives, of which making money is only one and not necessarily the primary one. Start-ups should not be based on the founders' getting rich fast, but on other visions that can motivate and sustain the companies and their future employees long into the future.

4. There is no single set of successful core values for a visionary company. Core values are all different. Therefore, start-ups do not need to copy other companies' values. They can be helpful as inspiration, but ultimately core values should be defined uniquely.

5. Core values and ideologies are tightly fixed and do not change over time. Start-ups, therefore, need to focus on enduring values and ideologies, not time-restrained or fashion-based ones.

6. Stretch goals are used as powerful drivers for progress that enable change and adaptation without compromising core values. They give employees excitement and challenge and create forward momentum. Start-ups should set visionary and measurable goals for the performance of the company, in order to set clear and unambiguous directions which can easily be understood and eventually shared by all employees.

7. Visionary companies, with their strong corporate cultures, are not great places to work for everyone. Either people fit in or not; there is rarely a middle ground. Start-ups often have weak, undefined cultures during their initial phase. They should not strive to make a culture that suits everyone. They should outline the culture of how they would like to be and

have that in mind when recruiting. If a desired trait is that everyone uses even his/her spare time to work, then a single mother, or a father with two small children and a wife who works full time will not fit in — not because of lack of motivation, but rather because of a shortage of spare time to be used at work. If the culture is based on a blue suit, white shirt, tie, and wingtips, a jeans-wearing genius will not fit in.

8. The best, most successful moves are made by experimentation, trial and error, opportunism or pure accident, not by brilliant and complex strategic planning. With apologies to Robert Storm Petersen, it is hard to write a strategic plan, especially one that concerns the future.

9. Most successful second generation CEOs are homegrown and internally found, not headhunted from outside the company. Look at GE and its executive succession.

10. Focus on internal improvement is much more likely than focus on beating the competition. All the various quality initiatives, six sigma and so forth, are directed at improving the process, not at out-marketing the competition.

11. Visionary companies think complimentarily and pursue seemingly opposite opportunities at the same time. They are not choosing A or B, but rather A and B.

12. A Vision Statement does not a visionary company make. To put it differently, **you** must have the vision and carry it; the vision statement crafted by your consultant is only a part of the solution.

1.4
Market Conditions in the New Economy

The e-Revolution made fundamental changes to "normal" business. Market circumstances are significantly more intense than those of the traditional market. The reason for this is, of course, among other things, the increased competitive conditions driven by the possibilities of the Internet.

We have identified some new, or changed, rules for the market circumstances of the economy with some inspiration from other visionary business strategists.[11] The last one is key to leveraging temporary competitive advantages open to new companies, and we shall spend a little more time on it.

- The market and the competition are global
- The market is becoming many "markets of one"
- Market segments are becoming transparent
- The "bricks and clicks" models are proliferating
- The market supports cooperation
- Most everything can be a product
- The cost of entry is lower on the Web
- Company valuation models are changing
- Timing is key, or "Internet time is real"

The Market and the competition are global
The Internet is global by definition. You are globally accessible from the moment your Web site is up. You are only a mouse-click away from any customer in the world who has a browser. However, so is your competitor. As long as you can handle the distribution and any legal formalities, you can sell to the world. Remember, however, that studies show that most of the Web will be in a language other than English within a few years, so you should start considering internationalizing your Web presence.

The Market is becoming many "markets of one"
The Internet allows companies to collect more information regarding transactions and prospective transactions than conventional commerce does, and current technology allows cost-effective use of this data. The net result of this is the capability for Internet commerce to customize browsing, shopping,

and overall customer service to specific customers or customer segments, leading to greater loyalty on the part of the customers.

Market segments are becoming transparent

The Internet automatically makes the market more transparent – at least in the B2C (Business to Consumer) space — as the total market is only a mouse click away. "Smart Shopping Agents" or "Bots" make the market even more transparent, as they scan the market for you, searching for the best price. Examples are www.mysimon.com and www.cnet.com. Ironically, however, one can argue that the Web has the potential for making pricing in the B2B less transparent, since trading on captive exchanges among invited suppliers can make the price setting quite opaque.

"Bricks and clicks" models are proliferating

As one should expect, the development of Web commerce is showing that the model is not "Bricks and Mortar" **or** Clicks, it is "Bricks and Mortar" **and** Clicks. Commerce models are evolving so that merchandise bought via the Web can be returned to the nearest store – for example, www.sears.com — and merchandise ordered via the Web can be picked up at the nearest store – for example, www.amazon.com and Circuit City. The evolution of these hybrid models will continue and will be the area of most interest and greatest long-term opportunity.

The Market supports cooperation

Your customer/prospect is only one mouse-click away from you, and he/she is also only one mouse-click away from another customer or prospect of yours. This has a number of implications, one being the possibility of their joining forces for shared buys – for example, www.letsbuyit.com — another being that opinions, correct or incorrect, about your service or products can be easily disseminated. See the many sites berating companies, www.arrivasucks.com, for instance.

Most everything can be a product

The fact that the market is global and electronic means that many things that are difficult to market off the Web, either because of form or size of local market, can be profitably sold on it. For example, there is a thriving market for PEZ dispensers on eBay. Information – content – can also be sold on the net, although there are still issues about pricing – and getting paid for – information.

The Cost of entry is lower on the Web

For the moment, the cost of entry onto the Web with a new business model/solution is lower than implementing a similar solution off the Web. This is what in many ways makes the Internet so interesting and creates so many possibilities for entrepreneurs: experimentation is possible without having to ship marketing kits to stores, train store personnel, and re-route delivery trucks.

Fully established companies will be put out of business if a new company develops and markets an innovative business concept/model, product/service and technology – *this is the rule of the "new" economy.* A "solution" does not, of course, have to be technology-related; it can be a product/service as well as an entirely new business concept/model, or perhaps just a new way of doing things.

Does this mean the best solution wins? Probably not more often than it happens off the Web; success depends on many factors. Many users would argue that Napster was the "best" solution for music distribution. The courts obviously disagreed.

Company valuation models are changing

Valuation of a company, as when it is put up for sale, is difficult, and it has been argued that the e-Revolution created valuation models and valuations that had no connection with reality.[12]

Although valuation methods used for regulated financial reporting purposes have not changed, different methods had to be developed to handle the dot.coms since buying and selling of companies does not stop. Expect the methods to change further as more experience is gained with these types of companies.

When estimating company value, the analysis is now often founded on a broad range of sub-values based on:[13]
- Financial capital (cash-flow, equity/debt, EBITDA,[14] *etc.*),
- Market capital (the product/brand portfolio, the position in the market, markets, sales process, the equity from the customer relations, *etc.*),
- Human capital (the leadership, people and their skills, motivation, capabilities, entrepreneurship, *etc.*), and
- Structural capital (systems, technology platform, management systems, processes, *etc.*).

The two most important drivers for the valuation are the new company's cash flow and the evaluation of the future potential of the company.

1.5
Market Timing

"Timing is everything" is an old saying that relates to many things, not the least the timing of market entry for a corporation. Enter too early, and nobody knows what to do with your product or service; enter too late, and your "me too" entry will have a much limited chance of success. To use a somewhat farfetched example, the Greek mathematician Heron — who lived from about 10 AD to about 75 AD – invented the steam engine, but it took until the 19th century before this invention found a niche as the engine of the Industrial Revolution.

In this section we shall look at issues of timing of market entry from the perspective of a company in the post e-Revolution space. First, we look at some common pitfalls and market characteristics, followed by a discussion of some areas of study for you, the company founder, and finally we look at how you operate on "Internet time."

Challenges of market timing

When are substantial numbers of customers ready to invest in new products? Some companies get it right, as when Nokia and Ericsson launched mobile phones about ten years ago. And some get it wrong. We have observed two typical market pitfalls that have taken their toll:

Customers' interest in buying and their actual buying behavior are not the same.

Actual demand for a product may not occur when the interest in the product by potential customers reaches an initial peak. Demand is when customers are actually ready to spend money and buy the product, which may be some time later. This is where many market analyses fall short and wrongly document that the time is right to go to market. The problem is that they measure interest in buying, not actual buying readiness, and can therefore go wrong. ToyCity (a former Danish on-line toy store that went bankrupt, now restarted in a different incarnation) is a prime example of someone's having done the basic market analysis and found high interest in buying toys online. Reality did not deliver high sales because potential customers were not actually ready to spend.

Moving in too early or moving in without significant customer value delivery can be your downfall.

The mobile phone space is a great example of this. Both WAP – Wireless Application Protocol - and 3G have created cash flow problems for the companies offering, or about to offer, services based on these technologies. Customers do not perceive a significant extra value and thus will not pay for the technologically advanced phones, given a choice not to sign up for services of little perceived value. The phone companies have had a hard time creating the cash flow to pay for steep investments in market development.

It is clear that profitable services requiring the technology of 3G, to use that as an example, will appear — the success of NTT's iMode shows it — but it is equally clear that it will take much longer than expected and that mobile services are fundamentally different than services on a browser on a PC display.

If you had gone to the market a while ago with phones supporting these technologies, you might have seriously hurt your business by the cost of the continuous product development required to supply competitive quality despite restricted market demand. Ironically, in certain markets the situation is now the reverse: mobile phone companies are delaying launches of services because not enough advanced phones are available.

Temporary competitive advantage

Being first can give you a **temporary competitive advantage**. The first mover advantage can mean that yours is the first product in the minds of the customers; you fill a previously empty space, potentially blocking out competitive products and possibly defining the market for a while. Motorola and the first mobile phones are one example.

Exploiting the first mover advantage means both developing the product/service and marketing it. This has a parallel to the classical market strategy for innovative companies like 3M. That company's strategy is to develop and market new inventions and then get out of the market when stronger competitors enter with a focus on competing on product quality, price, distribution, service and market communication.

A first mover advantage will not last without continuing product development and marketing, both of which cost money. This makes the situation difficult for start-ups. The timing of developing the business and going to market too early might kill the business by running it out of cash, and going in too late might make it much harder to prevail. You have to find the optimal time to market, and that is not always as soon as possible or when you have everything ready. Those times might be too early or too late.

Market Characteristics

Although every market seems to have a unique set of timing issues, there are two basic market situations: entering an existing market or entering/creating a new market.

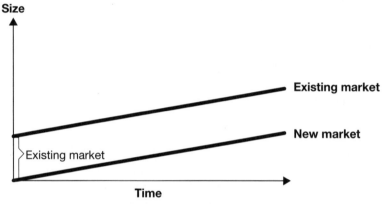

Figure 1.1   Market Types

Existing markets

Existing markets have a current size and structure already in place; the business model is well known by potential customers when a new company appears. Unless you are following a "me too" strategy, you will enter the market as a substitute with a materially different business offering or model. This is a **market development** situation.

Take, for instance, the market for buying clubs which LetsBuyIt.com entered in early 1998. The market had a certain structure, prior to leveraging the Internet opportunities, to bring single customers together to pool their buying. Aggregation of buying power for consumers already took place in existing organizations – for example, larger companies, co-ops, governmental and labor organizations — which secured discounts for their members on products and services: insurance, pensions, the companies' own products, and even normal consumer goods bought either through retailers, wholesalers, or directly from the producers.

The areas offering potential for market growth for LetsBuyIt.com were:

- Customers in the existing market through offering a better/easier/faster process,

- Prospective new customers reached via the Internet, and
- Supplying a much larger portfolio of products to either category of customers.

Growth potential also depends on the non-Internet-driven general market development. For this type of established market, the main barriers to entry are existing structures and habits and the possibility of existing companies' in the space leveraging the same opportunities as the entrant.

Amazon and Barnes and Noble are also examples: Amazon entered an existing market, the selling of books, where Barnes and Noble already had a substantial bricks and mortar presence.

New markets
Some markets do not have an initial size but are built virtually from zero — new markets or virgin markets. Take the intelligent set top box market necessary to view interactive digital TV: virtually no one had a set top box in early 2000 in Europe, and just a few TV channels broadcasted their content digitally. Today, most TV channels have launched their digital broadcasts, and the penetration of set top boxes is growing, as are the capabilities and services of the individual boxes.

For this type of virgin market the most significant barrier for entering companies is that customers must be educated to understand the offering and must be persuaded to change their current behavior in order for sales to take off and values to be delivered. In virgin markets competitors or companies with supplementary services can actually help each other in growing the market because they share the investment in increasing the learning curve and penetration of the new products.

Another significant barrier for virgin markets is the cost of product development. In a virgin market, product/services are developed not through marginal improvements but through initial creation or major modifications. Competitors with marginal improvements quickly come along. Therefore, the period during which a product is "new" and the company has an edge on competency based on specific product development is relatively short. Constant product development and continued market research are essential.

Issues in Timing Market Entry

Three areas are key when considering when to enter a market: its size, the competitive situation, and the life cycle of your product/service/technology.

Market size

When is there a market for a product or service? And at what time is it what size? Seemingly simple questions, but they are pivotal for the success of a new company trying to exploit a market.

The market size calculation relies on three elements: the initial or existing market potentials, the possible growth over time, and the risk of loosing the market by cannibalization from substitute products/services of the future. This is the basis for a realistic estimate of the potential incoming cash flow for your company. The evaluation of market size must then be supplemented by a realistic estimate of the expected value share (market share) the company can expect to obtain. This, in turn, relies on market strategy, which is individual for each company.

The timing consequences of the market size value are different for the two basic market situations:

For market development situations, it takes a shorter time for cash to roll in when potential customers already understand the basics of the offering, but, since the market is already established, the speed of growth must be expected to be slower than in virgin markets, and the total potential might not be as high as expected. This was the case for LetsBuyIt.com — an overestimation of demand.

For virgin markets, it takes a longer time to generate cash from the market value. Customer penetration has to be built for the category. People need time to understand what the product/service is, what values the new product can deliver, and if the price for the value is appropriate before they buy the product. Simultaneously, the product/service development needs large and continuous investments up front.

But if no market value is being developed in the early phases, there are other values being built: organizational competence, the experience of the personnel behind developing the product and market potentials, and the processes developed. Because of this, the company's early value is in know-how and experience and resides in the minds of the key personnel. This value can be leveraged (sold, hired out, leveraged by partnerships, *etc.*) if so desired. We shall expand on this below.

The Competitive situation

Who is currently making competitive products? When will they be able to deliver a customer value comparable to what you are trying to deliver? Who is on the way into the market, and when are they expected to arrive there? Key questions for understanding the right time to market with competition in mind.

In an existing market the cost for a competitor to evolve a product to compete with your entry may be lower than in a new market and the time may be shorter, all putting pressure on you to move. This was the challenge for Sony with the launch of its Playstation 2. Microsoft was on its way with Xbox.

For virgin markets, the right thing might be to delay market entry until there are other supplementary companies or competitors ready to help develop the market. That way you are not carrying all the costs of creating the market.

The primary driver of business values in virgin markets is market growth, not market share. For existing markets the main value driver is competitive superiority, which can partly be seen as market share and partly market growth focus.

The Technology

The concept of product life cycles (PLC) has gotten its second wind. For years, it has been considered an old, worn-out and much criticized theory of how to understand and develop market potentials. But Internet, software and hardware technologies are prime examples of the importance of understanding and using classical product life cycle[15] principles for planning how to time the actions necessary to be successful. The PLC concept can be applied to product categories (*e.g.*, soft drinks, phones), product forms (carbonated soft drinks, mobile phones), a product (Lemon Lime taste, WAP mobile phones) or a brand (Sprite, Ericsson Smart Phone). Generally, product categories have the longest life cycles, product forms have the highest correlation to the classic life cycle, and individual products, *e.g.*, high tech products like WAP phones or specific CMS product types, have the shortest life cycle.

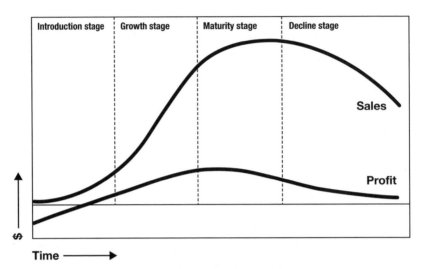

Figure 1.2   Product Life Cycle

The key new insight — especially relevant for companies that produce technology-based products — is not the product life cycle itself, but how to deal with extremely short product life cycles.

Take Content Management Systems: the early CMS were tailor-made HTML-based templates used by programmers to update Web sites. Then the technology brought out ASP/database-based templates, which could be designed in such a way that Web-site owners themselves could fill in and change some information on their sites. And now the CMS are becoming multi-platform CMS, which manage content for different applications such as Web sites for computers, WAP application for mobile phones, IDTV, and more. There are data management CMS and publishing CMS to cater specifically to back-end data management and integration and for front-end usability. The point here is that companies which spent substantial sums implementing a CMS of a certain generation will undoubtedly have to spend even more to implement another before too long.

The mobile industry is an example: going from voice units, to SMS/data units, to WAP applications, and then on to 3G and PDA integrated solutions. For Nokia's mobile phones, a standard product development lead-time is about three years, and the product life cycle is about one year. Talk about technology and time to market as critical factors! Also, within the mobile industry, most of the world's largest telecom companies invested heavily in buying and building 3G networks. Not only did they move in too early from the perspective of the market, as we discussed above, it now seems that local-ly-driven wireless networks – the so-called W-LAN's – are seriously challenging the competitiveness of 3G networks based on price/cost.

The expected life span of your product or service – and of your technology platform — with the initial technology must be estimated. When the technology is ready to deliver the planned product, and when the market is ready to absorb the technology and product (if ever) are key questions to answer. They will give you the market launch timing. The estimate of how long this market will exist will be based on this technology, or evolutions of it, and will have a significant impact on the net present value of the market size and on the calculation of how to profit from delivering customer value. This will also determine what level of cash you can expect from the market. By this, you can also calculate in which period you can expect what in-coming cash flow so you can estimate to what extent you can cover your costs and become profitable.

Startups on Internet Time

"Internet Time" is real. The Web allows companies to put up a prototype business model in a very short time and to revise this business model in response to real or imagined changes in an equally short time. Time to market can – and must, to maintain competitive advantages — be very short. This requires different ways of implementing change: do multiple things at once (multi-tasking) and/or let others do work for you (outsourcing).

Multitasking

Conventional automation projects before the Web typically had a planning horizon of eighteen to twenty-four months. This does not work for a Web project. The waterfall model of doing step one, followed by step two, *et cetera*, for a large project is being replaced by multiple smaller projects where the next one starts before the current one is finished, *i.e.*, multi-tasking.

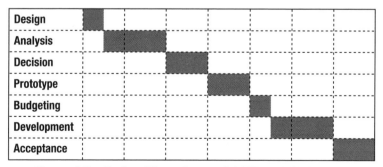

Figure 1.3   Project Plan – Sequential "Waterfall" Process

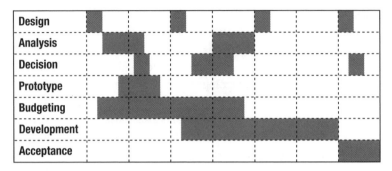

Figure 1.4   Project Plan - Multi-tasking

Outsourcing/partnerships

Using networks or partnerships to outsource functions — instead of building all the competencies and functions internally — is another way of getting ahead early. If time is important, who needs to hire and train an IT department which will be ready to perform in six months when you can subscribe to a hotline and get support service up and running in a couple of days? Or, if you need accounting systems, why not partner with a professional accounting firm in order to leverage the fact that they already have systems and personnel in place to handle your accounting from day one? Or why find and invest in your own premises when you can hire and share space in an office building where all the needed facilities are installed and ready to be used?
Outsourcing is often called "Business Process Outsourcing" (BPO). Many companies in the "new" economy are outsourcing all non-strategic business processes in order to be able to focus exclusively on the strategic issue; this is a characteristic trend of the "new" economy, including even processes such as logistics, production and marketing. An example is LetsBuyIt.com, which used third parties for almost everything — IT, logistics, finance, call center, *etc.* The core competencies on which the company was built are sourcing/buying and marketing/selling.

Timing is an important factor in how you start your company. If you are out of time and need to be in the market fast, you need to multi-task and outsource all non-strategic capabilities, building only the core competencies yourself. If you have more time, you have the comparative luxury of building more competencies in-house from the start.

1.6
Business Models
for e-Business

Somewhere out there is a bullet with your company's name on it. Somewhere out there is a competitor, unborn or unknown, that will render your business model obsolete. Bill Gates knows that. When he says that Microsoft is always two years away from failure, he's not blowing smoke at Janet Reno. He knows that competition today is not between products; it's between business models. He knows that irrelevancy is a bigger risk than inefficiency....
... The hottest and most dangerous new business models out there are on the web.

Gary Hamel[16]

...The definition of a business model is murky at best. Most often, it seems to refer to a loose conception of how a company does business and generates revenue. Yet simply having a business model is an exceedingly low bar to set for building a company....

Michael Porter[17]

Nothing like a little disagreement!

Why is there so much discussion of business models in the Internet space? One good reason is that it is natural to attempt to classify and create taxonomies for how business is conducted. A successful taxonomy creates shorthand for analysis and discussion and may, once experience has been gained regarding the success or failure of specific models, help entrepreneurs avoid or seek particular models.

A business model is not an inviolable totem; it is a tool. A business model for a company must constantly prove itself and should be discarded/modified if it stops generating value. A good example of a business model which, though considered very important in the B2B space, turned out to have limited applicability is the intermediary business exchange where, so the model went, companies would pay a transaction value-based fee to an intermediary for the privilege of trading on this exchange. The market showed that the model rarely worked.

Most new companies require new and innovative business models in order to be successful. The most attractive, accessible business opportunities for them can be found in the changing of society that opens up new market opportunities or in the spaces made available through a change in technology, not in existing crowded markets with traditional models and structures. A big, established company or industry is much like a tanker: it owns the sea today in its market, but it changes course very ponderously, even after orders from the captain. Moreover, once a change in direction has begun, it cannot be stopped by anyone or anything. New companies are more like speedboats: fast to change course and charge after new opportunities, but liable to run out of gas and lack the momentum and mass of a tanker to prevail.

Existing companies also have to rethink their business models, especially when they are in danger of becoming obsolete. A good example is the music industry, which will have to change its business model radically because of the possibilities for copying, playing and distributing music, for example, via the MP3 format on the net. It is not clear what this change will be, but the Napster experience showed the need for action.

Mapping and other demographic information delivery is another example of an industry in change. Conventional "Yellow Pages" were suddenly in danger of being marginalized due to the perception that all information is on the Web – and that it is all free. Examples of companies that have successfully changed their business model are the Danish Yellow Pages (De Gule Sider/TDC Forlag) and Krak.

Since new companies may not be able to compete within traditional parameters, they have to think differently and more creatively earlier on. One way to do that is to concentrate on the customer relationship. The ability to keep track of each customer's likes and dislikes is a winning edge in the "new" economy, one of the areas allowing you to achieve a lasting advantage in competition. Dell is a good example: when you do business with Dell, you not only get to configure your own computer, you also get very personalized service during and after the purchase.

It is important for existing as well as newly founded companies to analyze their existing business models and to imagine different scenarios of what future business models might look like, both for themselves and their competition. They must analyze whether or not the existing business model will fit in the imagined scenarios and which elements of the current model should be utilized, adapted, or dumped. Another important point to consider is what would happen if a rival suddenly changed its business model. How fast would your company be able to act and adapt to that change?

Microsoft *vis-à-vis* the Web is a good example: Microsoft did not embrace the Web for quite some time though its importance was growing and leading to commercial success for other companies. The company did not run the scenario for a while, so to speak. Microsoft finally did "get it," however, in time to change its business model and continue to prosper. DEC is an example of a company which, despite running the scenario, failed to change — to adapt a less proprietary operating system, UNIX, in place of its proprietary one, VMS. This cost it the company.

Value Chain

As information exchange capabilities have grown, leading to cost-effective opportunities for outsourcing, new versions of the value chain have appeared. They represent the continuum from all in-house to everything outsourced. The terms "value chain," "value network," and "dynamic market" are used as labels for different places on this continuum of business models. They represent redesign and optimization of a company's internal and external processes to achieve more effective and better positioning.

The value chain is the traditional business model, *i.e.*, one in which practically all a company's value-creating and business processes are internal. The concept encompasses all the value-creating activities within a company, typically in connection with a company's supply and demand side. It is possible, by analyzing individual steps of the value chain, to redesign and optimize the internal processes of a company to achieve increased efficiency and better positioning compared to the competition. This is often called business process reengineering (BPR). Also related to the value chain are "supporting activities" – activities that support individual processes in the company.

The value chain in a company includes both the movement of the actual goods or services and the information flows that facilitate/enhance that movement, the information or "virtual value chain."

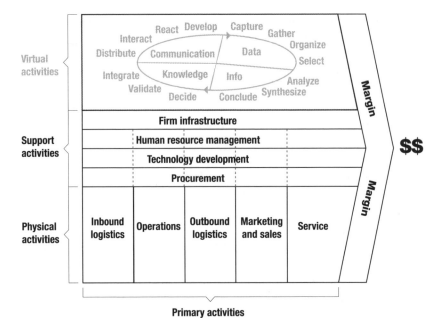

Figure 1.5 Value Chain

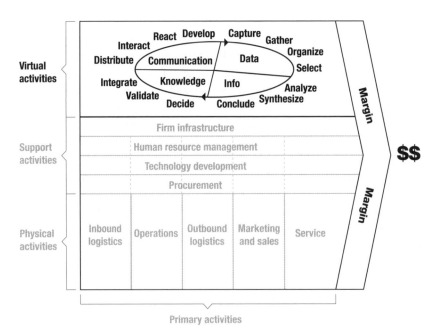

Figure 1.6 Virtual Value Chain

Value Network

The value network is an alternative to the value chain, describing a number of value-creating activities connected in a small network of both internal and external business processes. The idea of a value network is to establish close relationships between your company and a limited number of business partners, thereby gaining an optimal integration of the value-creating process.

The idea of companies' outsourcing their business processes and, with them, some of the value-creating activity is in fact not a new one. It has merely become more widespread, due to improved technology.

A value network has the following description:
- Deals primarily with a limited number of external partners
- The investment per partner is usually quite high
- Requires great commitment from the partners in the network.

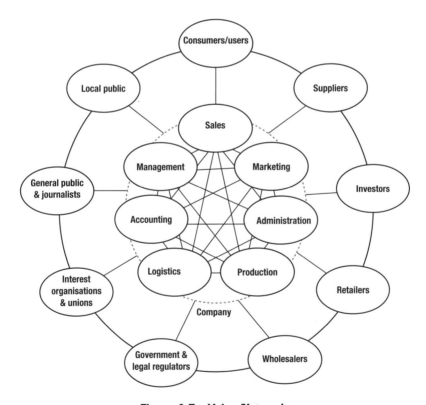

Figure 1.7   Value Network

Dynamic Market

A dynamic market is further along the continuum of business models. It describes a number of value-creating activities connected in an extensive, dynamic network of both internal and external business processes. The aim of a dynamic market is to establish a high number of business relationships to a large number of partners, thus gaining more flexibility and options for the value-creating process.

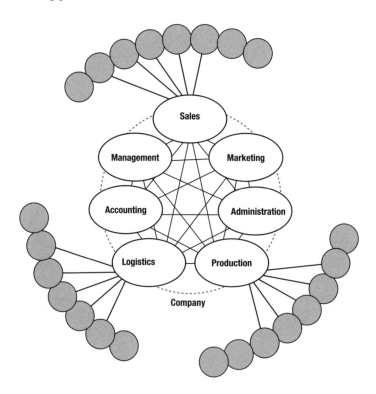

Figure 1.8   Dynamic Market

This model is widely used by virtual companies in the "new" economy. An example is a typical Internet banner exchange, which allows the company to advertise in an extensive network at an incredibly low cost.

A dynamic market has the following characteristics:
- Deals with a large numbers of external partners, meaning many external relationships
- The investment per partner is usually quite low
- Low or, at least, less commitment from partners in the dynamic market.

It is also possible to unite the models – *i.e.*, to select different realizations of parts of the value chain — and thereby utilize the advantages of all. Amazon.com is yet again a good example: the company uses a conventional value chain for fulfillment, picking, shipping, billing, *etc.*, and a dynamic network in its work with Amazon Associates.

Taxonomies of Business Models

To be useful, taxonomy must be exhaustive and consistent. Michael Rappa provides a set of categories of business models:[18]

- *Brokerage. Brokers are market makers: they bring buyers and sellers together and facilitate transactions. Those can be business-to-business (B2B), business-to-consumer (B2C), or consumer-to-consumer (C2C) markets. A broker makes its money by charging a fee for each transaction it enables.* [Examples: www.eTrade.com, www.Covisint.com]

- *Advertising. The web-advertising model is an extension of the traditional media-broadcasting model. The broadcaster, in this case, a web site, provides content (usually, but not necessarily, for free) and services (like e-mail, chat, forums) mixed with advertising messages in the form of banner or popup ads. The virtual ads may be the major or sole source of revenue for the "broadcaster."* [Examples: public search engines, such as www.google.com; news sites, such as www.cnn.com]

- *Infomediary. Some firms are able to function as infomediaries by collecting and selling information to other businesses. An infomediary may offer users free Internet access or free hardware in exchange for detailed information about their surfing and purchasing habits.* [Example: any site that requires customers to register, such as www.nyt.com]

- *Merchant. Classic wholesalers and retailers of goods and services (increasingly referred to as "e-tailers"). Sales may be made based on list prices or through auction. In some cases, the goods and services may be unique to the web and not have a traditional "brick-and-mortar" storefront.* [Examples: conventional retailers, such as www.sears.com]

- *Manufacturer. This model is predicated on the power of the web to allow manufacturers to reach buyers directly and thereby compress the distribution channel (i.e., eliminate wholesalers and retailers). The manufacturer model can be based on efficiency (cost-savings that may or may not be passed on to consumers), improved customer service, and a better understanding of customer preferences.* [Examples: computer manufacturers, such as www.dell.com and www.ibm.com]

- *Affiliate. In contrast to the generalized portal, which seeks to drive a high volume of traffic to one site, the affiliate model provides purchase opportunities wherever people may be surfing. It does this by offering financial incentives (in the form of a percentage of revenue) to affiliated partner sites.* [Example: the use by Amazon.com of Amazon Associates]

- **Community.** *The viability of the community model is based on user loyalty (as opposed to high traffic volume). Users have a high investment in both time and emotion in the site. In some cases, users are regular contributors of content and/or money. Having users who visit continually offers advertising, infomediary or specialized portal opportunities. The community model may also run on a subscription fee for premium services.* [Examples: an investment site with which some investors almost became emotionally involved, www.motleyfool.com; almost any site centered around a shared interest, such as The International Mountain Biking Association, www.imba.com]

- **Subscription.** *Users pay for access to the site. High value-added content is essential. Generic news content, viable on the newsstand, has proven less successful as a subscription model on the web. Some businesses have combined free content (to drive volume and ad revenue) with premium content or services for subscribers only.* [Example: job search sites requiring a subscription to view certain job leads, www.geoweb.info]

- **Utility.** *The utility model is a metered usage or pay as you go approach. Its success may depend on the ability to charge by the byte, including micropayments (that is, those too small to pay by credit card due to processing fees).* [This model has not reached its full potential yet, partly because there are few micropayment models implemented. A current example is the archive of articles on most newspaper sites, for example, on www.nyt.com]

This set of categories, albeit quite exhaustive and useful, shows how the area is still unsettled. For example, the Open Market Exchange and the general Advertising model have been shown lately to be quite limited niche models.

Inverted business model

The last area related to a company's business model we are going to discuss is cannibalization of the business model – a quite controversial area. Several phone companies offer free calling in exchange for listening to commercials during the call, and several – actually most — newspapers offer the news free on the Internet.

This is difficult to categorize, the argument having been made that it is not a business model at all and that, for example, the availability of free branded – by the newspaper – news is a temporary phenomenon. In the future, the argument goes, there will undoubtedly be a free front page with regular news, but value added services, such as movie reviews by the newspaper's popular movie critic, will not be free. Reading them will likely require a micropayment or a subscription.

Other inverted business models that were tried earlier turned out to not work at all, one example being free Internet access. An inverted business model must, to be successful, lead to long-term competitive advantages that can be monetized in a manner different than today's business model.

1.7
Objectives and Strategies for e-Business

Business objectives and strategies
Companies with market success have a strong positioning strategy. On top of this, they apply business strategies, amongst which use of the Internet is one and often a key one. But use of the Internet has now penetrated most of the larger companies. The net will be much less prominent within the coming two or three years. It will just be there, everybody will use it and have it be an integral part of their business strategy, and the next novel/exiting new business models will be built in another part of technology and business.

This is just like what telephones must have been late in the 19th century and what fax machines were in the middle of the 20th. Within two years pretty much every company will be on-line, the Internet will be part of their system, part of their marketing, part of their information and supply chain, and it will just be there. People who have Internet expertise and/or can quickly establish Web sites are going to be perceived as less valuable and will get paid less well for those skills.

This has already hit a list of Web agencies and Web consultants hard (*e.g.*, FramFab, Icon Medialab, Cell, Agency.com), especially in regions where the Internet usage is the highest in the world, Scandinavia and the USA. This trend is spreading across Europe just now. Users are becoming much less intimidated, much more familiar, and much more able to bypass the intermediaries. Businesses are being created to enable the customer to handle functions that once would have required a Web consultant. Virtual wallets are one example: consumer information will be stored in one place for him/her to use across the Web for purchases.

We are going to return to normalcy, which is to say some other technology will be the next hot thing – as Mobile is trying very hard to be right now.

The Strategic Planning Institute (SPI) documents from its PIMS database that the ROI in smaller market segments (= niche markets) is almost three times higher than in larger segments. Another study of mid-sized companies[19] documents that the most profitable companies are fast changing, high-value-adding creators of niche markets. As a new company you must aim to be the best at something specific rather than good at many things, preferably with a product/service that in one way or other is considered unique by customers. Take Content Management Systems for Web sites (*e.g.*, Web500/Periscope or the like), ERP systems (SAP, Navision, *etc.*) and CRM systems (Siebel, *etc.*). These companies and products prove that it can be better and more profitable to focus fully on becoming best at something (making the best system), letting partners do the selling/consultancy/implementation, than to develop merely a good system while doing the Web consulting and implementation work oneself.

For a "new economy" start-up company, the first real challenge is to define the company's basic positioning strategy. The first task is to look at the industry in which you are operating. The "new" economy we would call an emerging "industry." This phase of this particular phenomenon is one in which experimentation has really got to be part of any way of competing. An example: Yahoo is a company that quickly and early made a commitment that it was going to be a media company, not a search company. Its managers had a set of principles that they've been radically applying ever since they started, and they're constantly experimenting with, if you will, the details of the product offering, the service offering, and so forth. Yet the basic positioning of the enterprise really hasn't changed. That's a fundamental distinction that is often lost in the discussion of strategy. Somehow people see strategy as something that is a fixed way of doing things. If you're changing, then you don't have a strategy, or so they think.

Our conception of positioning strategy is that it defines a general direction in the marketplace. Within that direction you're constantly improving your capacity to deliver on it. Take Reuters, which is an excellent example of applied strategy. Reuters started out with carrier pigeons, but the purpose was to deliver physical information. As new approaches for delivering information evolved, they added them to their product. Reuters is constantly experimenting, thus you might say they don't have a strategy at all. The reason they are so good at what they do is that they *do* have a strategy: they know what their fundamental position is, and they're constantly screening and searching for ways of delivering on that.

You, too, will need to find and select your fundamental position strategy and then constantly find new and better ways to deliver on it. We recommend that you make a strategy for what business you truly want to be in, just as Yahoo and Reuters did. A strategy should be tied to reality by a set of relevant measurable goals that can quantify the objectives and bridge the gap from conceptual thinking to reality. Then you work out your strategy by planning and selecting what actions you are going to take to reach the goals set and what resources you will need.

Research on successful and unsuccessful e-Business initiatives[20] helps our understanding of the basic mistakes made by many companies. The biggest overriding mistake of many "new economy" companies is to see the Internet as a lasting competitive position by itself. Boo, Dressmart, and Boxman are good examples of that. The business objective of doing something on the Internet is not enough by itself. Soon everyone will have Internet-enabled their company and business processes, so leveraging the Internet will be, at best, only a short-term temporary competitive advantage. The right thing to do is to leverage Internet opportunities to strengthen business strategies.

Dot.com companies ignored that principle prior to the market crash — their only focus was on growth — and even old economy companies forgot what they stood for when they designed their Internet businesses.

Porter lists six principles of strategic positioning which are paraphrased below:

1. Focus on value. A strategy is only effective if the objective is based on generating superior value for the owners, *e.g.*, superior long-term return on investments. Other main objectives like growth, market share, number of club members, number of Website visitors, *etc.* will lead the wrong way, as they have for a number of dot.com companies. Instead of focusing on delivering profitable value or profitability, focus has been on market share or turnover. Using high rebates or free offers, many companies have killed their own market potentials. For example, some newspapers and magazines, which usually charge a minimal fee for their content in physical paper form, are offering the same news faster free of charge on the net, relying solely on advertising to pay for all content creation. The on-line business model cannot pay for the cost of operating an on-line

newspaper; in fact, it costs the company money every time somebody goes on the Web site – he or she does not buy the paper.

2. Deliver unique customer value. To thrive, you need to deliver value in a way that is different from that of your competitors. To sell everything to everybody is destructive thinking because it often leaves you with price as your only competitive tool. You need to be best at something: serving a special type of customer, delivering a superior specific product or service, having the fastest delivery, having the best customer service, or the like. If IKEA had decided to become just another furniture producer, IKEA would not be what it is today.

3. Be yourself. Execute the business process in a way that makes sense for your organization. This will ensure that you are leveraging your organization as a competitive advantage. Everybody knows the "best practices" the consultants are selling, so if you use them you will just be one of many.

4. Concentrate. When deciding on a strategy, you are consciously deciding what opportunities to pursue, thus also deciding what opportunities or strategic directions to ignore. If you are not selective in which opportunities you pursue, you will struggle to find a competitive advantage.

6. Make sure your company works as one. The different activities in your company must strengthen each other. Product design must support production, and both must strengthen service/after-sale initiatives and marketing communication. Such an integrated system not only increases profitability but also makes the strategy harder to copy for competitors, because the latter must then copy a full system of integrated and inter-depending actions. There is still no substantial competitor to IKEA because the smart integration of product development, logistics, economic behavior, family friendliness and marketing goes hand in hand. This point also holds true for Hennes & Mauritzs, which has secured strong integrated system synergies and has the same positioning strategy in clothes as IKEA has in furniture.

6. Be patient. You have to stick to your basic positioning strategy because it takes time to build up internal processes, competencies, brand, and market reputation. To reinvent or re-launch a company with a new strategy destroys the continuity and can cost a lot of money. Even the decision to change a brand name can cost you the millions that you have invested in brand equity. Mobilix has invested millions in its brand name in Denmark and is now struggling to build another brand name, Orange, at additional cost — almost double the money for the same quantity of brand equity. That may not be the smartest thing to do. It is crucial to continuously improve the business and value propositions, but it has to be guid-

ed by a basic fundamental positioning strategy which is fixed as long as at all possible.

Strategic Positioning

Competitive advantage is often determined by the strategic position chosen for a company or a product/service/brand. The more unclear and complex the choice is, the weaker the positioning strategy. From analyzing a long list of successful companies, five clear winning positions appear in an open market segment, as shown by the positioning star:

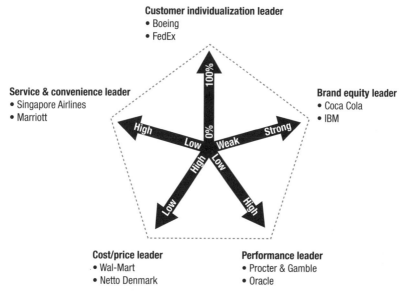

Figure 1.9   The Positioning Star

It is possible to pursue all five dimensions but impossible to be the best and a leader in more than one. So a positioning strategy should focus on selecting a balanced market approach for the different dimensions, but with only one dimension as the key driver.

Service and convenience leaders are typically companies like Singapore Airlines with its commitment to the absolute best flight experience of any airline. Marriott hotels also have the same intense focus on delivering the most pleasant stay at the best location of any hotel chain in the world.

Cost/price leaders are typically companies like Wal-Mart, which through their buying power and retailing concepts have the lowest prices. Brand equity leaders are the strongest brands with the highest level of attachment and sympathy, like Coca Cola and IBM. Customer individualization leaders are companies which have the best tailor-made products for individual clients. Typically, companies like Boeing and FedEx have the leading position in personalized products and services, but consultancies like McKinsey are also high on the list of leaders in this dimension.

Procter & Gamble produces performance-leading products, *e.g.*, Ariel detergents. The firm will not launch a new product unless it scores better on performance or, at minimum, equal to the best-performing product in the specific category. Ariel is a strong, well-known household brand. There are a list of line extensions for different types of users, a hot line telephone service, competitive prices and occasional special discounts. But Ariel's leadership position is driven by being a product performance leader.

Many "new economy" companies have thought of the first mover advantage as a positioning strategy, but history shows that this is neither a lasting competitive advantage nor a successful market position. 3M is typically a company which has at its core business innovation. But its positioning strategy is not to be first in a category, but to have the best (and often only) product in a specific category. When competitors enter the category and perhaps within a year or so produce a better product, 3M retreats unless in the meantime it has invented an even better product. 3M's positioning strategy for most of its products is thus a type of performance leader strategy.

Strategy and the e-Business Ladder

In the following section we shall go through transformation and reengineering strategies, one by one, but consider first the steps usually found on the e-Business "ladder." The e-Business ladder represents progressively higher involvement by a company with the Web. It is also a useful tool for comparing one's self with competitors.

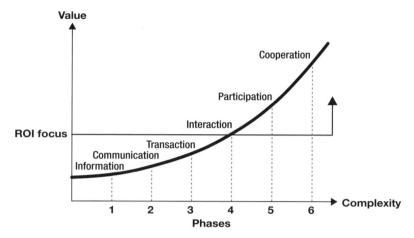

Figure 1.10 e-Business Ladder

The steps are:

1. **Information**: The company has an electronic presence on the Web and is visible, like a business card. The results are company awareness.

2. **Communication**: The company is able to communicate with prospects on the Web. This includes traditional marketing communication in order to make the company and its products interesting to the viewer. The results are company and product understanding. Communication can also include product information, user manuals, and purchasing information. It is typically impersonal, *i.e.*, does not include customer relationships.

3. **Transaction**: The company engages in simple transactions like the selling of products and provision of services, or providing brochures or product manuals on demand. The result is the exchange of goods or simple sales.

4. **Interaction**: The company creates a closer relationship between buyer and seller, like securing electronic data integration (EDI), where standard transactions are accompanied by automatic ordering when stock is low, a printout of an invoice is automatically created when a transaction has occurred, or a record of buying history is maintained. The result is automation of processes leading to savings in process cost and manpower resources.

5. **Participation**. Participation means, for instance, establishment of e-Marketplaces where an industry's buyers and sellers interact in one universe, with one system to effectively organize their participation. The result is leveraging of industry synergies in how to organize commercial relationships, making commerce and trading more effective.

6. **Cooperation**. The company implements a strategy that ties the customers ever closer. An example is Dell, where customers participate in the creation of the product. The result for the customer is an opportunity to tailor

the product to fit his/her specific needs, for the seller, an opportunity to produce the product when it is ordered and bought — the ultimate personalization. Additionally, the company may seek to outsource non-core business from the customer.

Most companies today find themselves in the earlier phases of e-Business strategy development and e-Opportunity exploitation. They have presented their company on a Web site, and maybe even offered their products for sale through an online shop. But at the same time, the discussion of cost/benefits or ROI on their e-Business investment has not yet kicked in, and e-Business is seen as that, "e," and not as an integral part of the whole company undertaking.

Strategic considerations for established "old economy" companies

There are two general e-Business strategies for physical, existing companies: transformation and reengineering. The former revolves around creating a whole new business model, products/services and organization based on the net by digitalizing (automating) the value chain and all business processes, whereas the sole purpose of the latter is to improve and make more effective some or a few of the business processes by digitalizing them – "electrifying" them. The object of the latter strategy is therefore not to change completely the company's business model, *etc.*, but to implement greater cost effectiveness and/or throughput. If you are operating with a fully virtual and newly started dot.com start-up, you will, of course, not be using either of these strategies, but rather setting up – engineering – a business on the basis of the "new economy" opportunities that you have identified as your business idea.

The two strategies framework is therefore relevant only for existing physical companies.

	Business Initiatives (External focus)	Business Processes (Internal focus)
Strategic Change (Substantial business strategic values)	**Revised Business Model** - New vision/mission - Aggregation	**Revised Organization** - Customer management department - Outsourcing - Networking
Improvements (Support to initiatives and current processes)	**Higher turnover** - Increased sales - Brand equity - Loyalty/Satisfaction - New/improved products - Larger distribution - Better customer knowledge	**Cost reductions** - Self service - Resource optimization - New processes - Information sharing/ Knowledge Management - Training/e-Learning
Operational Savings (Short term cost reduction and resource efficiencies)	**Access and distribution** - Promotion participation - Materials on-line (Brochures)	**Handling** - Better control and handling of current processes

Transformation brackets the first two rows; *Reengineering* brackets the lower rows (vertical labels at left).

Figure 1.11   Strategic Frameworks

The successful e-Business operations we have worked with share a set of principles by which they have managed to profit and prosper:

1. **e-Business is not marketing**. e-Business in not a marketing assignment; it is a major business opportunity that needs direct top-management involvement and a separate organization with cross-functional participation. It can be a catastrophe to make a marketing department responsible for e-Business initiatives.

2. **Value-based objectives are outlined**. The business case for the e-Business strategy and the resulting expectations in terms of ROI or cost/benefit calculations for the e-Business initiatives are laid out explicitly.

3. **Integration**. The e-Business strategy involves not just the company itself, but also close contact with and the cooperation of key stakeholders like customers, investors, suppliers, mass media/journalists, consultants, and industry partners.

e-Business transformation strategy
The aim of a transformation strategy is to create a whole new business model, new products/services, and a new organization based on the net by digitalizing (automating) the value chain and all business processes, thereby creating new products and services throughout the value chain.

This is, naturally, a long and tedious process for any existing company as the changes affect everything and everyone. You may encounter difficulties with your employees if they are not included in the project and given some kind of influence. But, having said that, there is no doubt that this strategy will help give your company a secure position in future competitive situations. And in some (probably most) situations it is simply a necessity for survival in the future market.

e-Business reengineering strategy

As opposed to the transformation approach, the purpose of the e-Business reengineering strategy is to improve and increase the effectiveness of the company's business processes by digitalizing them. *In popular terms, we "electrify" the value chain.* So the e-Business reengineering strategy does not aim to change a company's entire business model, products/services or organization, but merely to cut costs and/or increase the productivity of the company.

This strategy is still often preferred to the e-Business transformation strategy as it is far easier and quicker to implement and the results are, in the short term, much better and more easily measured. The problem, however, is that this strategy is often more a "patching" solution than an actual method of adapting a company to future competitive situations. Again, this depends on the company in question and the market in which it operates.

Choosing a strategy

Which strategy to choose for your company depends on many different factors and conditions, including the following:

- Business model
- Employees
- Competition
- Customers
- Products and services
- Qualifications/Readiness.

Important competition parameters of the "new" economy are qualifications and readiness.

Qualifications, rather than the actual product array, are often the basis of a company's competitive strength in the "new" economy, making them key factors. They force a company to evaluate its current qualifications and readiness and decide whether or not it will be able to meet future demands. If not, the company will have to implement new qualifications along the way and make them an integral part of its e-Business strategy.

The heaviest factor in choosing a strategy is probably readiness: whether or not management can face delving into a completely new strategy via the e-Business transformation approach, thereby transforming the company to suit the future.

1.8
Amazon.com
- The first big e-Business start-up success – or is it?

Is Amazon a success? If you measure Amazon by its conventional GAAP financial reports, the answer would be no. As we discuss below in the section on value, the shareholders' deficit has grown by approximately one half billion dollars in twelve months. If you measure Amazon by ...

- having blazed a trail in the Internet economy,
- having created a novel business model which it continues to refine,
- being profitable within its original core sector – selling books, and
- having created a brand, the value of which is probably higher than the shareholders' deficit,[21]

the answer is unquestionably yes. In other words, the jury is still out.

The new objectives and strategies around being the world's first and biggest global market for any kind of product still need to prove themselves. Large cash flows from the base business are being transferred to support the new strategy.

Amazon.com took advantage of the business opportunities on the Web at an early stage and created a business model that is not only well adapted to the Internet but takes maximum advantage of the opportunities it offers. The most obvious ones are virtual distribution and convenience to customers. Amazon.com makes a large variety of books available to everyone, 24 hours x 7 days a week x 365 days a year, just a few clicks away, and delivers them to the doorstep of the customer. That had not been done before, and a lot of customers were attracted to this higher value the new book retailer was offering.

Amazon.com is still the world's biggest on-line bookstore and still has a head start over its competitors, including Barnes & Noble, Waterstone, Borders, *etc*.

Their primary customer group today is, of course, readers buying their books, and their secondary target groups are publishers supported by Amazon.com's "Advantage Service" and resellers supported by "Amazon Associates." What makes these services so interesting to us is that they have broken the traditional book-publishing value chain, which can be described as follows:

- Author
- Publisher
- Distributor
- Bookstore
- Reader.

As we discussed earlier in this chapter, the company has configured a combination of a conventional value chain, a value network and a dynamic market, allowing the parties involved to assume different roles depending on the value functionality they wish to offer. All the strategic processes are, of course, in Amazon.com's possession:

- Customer relationship management (CRM), *e.g.*, customer optimization
- Information management, *e.g.*, catalog information
- Transaction management, *e.g.*, payments
- Logistics management, *e.g.*, shipping and delivery administration
- Sales interface, both directly via their own catalog and indirectly via their Associates.

The Advantage Service program is a service for publishers, allowing them to integrate their books' information into Amazon.com's catalog. The greatest advantage for the publishers is, of course, that they can easily sell their books via Amazon.com and gain access to its huge customer database. Apart from that, Amazon.com offers stock management and many other functions without a start-up fee or service charges. The publisher, however, must pay 50% to 60% to Amazon.com for arranging the sales. Amazon.com estimates that in the USA alone there are somewhere between 10,000 and 50,000 independent publishers, a large market.

The Amazon Associates program is a service for other on-line bookstores or in general anyone who would like to sell books on-line. Amazon.com offers Amazon Associates the use of its catalog while Amazon.com handles the ordering, handling, shipment and payments. The set-up is extremely easy and fast, and again there are no fees or service charges. An Associate receives up to 15% in commission per sold unit. This program makes the on-line bookstores value chain service providers to Amazon.com by acting as marketing units for the company and providing access to the books in their catalogs.

Amazon.com uses its primary customers (book readers) to review books, which, by the way, is a huge success.

Amazon.com probably has the best understanding and implementation of e-CRM so far. Among other things, it conducts customer analyses that give each customer an "interest profile," allowing Amazon.com to suggest specific books of interest to him/her.

Amazon.com's marketing strategy is to have the most extensive catalog, to have the widest distribution available to its customers, and to have the most well-known brands. These objectives have been reached to a large extent, and, we might add, in a mere four years!

1.9
Customer, Company, and Shareholder Value

The discussions above of value-based company creation and of Amazon.com as an example of a successful start-up in the Web space are a good lead-in to a more general discussion of value: customer, company and shareholder value.

The 10Q filing made by Amazon.com on October 30th 2001 contains the following information:[22]

	September 30th 2001	December 31st, 2000
Total stockholders' deficit	$(1,453,994,000)	$(967,251,000)
	Nine Months Ended September 30th, 2001	Nine Months Ended September 30th, 2000
Net loss	$(572,364,000)	$(866,133,000)

On September 30th, 2001, there were 371,766,000 shares outstanding;[23] the share price was $5.97 on September 28th, 2001 and $6.01 on October 1st, 2001.[24] In other words, the market valued Amazon.com at somewhere around 2.2 billion US$, while taking into account a shareholders' deficit of 1.5 billion US$. Barring "irrational exuberance," this market value reflects something not shown in the GAAP financials.

Customer Value

Let us start by looking at the concept of **customer value**, and begin with an example: a press release from i2 – a supply chain automation company – dated October 25th, 2001 states:[25]

The report[26] states that as of June 2001, the Cumulative Value achieved by customers who have successfully implemented i2 solutions is estimated to be approximately $29.9 billion US....

and further

In 1995, i2 adopted as its mission, to provide $50 billion in value to its customers by the year 2005. Miller-Williams, a customer research firm specializing in value and expectations metrics, started in 1997 to measure and certify value results with i2 customers. Over the past five years, cumulative customer value from i2's solutions has compounded rapidly such that in

October of 2000, i2 revised its mission to increase the value provided from $50 billion to $75 billion....

These figures exceed by far the cumulative sales by i2, so they represent something else: the value – based on a set of metrics defined by i2 and the company doing the auditing — that i2's customers obtained through the use of i2's software.

The model used to calculate customer value in the i2 example is somewhat involved, and one should expect that models will vary among industries and products.

A simplified model for the general case of calculating customer value obtained by a company's customers will have the following components:

- **Reach**: how many customers the company reaches
- **Value proposition**: the worth of the offering to one customer (the component that will vary by industry and product)
- **Frequency**: how often one customer buys on the average per unit time, a year
- **Time**: the time span over which the calculation is being made, how many years

In other words:

Customer value = reach * value proposition * frequency * time

This calculation, or a similar one adapted for the i2 product set, is what led to the US$ 29.9b number above.

Value translates into turnover and then to profit by the ability of the company to turn value delivered into profits earned, illustrated by the following two formulas:

Turnover = (value * price) – credit time
Profit = turnover – cost

Turnover within a given period equals the total value delivered times the price charged for the value – *i.e.*, what the company charges per unit of customer value — minus the value delivered which is not invoiced within the time period of the turnover calculation. And, simply speaking, profit equals the turnover generated minus all the cost. A company can thus derive a projection for obtainable profit by using a market analysis identifying the value proposition for a customer segment and the size of that segment.

Knowing your customers' value proposition well helps you with pricing and with determining whether there is a business in selling the product or service. Many companies sell their products too cheaply, thereby not capitalizing properly on the customer value delivered, or attempt to sell into a market where the combined value proposition and customer reach is not large enough to justify the effort.

Take, for example, the free news media on the Web: you can get news for free on the Web faster than you can via your daily newspaper, which costs money. A better pricing model would take into account the cost (production price or direct product profitability) and also the perceived value of the product by customers. In fact, the jury is still out as to whether users perceive a high enough value in an electronic version of a newspaper to be willing to pay for it, the *Wall Street Journal*'s being the only example thus far of a newspaper making money on an electronic version.

Many companies, especially "new economy" companies, market products for such a small group of interested customers that the cost to make the product is higher than the price paid by the customer. There have to be enough customers who get a high value to support a high price.

How do the customer value, turnover, and profits relate to company value and shareholder value? The central concept is that investments (or capital employed) yielding returns greater than the cost of capital will create shareholder value, while those yielding less will decrease it. Returns are not just cash money today — they can also be future cash returns in the form of a stronger brand, more loyal customers, better core capabilities of employees, and a host of other value drivers of a business — but they must be cash returns at some point in time.

Company Value

Many traditional companies are managed basically by focusing on the account or book value, *i.e.*, **company value** equals assets minus liabilities, as defined in conventional financial reports. The major problem with classical book value is that intangibles like the brand value, the value of the personnel's satisfaction/motivation and skills, and the value of customer and supplier relationships are not included. Depending on the industry, this may be a very shortsighted view, one that does not take into account future values and opportunities.

Shareholder Value

Many venture capitalists, other professional investors, and financial analysts are using **shareholder value** calculations to estimate the value of a company, which translates into the estimated company market value or stock price. When a company is overvalued (the company value or stock price is higher than the shareholder value calculated), investors tend not to invest or to sell, and when the company is undervalued, they tend to invest/buy.

The principle of the shareholder value method is that a company's or enterprise's economic value — measured by its company value or share price — is determined by the sum (net present value) of all its anticipated future cash flows, adjusted by an interest rate known as the cost of capital and debt. Cash flow is therefore the key concept behind shareholder value, not turnover and not profits. They are important elements but not core measures of value for a running business. The enterprise value has three basic components: the forecast period value (present value of cash flow within the forecast period, normally 4-10 years), the continuing value better know as the terminal value (present value of cash flow after the forecast period), and the value of other investments, *e.g.*, stocks in other businesses, securities, or investments outside the normal operations. So:

Shareholder value = present value of cash flow within forecast period + present value of cash flow after forecast period + present value of investments – present value of cost of debt

Cash flow = net income – (cash tax + incremental working capital + incremental fixed investment)

Cash flows which are relevant for the value components are the incoming cash flow: net income, less the outgoing cash flow determined by tax, incremental working capital, and incremental fixed investments.

For new companies and especially "new economy" companies, the present value (PV) within the forecast period tends to be very small, so the focus is on the continuing values. This concept is very important for marketing too. In companies that have identified new market opportunities, it usually makes sense to spend heavily on new product development, developing the brand and opening up new markets. In this way, they pre-empt competition and build a leading strategic position in the industry. While such strategies generate value, they absorb rather than generate cash in the formative period or short run. Aggressive marketing strategies may well lead to minimal profits and negative cash flow in the first years, while simultaneously creating enormous value, which is reflected in the high figure for continuing value and in a rocketing share or company price. Microsoft, Intel, AOL, Nokia and Dell are examples of companies that have followed exactly this pattern. In contrast, companies with high profits and large cash flows tend to be mature businesses.

Valuation Challenges

These financial values are the objectives you should pursue as a company. But in order to achieve faster sales growth or higher profit margins, thereby improving the present value, you need strategies that relate to the drivers of shareholder value. For a typical business, there are three sets of relevant value drivers[27] that significantly influence shareholder value.

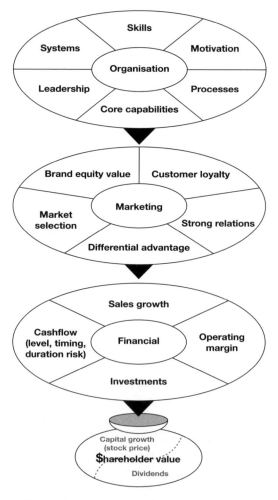

Figure 1.12   Sources of Shareholder Value

It's easy to boost cash flow or economic profit in the short-term by cutting back on long-term investments and marketing support; this is a common short-term problem solver. But such actions will result in a decline in the continuing value of the business and eventually in the share price. To determine whether a strategy makes sense, long-term cash flow or economic profits have to be estimated and discounted by the cost of capital. As we have discussed above, the intangibles like brands, skills, customer and supplier relationships are often the primary assets, at least in the beginning.

Creating a credible estimation of shareholder value requires attention to the areas listed below. Obviously, the more effort you put into this, the better the result. Not only will the company valuation be done properly, but — equally importantly – the executive, the owners, and the investors will be in agreement about the valuation.

- Forecasting future cash flow
- Determining the cost of capital, now and in the future
- Estimating the terminal value
- Determining the baseline valuation from where you start
- Identifying the opportunities for growth
- Predicting the stock market expectations for your industry vertical.

...And Next...

This chapter set the framework for creating a company in the post "e" era. We looked at business models, at whether to start fresh or modify, and at the meaning of value in the corporate context. Read on to start the process. First, how to get an idea for a business.

Chapter 2
The Business Idea

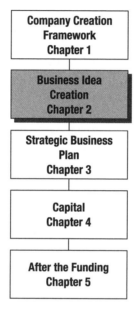

Success is 1% inspiration and 99% perspiration — with apologies to Edison

2.1
What is a Business Idea ?

To start a company you need a company idea, but to start doing business you need a business idea. The company idea and the business idea should be two different things and, for visionary companies, they are in fact very different. A business idea is an idea for a product or a service that can generate value for a customer and by doing so can generate profit for you. A company idea is an idea for how you can create a full business system in which the business idea can thrive. You might have a company idea but not a business idea when you start, like quite a few of the visionary companies, but you need one or more business ideas that create value for customers in order to be successful – make money.

There are two general archetypes of entrepreneurs: the market-oriented entrepreneur and the technology-oriented entrepreneur. The market-oriented entrepreneur focuses on market relations and customer needs in the business idea, whereas the technology-oriented one focuses on the product or technology there. The market-oriented entrepreneur's major challenge when defining the business idea is to consider whether his business concept is possible to pull off and what technology it will require. The technology-oriented entrepreneur's greatest challenge is to find out whether or not there is a market for his technology/product and where and how it can be implemented.

All entrepreneurs we have met have had, without exception, some structured thoughts about what they want to do, the foundation for a business idea. Some made it big, some made it big and then small, some never made it, and some were bought for a high price. Examples abound of successes and failures, names in Denmark like InCite/InCorp, ProActive, Visionik, and names in the U.S. like pets.com, and toys.com – failures — or eBay, a success. All entrepreneurs think their ideas are great, but reality can be brutal sometimes. The reasons for failure or hardship are many: maybe they were wrong about the idea, maybe the timing was wrong, or maybe they were just out of luck. Think of LetsBuyIt.com or Last-Minute.com: were they great ideas that didn't make it, or less than great ideas carried forward in the excitement of the dot.com era until they ran out of venture capital and cash?

Many ideas — neither great nor unique — make it one way or another through the incredible commitment of the entrepreneurs and the resources of the investors. But these mediocre ideas are soon the root of many company problems, the source of struggles to become profitable and healthy, and the reason behind many bankruptcies. The entrepreneurs behind these companies would have been better off using their energies and the investor's resources on great ideas, and therefore should have had guidance in evaluating whether an idea is truly great or not so great.

On the other hand, many great ideas never make it. Somewhere along the line they are choked by bad planning, shortage of funds, bad luck, de-motivated employees, or one of the many other reasons for not reaching their full potentials.

The fact is that some of the companies were built on ideas that were not business ideas. They were just thoughts on how the world should be, not ideas on how to deliver superior value to customers. A thought is just a thought, but a business idea embodies the promise of potential.

An idea is many things but, generally speaking, is …
- a transcendent entity that is a real pattern of which existing things are imperfect representations,[28]
- a new thought strong enough to change the status quo,
- something to make the strange familiar and the familiar new,
- a surprise with the element of inevitability, a shock resolved by relevance,
- a fresh perspective with roots in fundamental truths,
- a new combination of old elements,[29] and/or
- a connection between two or more things that creates a distinct new entity and new opportunity.

The good business idea can come from many sources, but it must be evaluated: can it be implemented?, how much value can it create for potential customers?, and to what extent is it different and better than what is on the market already?

2.2
The Business Idea in Context

Your business idea(s) will begin to describe the "what" of your future company. You will put much effort into expanding and detailing your idea until it becomes, in order, a strategic plan, a funding event, a company and an operational plan. However, even before you get to those steps, you need to understand where you are going and how best to check your direction during the process.

A good first step is to see whether your business idea includes the fundamental areas of business and whether it can be converted into a Mission Statement. (We cover mission statements in more detail in Chapter 3, but it is useful to begin thinking that way early.) A mission statement is a short (typically a few sentences), concise description of what your company does, such as "my company does xxx," or "my company builds yyy," or "my company is the zzz." It is important for you as the start-up entrepreneur to have a statement that lays out the foundation for your idea, delimits the business area, and lays out guidelines for how the business can be developed in the long run. You will use this mission statement everywhere — in the elevator, as the second slide in your fund-raising presentation, *etc.* The business fundamen-

tals, however, encompass more than the mission statement alone, including —
at minimum — needs/values, competence, and competition. You can do a
quick check of your business idea by seeing whether it covers those three
areas. If it doesn't, you need to change it. Don't make it longer; make it
clearer.

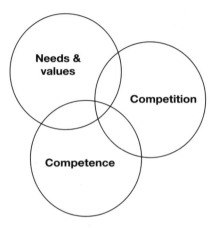

Figure 2.1   Business Idea Mix

Need/values
You should describe which needs you are striving to cover, with what values,
for whom, as well as how you are planning to cover them.

Competence
Special competence should be described, including the competence of the
team in relation to the current project. The total package must match the
needs and desires of the market.

Competition
Traditional companies analyze competitive matters through the use of
Michael Porter's 5-forces model[30] that outlines five types of competitive
forces:
- Industry competitors – rivalry among existing products/firms in geogra-
  phically defined areas
- Threat of new entrants
- Bargaining power of buyers
- Threat of substitute products or services
- Bargaining power of supplier(s).

Many strategists of the "new" economy have criticized this model, as it is
meant for businesses of the old economy where competitive conditions

were/are different. With the addition of two additional "forces," however, it has proved very useful for today's e-Business situation. They are the rapid obsolescence of digital technology and globalization – both driven by key features of the Internet.[31]

Digital technology

The power of digital technology and the speed of evolution of the next "killer app" have multiple impacts: a competitor can come out of nowhere with a new technology and make your products obsolete – think, for example, of the growth of optical networking components — and the life-spans of existing technologies are so short that constant product evolution is required.

Globalization

The Internet is global, which in effect means that you can no longer be considered a local, national or international player, rather a global one – or at least you have the option to become that in a much greater sense than earlier. It also means that you may encounter new and unforeseen competition that was not possible earlier on. The geographical barrier to entry has been low-ered dramatically.

In many markets there is a conscious attempt by the dominating companies to regulate the level of competition along with the amount of influence of the customer – think, for example, of the high fashion brands. With globalization it has become extremely difficult for these companies to retain their control, as the Internet has put power in the hands of the consumers. It also means that companies now need to think entirely differently, as their niche in the market can be threatened "overnight" by a newly-started competitor on the other side of the globe.

2.3
How to be Creative

The charter of the entrepreneur is to be able to spot big new business ideas. Some people have more natural talent in this area, but all of us can improve our capacity. Stimulating creative thinking – a necessity for coining a great business idea — is possible. That is why we have included this chapter in the book. The way to do it is threefold: firstly, we need to learn to think more creatively every day, all by ourselves; secondly, we need to create an environment that fosters creativity; and, last but not least, we need to be able to work together as a team to create and develop new ideas.

Our brains constitute enormous storehouses of materials used to generate ideas. The total sums of all things we have seen, touched, felt, read and learned, all the way from when we were kids, are up there, great reservoirs of knowledge. Thus all people have enormous capacities for creative thinking based on stored knowledge.

But we have made it hard for ourselves. Typically, the older we get, the harder it becomes. Adults are supposed to make decisions and expected to do the right thing. Adults function in very regulated systems: we pay bills on time, we go to work every day, we eat at the same time everyday, *etc*. As parents we have, with the best intentions, developed our school systems to train kids to think and function like adults, the faster the better. We learn that there is a right way to solve a problem and a wrong way. Slowly but surely, we lose our connection to spontaneous, free thinking, the creativity of our childhood. This is why millions of books are written and sold and billions of euros have been paid to expensive consultants for help.

The best advice for creative thinking is to reestablish the child's way of thinking. As adults we tend to approach problem-solving on the level of the analytical *vs*. heuristic/creative and the evaluative vs. generative. Analytical thinking is our most common approach. It teaches us to follow the path until the solution is in sight with a strict process drive. Heuristic thinking is to make the connection between, say, 3 different possible solutions, where 1+2+3 = "the creative solution." The generative approach is different from the evaluative process in that it is a continuing spiral of generation, evaluation, generation, evaluation, generation, evaluation, *etc*.

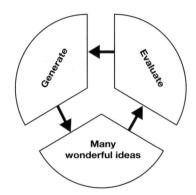

Figure 2.2   Business Idea Generation

The generative is accompanied by the evaluative because no idea is perfect; most ideas occur along a spectrum from worthless to flawless. The goal is to move ideas along the spectrum as far towards the perfect as possible.

From many sources, but especially from industries with a strong focus on creativity — communication and advertising – we have distilled seven principles of creative thinking that have helped companies unleash creativity and increase the quality of idea generation. They can be a good platform from which to start your development of a business idea:

Expand your horizons
Expand your platform of knowledge and experience. Use creative elements like visits to unlikely and exotic places, read books, study history, get a new hobby, take up a new sport, take a new way home from work everyday — anything that can help you to learn something new everyday. Creativity is a daily exercise and frame of mind, but new inspiration has to come from exploration. An interesting fact is that many significant scientific break-throughs come about when scientists switch fields. You have to know your field or business, but do not let this get in your way of seeing things from a new perspective.

Look for relations
Ideas are often new combinations of old elements. Broad knowledge and experience can help. Just think of Velcro, a new, strong competitor to buttons and zippers, or Federal Express, the first modern courier service in the U.S. Think about cyberspace, the linking of cables and computers in an anarchistic, decentralized network. The ability to see relationships leads to identification of general principles, underlying truths, and real customer insights. The use of metaphors and analogies can help, so look for relationships in other areas from your general knowledge. They can reveal a relationship in the new area you are exploring.

Be and act like a kid.
Heraklit once said, "Man is most nearly himself when he achieves the seriousness of a child at play." Kids are naturally creative, but in school they lose most of it because of neglect and devalued imagination. Adults often make virtues out of consistency and rigidity, which often leads to unnecessary focus on details, precision, and too much self-censorship. In some ways, man is the only species on earth that is so intelligent it can learn to be stupid.

Make sure it's fun

Try to be silly. Humor is the most fertile environment for creating ideas. Park the practical and sensible part of your brain somewhere at least once a day — find the kid in you. Some ideas might seem absurd but, as Einstein once said, "When there is no hope for the idea, celebrate absurdity."

Break every rule

Kids go beyond the rules and regulations in order to explore. To maximize strategic freedom of thought, you need to go beyond the rules of your own game. You need to work without prejudice and limitations. Kill the sacred cows. And make no assumptions when you start. Picasso's revolution in art came from the principle that every act of creation is, first of all, an act of destruction.

Think oppositely or "wrongly"

Don't be scared to do things wrongly. And let others do things wrongly too. When growing up, we try to be right all the time by editing our behavior and thinking before we speak. This attitude is guaranteed to kill an idea before we even know we have one. Take the chance or chances and reward risk-taking. As Einstein also said, "Anyone who has never made a mistake has never tried anything new."

Stay at it

Don't stop after you have found one idea. Nothing is more dangerous than an idea, if it is the only one you have. For every problem there is at least one solution that is simple, attractive and ... wrong. Always look for the second and third right answers and generate many ideas, a pool of different options, before deciding on one to follow.

2.4
Techniques for Innovative Thinking

If you need to develop an innovative business idea, there are a number of techniques you can use. We have often found inspiration in four lines of thinking – "milk production,"[32] removing the value barriers,[33] finding new combinations, and maximizing the strategic degrees of freedom — in order to come up with new business ideas, products and services that can achieve maximum differentiation from the competition. But the biggest insight of all is that analytical thinking is just one out of many ways of to come up with a great business idea. Creativity is often restricted if analytical thinking is its sole or primary basis, and creative thinkers are rarely found amongst analysis-minded business professionals with business school backgrounds.

Milk production

This technique of imitating a cow recognizes that ideas appear on the surface of the mind, but are built on a foundation in the subconscious, *i.e.*, through rumination. All idea creation follows the same process, either consciously or unconsciously. It's a technique that can be learned and controlled and, once learned, increases the ability to produce.

Figure 2.3   The Milk Production Technique

Stage 1: Grazing

No browsing, no milk. Gather the raw materials, the more material the better. Obviously, make sure that no one else has already implemented your initial idea successfully.

Stage 2: Chew and observe.

Speculate. Work the information over in your mind and look for relation-ships. Listen for the meaning instead of looking for it. Write down practical ideas and try to fit the puzzle together until you reach the "hopeless" stage.

Stage 3: Digest
It's time to distill the speculations, to incubate. Walk away from the problem and let your subconscious work. Leave time for inspiration to arise, for the crystals to appear.

Stage 4: Milk making
The idea appears, invariably when you least expect it — in the shower, walking the dog, when you are half asleep. It bubbles up from the subconscious if you let it. Don't overwork your brain with other tasks, cannibalizing your mental energy.

Stage 5: Milking
After the elation of discovery, the cold gray light of dawn sets in. You need to make the idea fit the practicalities. Don't protect the idea by hiding it; instead, nurture and improve it and expose it to others. Good ideas have self-expanding properties, and others may see possibilities you have missed.

Stage 6: Aggregation
You need to use a group to create a lot of milk, to create big ideas. None of us is as smart alone as all of us are together. Aggregation fosters innovation and teamwork, it gains greater commitment through the use of others' ideas, it identifies correct roles and responsibilities, and it increases the odds for a win/win outcome. To aggregate successfully, you need to follow a few guidelines:

- Do proper planning. First outline the objective, what you want to do, and the headline. Then do an analysis of why there is a problem or opportunity, what its history is, why it is your responsibility, what you have thought or tried, what would be the ideal solution, and whether the problem/-opportunity should be reworded.
- Separate process from content.
- Assign roles and responsibilities.
- Be generative vs. evaluative. Be careful not to subject new thoughts to criteria that lead to over-quick go/no-go decisions. This might kill a great idea.
- Apply in/out listening.
- Do headlining.
- Apply developmental thinking, with itemized responses.

These can be put into a simple task headline and analysis form that you can use directly:

A. Task headline (a one-sentence statement that reflects what you want to work on. To give the session an action orientation, it's recommended that you start the statement with words such as "devise ways to ...," "develop a strategy for ...," "generate alternatives for ...," *etc.*)

B. Analysis (enough information to get the group — or if working alone, yourself — going and answering the questions below. Ideally, the entire analysis should take no more than three or four minutes.)

B1. Why is this a problem or opportunity?
B2. What is a brief history of the problem/opportunity?
B3. Why is this your responsibility? What is your role (decision maker, implementer, or the like)?
B4. What have you already tried or thought of? (notes to keep yourself from reinventing the wheel and to give examples of what you are and are not looking for)
B5. What would be the ideal solution?
B6. As a result of this analysis, do you want to reword the problem/-opportunity? (Has an underlying issue surfaced which is the real problem?, is a prior idea perfect but needs to be sold differently?, *etc.*)

Removing Value Delivery Barriers

Figure 2.4   Removing Barriers

About ten years ago there was a push in most countries to get people to have a fax machine at home. It was believed that price and size (technology) were the major barriers to a large customer demand. So the fax companies made machines the same size as laptop computers and priced a fax equal to a small TV set — but still no demand. One player – Sharp — analyzed the customer situation and concluded that most people's objective in buying a fax was the desire to send documents accurately and easily, but potential customers considered fax machines neither accurate nor easy to use. Why? Because small letters became illegible, rows were sometimes skipped, heat-sensitive paper was required, paper came out rolled up, messages were not received because of being out of paper, two phone lines were necessary, and the machines were noisy at night. These problems could be overcome by securing error correction functions, adapting the machines to the use of regular paper, building in room for a spare roll or increasing memory, adjusting the system so one telephone line could be used, and incorporating a sound mute at night. The solution was an improvement plan for the product and an imaginative communication campaign with TV commercials demonstrating the accuracy and ease of use of the new fax. Within months, sales of the new Sharp faxes soared, and Sharp soon became the no. 1 fax supplier to private homes.

In customer value delivery there are often bottlenecks that cause a difference between the value desired by customers and the value propositions of existing products and services. A great business idea can be coined by closing such a gap. To profit from understanding this market potential, you need to identify the bottlenecks through a rational, analytical process and then apply creative minds to solve the problems and to communicate the business idea to potential customers. The following five-step innovation model can be used to develop business ideas or to secure an understanding of whether or not a given business idea is set on a strong customer value foundation:

- **Correct understanding of potential customers' core objectives** — send documents accurately and easily

- **Key obstacles to purchase** — neither accurate nor easy to use

- **Customer objections** – small letters become illegible, sometimes skips rows, requires heat-sensitive paper, paper comes out rolled up, fax not received because of being out of paper, two phone lines necessary, noisy at night

- **Possible product improvements** – add error corrections functions, permit use of regular paper, build in room for a spare roll or increased memory, adjust so that one telephone line can be used, mute sound at night

- **Key communication idea for customer interface** – communicate improved accuracy and ease of use through TV commercials.

This model can be used to structure the development of a business idea, especially if it is for a product or "tangible" non-complex service.

Creating convergences

Figure 2.5   Convergence Model

Many new business ideas are often combinations of known elements.[34] Mitsubishi put the microwave in the oven range to overcome the space problem. Bang & Olufsen combined remote controls for the TV, radio, VCR, CD-player, *etc.* into one. Ericsson is combining mobile phones and digital assistants into a new handheld device. CMS for Web sites, WAP solutions, IDTV, *etc.* are being combined into multi-platform CMS by, for example, Trippledash and Agency.com.

Elements can vary, but elements to combine could be existing products with existing functions, existing packaging, *etc.* Take, for instance, TV innovations:

Existing product	Other product	New product opportunity
TV	Set top box	Interactive digital TV
TV	HiFi	Multimedia center
TV remote control	Light switches	Appliances remote control
TV	Computer	Leisure work station
TV	Gameboy	Entertainment center with docking station

Maximizing strategic freedom to deliver customer value

If you work from scratch, then everything has to be set up and you have the ultimate strategic freedom to design your business idea and business system any way you like, as long as they can realistically generate profitable value. Strategic freedom is freedom in the conceptual development of how to deliver value in new and innovative ways.

You, a coffee producer, might want to coin a new business idea for coffee makers. Customer analysis shows that customers use coffee makers because they want superior taste in their coffee. The key strategic elements in making superior coffee are: the quality of the water, the beans, the grinding method, the time between grinding and the pouring of water, the temperature of the water being poured, the time and quantity of air contact from when the coffee is ready until it is drunk, and the temperature of the coffee when it is being poured and drunk.

For maximum strategic freedom the company needs to control all the elements, but for practical reasons you need to decide what you want to control and compare this to what you actually control. As a traditional producer of coffee brands, you only control the beans. Amazingly, most coffee-maker user manuals just say, "Pour water," not mentioning the quality of the water, the beans, or the distribution of ground coffee. Indeed, current user manuals say nothing about the taste of the coffee, which is what customers want to know about. The only benefit coffee-makers deal with is that coffee can be ready in 5 minutes vs. the usual 15 minutes for percolators.

Based on this type of analysis, one idea would be to include a grinder and a de-chlorinator within the coffeemaker. (The company that did that sold over two million units.) Another idea would be to make a closed brewing system with no airflow before the coffee is poured from the can. The can itself would include an airtight lid that opens automatically when coffee is being poured.

The point of the story is this: you need to understand what customers are really looking for, you need to find out how many different ways you can deliver on it, and then consider if the value delivery is, in fact, cost effective. By doing so, you are maximizing the strategic degrees of freedom:[35]

Understand the customers' objectives
Coffee makers are used because people want to drink good coffee.

Find ultimate values
Key question: what is good coffee? Key answers: good taste, pleasant aroma, hot.

Develop product/business ideas based on maximum strategic freedom
Draw out the taste of the coffee beans better, grind coffee beans visibly and let out a little aroma from the grinder, control the thermostat function to optimize heat, coat the can, and put a covering lid on.

Estimate investment in development, production, distribution, marketing, turnover and profit potentials for ideas.
Figure out if any/all of the above is doable, with a reasonable resulting profit.

Expanding the business idea with a Customer Value Mix
When you conduct customer analysis, it is quite easy to analyze the rational decisions and objectives of potential customers. But be careful: key decision-making or buying is not done purely for rational, conscious reasons; in fact some products or services are not selected based on rational reasons at all but rather for other reasons. Today, many customers believe that there are many products that can satisfy their needs; they all deliver performance in more or less the same way. Decisions between possible suppliers are then driven by other values.

Rational   Sensual   Emotional

Figure 2.6   Customer Value Mix

You need to make sure that you understand the more hidden factors of potential customers' buying behavior, those based on their sensual and emotional values. A host of studies of consumer behavior document three basic levels of values that customers experience. They can help you plan the full scope of your value proposition:

- **Rational values** — *e.g.*, performance, speed, cost/benefit relationships, time of delivery, usability, service level, durability, and quality,

- **Sensual values** — the experience or contact with the product, *e.g.*, the feel, taste, smell, looks, design, sound,

- **Emotional values** — *e.g.*, attractiveness, brand, imagery, specific feelings (*e.g.*, safety, reliability, trendy, modern/old-fashioned) and signal values.

Rational or material values are often in focus, especially when technology-focused entrepreneurs develop products or services and the customers are professionals (B2B). "The new software can do this or that, isn't that great?" is a common line used to describe the value delivered by a technological entrepreneur.

Most entrepreneurs overlook the sensual and emotional values of a product or service. Take computer producers, for example: up until the launch of the iMac, most computers were square, gray, boring boxes of technology with purely functional features. The iMac design put an extra esthetic value into the game and has taken huge market shares, even though the technology is a niche platform *vs.* the Microsoft PC/Windows technology.

When analyzing customer objectives, a means of revealing non-rational values must be included to get a full picture of the customer situation. This insight underlies many of the world's most successful brands like Coca-Cola, Oracle, Miele, Mercedes, Intel, and IBM. Sensual and emotional values are often harder to copy by competitors than rational values. Coca-Cola has been out-performed many times in taste tests by other colas like Pepsi, but is by far the most preferred soft drink worldwide because of the specific taste, look and feel of the bottle, and the attractive imagery that goes with Coca-Cola.

Oracle is by far the largest brand in high-end databases even though others sometimes out-perform it in tests of price/performance. What Oracle delivers to customers on top of its technology are safety, reliability, and reassurance that other high-profile companies also use Oracle, all emotional values.

A host of brand studies documents that it is the sensual or emotional values that secure brands' strong long-term positions, whereas the rational are often only short-term advantages. The essence is that — however you plan what values you are going to deliver – in fact you deliver a mix of all three types. Rational values are often faster to build and more visible but at the same time more short-lived than sensual and emotional values. Successful brands often sustain long-term competitive advantages by delivering unique sensual and emotional values. High-tech brands built on rational values are quickly out-performed by other competitors and can only expect to gain a temporary short-term competitive advantage.

2.5
Checking Your Idea(s)

Now you have one or more business ideas which you have fleshed out and which make sense to you. It is time to do a sanity check with some friendly outsiders — not too friendly because you want honest advice, but friendly enough that they will take your idea(s) seriously. Realize that it is difficult at this stage for outsiders – even the most experienced strategists — to evaluate your business concept: your strategic business plan is not yet developed, and an analysis of the work has not yet been completed.

Nevertheless, it is still crucial at this stage to outline the full business concept by performing a general analysis of the three most critical elements: the business idea, yourself and the team, and the necessary technology. The reason, of course, is that nobody wants to waste a lot of time on a start-up that will not last. A strong business concept is a threesome: a strong business idea in its own right, a solid team, and a set of processes and procedures that will work. The paragraphs below are not a complete checklist. You should add whatever additional points/areas of relevance that seem pertinent to your specific business idea(s). Most importantly of all, be open at this point. The more you discuss your idea(s) now, the better the end result will be.

By the way, if you have not gathered a team yet, it is even more important that you have one or more outsiders whom you trust look at your idea(s). This may seem painful, but it will help you immeasurably in the long run.

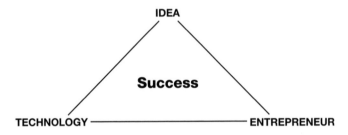

Figure 2.7   Business Concept Creation

The Business Idea

Most business concepts spring from a public need or demand (with a few exceptions, of course). The developmental techniques and content of a business idea are already described above. With the business idea outlined, you can evaluate the potential of your business by taking a critical view of the following elements as they appear in your business concept:

Areas of potential use

Describe what uses your business concept has and how/why it is different from those of existing suppliers on the market.

Uniqueness

Which unique qualities does your business idea have for the potential customer, and how many unique advantages does it have?

The market(s)

How great is the volume and concentration of the market(s), *i.e.*, how many people need your product and are their needs sporadic or constant? You should also consider whether the market is homogeneous – characterized by standard solutions, or heterogeneous — characterized by differentiated, individual solutions. The maturity and stability of the market are also important, analyzable elements. Is it a brand new market, a pioneer market, a growing market or a saturated market?

The customers
How great a value does the business concept bring to the customer, and is it a low- or high-focus area? The general loyalty of the market/customers should also be looked at in order to evaluate the potential for switching.

Covering a need
How is the need that created your product being satisfied in the market today, with what value mix, and what will that need probably be like in the future? It is important to analyze and evaluate all of the different needs your product or service will be covering. Make sure to separate the product features from the customer benefits and needs. There is no customer need or demand for an 8 and one-half millimeter drill; the customer's desire is to make an 8 and one-half millimeter hole. Some entrepreneurs, especially the technology-driven ones, have a problem seeing this difference. A product is not superior or competitive in the mind of a potential user because of a set of unique features or attributes. What makes it an interesting product is that it addresses a specific need in a unique, different, more entertaining, or cheaper way and by so doing can deliver superior value to the customer.

The Entrepreneur
It is very difficult to analyze yourself because we are subjective, not objective. If you have all or part of your team, use each other – when possible — to evaluate human aspects. At a minimum, you should take the following pointers into consideration:

Economy
Finding out how to finance your project is, of course, a crucial factor, determining also on which financial level your business concept lies – if it's a realistic one at all. Key questions are: can you finance the development up to the point when you can expect capital from external partners, or, are you willing or able to finance the start-up process further than that yourself?

Technology
You should analyze and evaluate whether you and your team can develop your business concept both from a business and a technological point of view.

Yourself and the team
This is where it gets tough – analyzing and evaluating one's self. You should look at professional expertise, but not forget the personal qualities.

Reputation
Your reputation is of importance in customer- and supplier relations, in competition, and among partners in general. Do you have the credibility needed?

Network
A personal and business network is immensely important. Your personal network must be evaluated, and you should determine whom you can rely on in the starting phase.

Family
Being an entrepreneur means a lot of hard work, no matter how great your idea is. Therefore it is critical that your closest relatives express their acceptance and support prior to starting a project.

If you are on your own in the first phase of the project, have a second party — whom you trust and who will give it to you straight — evaluate the points above.

The Technology
The last area to analyze and evaluate is the technology for your business idea. The problem with technology is often underestimated, both by market-oriented entrepreneurs and by technology-oriented ones, though for different reasons. The market-oriented entrepreneur may not understand the complexities of a new or different way of doing things because he/she is not technologically oriented, while the technologically-oriented entrepreneur may "know it all" and think that, because it is easy for him/her, it will be easy for future users. In either case, a mistake results that can have fatal consequences as technology becomes ever more important, whether in "e" or not. Appropriate technology is really what keeps business running. Remember to analyze and evaluate the following technical elements:

Complexity
How complex is the technology you (not your customer) will be using in your business? The advantage of highly-complex technology versus low-end technology is that it is not easily copied, but, on the downside, it can be difficult to obtain qualified craftspeople for the job, internally or externally. Look at the total life-cycle cost of the technology — what it will cost to implement and what it will cost to maintain. Is your team ready for it?

Functionality
Which functions should your project have, and can they be developed in a timely and cost-effective fashion? If the functionality is very complex, can you phase the development so that you start with a simpler implementation?

Intellectual rights
Is there any part of the technology that can be – or already has been — protected by patent or copyright, *etc.*?

Life span
Where in its life span is your technology, and how long will it last? Is it "bleeding edge?"

...And Next...
This chapter covered the development of a business idea, how you define and describe your vision and – hopefully – your passion for the next little while. Now you've got to sell it! Read on for how to create your Strategic Business Plan.

Chapter 3
The Strategic Business Plan

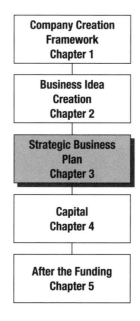

Create opportunities instead of just reacting to them – that's what strategic planning is all about!

Main Entry: **strat·e·gy**
Function: *noun*
Inflected Form(s): *plural* **-gies**
Etymology: Greek *stratEgia* generalship, from *stratEgos*
Date: 1810
1 a (1) : the science and art of employing the political, economic, psychological, and military forces of a nation or group of nations to afford the maximum support to adopted policies in peace or war (2) : the science and art of military command exercised to meet the enemy in combat under advantageous conditions
b : a variety of or instance of the use of strategy
2 a : a careful plan or method : a clever <u>stratagem</u> **b** : the art of devising or

employing plans or <u>stratagems</u> toward a goal
3 : an adaptation or complex of adaptations (as of behavior, metabolism, or structure) that serves or appears to serve an important function in achieving evolutionary success <foraging *strategies* of insects>

Merriam-Webster

In Chapter 3, we shall take a look at how to develop and structure a strategic business plan, why we need it, and what we will be using it for. This is an essential part of starting a company and running it later on. No strategic plan — no money, no company. You will use it to raise money, to recruit with, and to remind yourself every so often what it is you are doing, particularly at moments of self-doubt. The strategic plan is a living document. As you go forward getting funding and starting your company, expect to change it to reflect current reality.

3.1
Introduction to Strategic Planning

What is Strategic Planning?
In its simplest form, strategic planning is a roadmap of getting from one place to another in a structured and orderly fashion. Our perception of strategic planning involves a strategy that is as simple as possible, so that it may be easily communicated, incorporated and put into action within the organization.

Strategic planning is somewhat like the planning of an airplane flight — you want to get from point A to point B in a structured, orderly fashion with the flight as smooth as possible. Would you even consider getting on a plane if you knew the pilot hadn't planned the flight or – even worse – was not in control of flying the plane? Of course not! However, thoughtless business executives do it all the time — starting without a Strategic Business Plan, that is.

Let us briefly take a look at the planning process a pilot would go through before taking off; look for the business parallels in parentheses.

First, the captain (CEO) goes through the names of the crew (the management) and the passengers that have checked in (the employees) on the flight in question (strategic business unit — SBU). He then meets with his co-pilot (COO) and the planning (strategic planning) begins. The first task is to calculate the amount of fuel (liquidity) the plane (the company) will need. Subsequently, the weather (competition) is examined at the destination (the market) and at an alternative airport (alternative market), preferably close to the main destination. They would also consider whether or not they would have the wind against them (market situation), and how heavy the plane is (size of the company) — the heavier the plane, the more fuel (liquidity) will be needed. Next, the pilots study the "notam" (market conditions), an old expression that means "notifications to airmen." It informs the pilots (CEO and COO) of technical installations (special market conditions) at the airports (markets) and along the route (the strategy) and whether there are any repairs (bad market conditions/access barriers) on the runway (core product) that may influence the flight (SBU). It would be unwise to make a flight towards an airport (market) where the runways (core products) are closed (out of date, *etc.*).

The pilots (CEO and COO) then enter the course digits (individual areas of the strategy plan) into a computer. It outputs information on the weather (competition) and notams (market conditions) on a number of airports (markets) along the course (years of the business plan), plus the estimated weight of the plane (size of the company). Weather (competition) information is provided as a type of code (conclusion), and there are strict requirements for how good it must be depending on the plane's (the company's) and the airport's (the market's) equipment (market value/potential). At least one alternative airport (alternative market) must be planned that you can fly to (change strategy to) if landing at the original destination is impossible (negative changes in market conditions) and the weather (competition) at the alternative airport is better than that at the original destination. If the weather (competition) at the destination (market) is very bad, you will need two alternative airports (markets) and therefore even more fuel (liquidity). Apart from enough fuel (liquidity) to get to the destination (market) and further on to the alternative airport (alternative market), you will need a backup supply (alternative strategy and liquidity) of 5%, plus an additional 30 minutes of flight time. It is up to the captain (CEO) to decide whether or not to bring even more fuel (liquidity).

When the pilots (CEO and COO) have decided how much fuel (liquidity) to bring, a flight plan (strategic plan) is printed with the course (the time period) calculated with the amount of fuel (liquidity). Simultaneously, a message is sent to the station (administration employees) stating how much fuel they will be taking on (stake), after which the station makes sure it happens (operational execution).

The weather (competition) should be monitored along the way to make sure it is consistent with the plan (strategic plan). Fuel (liquidity) consumption should also be paid attention to; if more than expected (budgeted) is used, a re-planning (change of strategy) or, at worst, a temporary landing (total change of strategy) and refueling (new liquidity) may be required.

Obviously, flying a plane and running a company are two completely different things, but there are some interesting parallels. Though you do not need a pilot's license to "fly" a business, you will suffer quite unpleasant consequences if you do not take the development, execution, and maintenance of your strategy as seriously as the pilot does the planning of his flight.[36]

Anyway, back to reality. The three primary stakeholders in a business are usually the owners, the employees and the customers or future customers. The owners' primary interest is the Return On Investment (ROI), whereas the employees focus on their own personal development and finances and the conditions under which they work. The customers focus both on the products and/or services that meet their needs and on their general relationship with the company.

The strategy process has three general steps:

- Setting the guidelines for the strategic business plan;

- Developing the strategic business plan;

- Implementing, executing, and modifying the strategic business plan.

A successful strategy is characterized by the participation of all members of the organization, from management to the operational level. All members of your organization must be well aware of the mission, must buy into it, and must — to the degree they are able – provide feedback based on their day-to-day experiences in the market.

The development process for the Strategic Plan must – as must the plan itself – be both proactive and dynamic: proactive, in the sense that you should have a well-defined strategy in mind and stick to it, and dynamic, in the sense that the market, the technologies, and the economy as a whole change rapidly and you must continuously re-evaluate the situation to ensure that your underlying assumptions are still valid. If they change, you should rethink your plan. It is of no use to have a stagnant strategy — often seen in the old economy, not allowing for adjustments and modifications. The new economy moves too fast for that.

Before you start the actual business plan, it is important to have a brainstorming session in which you contemplate the company's stronger and weaker sides. This is a process of getting to know your company.

The first overall questions you should ask yourself as an entrepreneur are the following:

- What are our core qualifications and what business should we be in?

- Who are our customers and why should they be loyal to us?

- How and why is our business concept going to create added value, and how do we plan to make money out of the added value?

After that, you should analyze your stronger and weaker sides, as well as go through the following points:

- What is the mission (purpose, or where am I heading)?

- What am I especially proud of about my company?

- What can motivate my employees?

- What are my core products/services?

- What are my strategic business processes?

- What are my non-strategic business processes?

- What can and should be outsourced?

- Who are my potential business partners?

- How many SBU's do I have?

- How financially secure am I?

- How dependant am I on the different products/services?

Please note that the above is in no way a complete checklist, just a few words for inspiration. The appendix contains a structured set of questions that one of us has used to facilitate this process.

The Strategic Business Plan

Many entrepreneurs start their company without first developing a business plan – big mistake! Starting a new company requires thorough preparation and planning, which is just what a business plan deals with. If, for example, a newly started company needs venture capital, a business plan is actually mandatory. This should not be the only incentive to develop a plan, however, since it is also a strategic navigation tool and an investigation of the business concept.

Developing a business plan is a time-consuming process that forces participants to thoroughly examine all aspects of the business concept. This is one of the advantages of developing a business plan before getting started: no stone of the business concept is left unturned. This usually results in both modification of the original concept and validation of it.

It is not easy to develop a business plan, as you constantly need to stay creative and analytical. The process usually involves a great deal of research as well, both before and during creation of the plan. We will inspire you on that subject at the end of this chapter.

To create a Strategic Business Plan:

- You must have a purpose,

- You must know where you are heading,

- You must know where the market is heading,

- You must have an objective,

- You must have a plan and timings,

- You must monitor your progress,

- You must modify your efforts along the way according to your plan, and

- You must modify your strategy according to the market situation.

A business plan helps you to estimate the business concept and the market and helps you to understand the workings of a rising enterprise. Developing such a plan is a systematic process in the creation of a company and, at the same time, a tool for the final decisions on and details of a company start-up. It is also usually a process in which new information and ideas evolve, resulting in some redesign of the original business concept.

In order to end up with a sound business concept that is adapted to current market conditions and circumstances, it is very important that the basic idea and accompanying assumptions — the concept — are the point of reference for the business plan. It is also important, however, that the business plan be dynamic, *i.e.*, that it can be changed and adjusted along the way as new information and conditions arise. The goal is to be flexible without losing one's bearings, thus ensuring that the company is always well-adapted and constantly in touch with its original plans and objectives.

As a final remark, if your business concept involves products and/or services that are not homogeneous, you may benefit from using several different Strategic Business Units (SBU), making separate strategic business plans for each SBU. If starting a business is like juggling, starting a business with multiple heterogeneous units is like juggling bowling balls, meat cleavers, and lit torches at the same time: you have to handle each one differently.

The Process of Developing a Strategic Business Plan
There is no instruction manual for creating a business plan. However, the usual process for a new business concept is to work towards the objective, starting from the business idea and going step by step, dealing with expected – and unexpected – issues, uncertainties and possible risks along the way. Expect both the strategy and the objective to evolve as you go.

With *existing* business concepts, on the other hand, you will in most cases be able to work backwards from the objective in a systematic and logical way since the objective can be relatively clearly defined from the beginning.

Not surprisingly, e-Business projects are typically developed according to the first method, as the Internet market is currently in an explosive phase of development and is sometimes quite unpredictable. Also, a lot of new e-Business projects are quite innovative. They involve a learning process in which insights and logic are developed underway, also in further strategic work.

Typical e-Business projects are therefore not developed as systematically as traditional ones. In turn, their strategic planning and processing are very different from the ways of the "old" economy.

Before we go any further, some general advice and guidelines for developing a business plan:

- Your business plan must be comprehensible and written in a manner that allows the target group to properly understand it.

- Your business plan must have a logical structure.

- Your business plan must focus more on the future than the past.

- Your business plan must not be too optimistic; it should convey a realistic image of the project.

- Your business plan must openly discuss the risks and challenges the company is faced with and include details on how to overcome them.

- The business plan must deal with who is going to run the company and make sure there is an efficient and qualified management team.

- The business plan must plainly demonstrate the investment potential of the company, with details of what investors will gain from it in the long run.

- Last but not least, your business plan must be as simple as you can make it. The sooner the reader gets to the "Aha, but of course" moment, the better.

To gain a better sense of perspective, you might want to write down the business plan step by step, based on a pre-defined structure, and mark off any areas along the way that are either not quite settled yet or lack information of some sort. You can then revise these areas later on when you have gained sufficient information.

During the process of developing a business plan, it will go through a period of frequent modifications and adjustments based on newly acquired information and analyses. This may lead to a total redefinition of the business concept when the plan is finished or, at worst, a conclusion that the business concept in question is not valid at all.

However, it is very important to evaluate the business concept and define the company's business foundation before the business plan is executed. Basic information on, for example, market conditions should also be produced before development on the business plan begins.

It is also important to observe the process of creating a business plan. It's a great chance to find out what individual participants are especially good at and in which areas they complement each other.

Areas a Business Plan applies to

While a business plan has many different applications, in general the following areas are key:

- As a strategic navigational tool,

- As a communication tool,

- As a decision support tool.

A business plan is a strategic navigational tool that ensures your company stays on track, a communications tool that informs partners internally and externally about the company's mission and strategy, *etc.*, and a decision support tool that helps you make the right decisions along the way.

Strategic navigational tool

A business plan is a strategic navigational tool that describes the company on a strategic level and builds the overall framework for the company's development. Its primary purpose is to give the company a tool to guide it in the right direction towards its objectives and to raise funds, if appropriate.

The predefined activities in the Strategic Business Plan must be brought down to a tactical and operational level in order to plant the business plan firmly in the organization and distribute responsibility to the right employees, especially in areas concerning production, product development, and marketing. Thus the strategic plan will include some operational planning for the first periods covered.

Please note that for smaller and medium sized businesses it is often all right to merge the tactical and operational plans; this depends on the company in question and its complexity.

Communication tool

Another important application of a business plan is its use as a communication tool, both internally within the company and externally with the rest of the world, including business partners, investors, suppliers, financing sources, *etc.*

It is essential that the business plan is adapted to the target group in question, in both content and language. An investor, for example, will typically prefer a business plan that offers a quick outline of the company with supplementary in-depth documentation.

If the company is using the business plan to acquire funding from venture capitalists, the plan will be a means of communication aimed at reaching that objective. If so, realize that venture capitalists look primarily at the following issues regarding an unproven business entity:

- A unique and "unbeatable" product or service,

- An experienced management team,

- An ROI that exceeds their internal hurdle rates.

Decision support tool

A business plan is also a tool that can help a company make the right decisions.

Using the business plan this way is not intended exclusively for management; any employee should be able to look at the business plan and use it to make decisions every day. Before you can achieve this, the plan must be firmly rooted in the organization so everyone knows it and thus knows where the company is heading.

3.2
The Structure and Contents of a Strategic Business Plan

There is no predefined structure for a Strategic Business Plan. However, based on our many years of experience, we have been able to come up with the framework shown in figure 3.1. The figure will be the basis for our business plan walk-through in this chapter. Please note that the points can be listed in the plan in whatever order seems most logical and comprehensible to the recipient/reader. In fact, it is usually a good idea to find out whether the group(s) to whom you are going to present this have any particular idiosyncrasies regarding presentation. If so, format at least the presentation that way, and, as necessary, reformat it for the next audience.

EXECUTIVE SUMMARY	Company Profile and Mission Statement Company Overview Market Description Objectives, Strategies, Strategic Activities and Goals Resources Marketing Strategy Financial Plan Conclusion
1. COMPANY PROFILE AND MISSION STATEMENT	The Business Concept The Company Profile The Mission Statement
2. COMPANY OVERVIEW	Legal Business Description Organizational Structure Board of Directors Management Team Key Personnel Strategic Alliances
3. MARKET DESCRIPTION	Market Definition Customer Profiles Competition Company Positioning Risk
4. OBJECTIVES, STRATEGIES, STRATEGIC ACTIVITIES AND GOALS	Objectives Strategies Strategic Activities Goals
5. RESOURCES	People Facilities Equipment
6. MARKETING STRATEGY	Overall Marketing Strategy Competitive Position Product/Brand Channels Pricing Customer Communication and Interaction
7. FINANCIAL PLAN	Assumptions Financial Statements Capital Statements Exit and Payback Strategy
8. SUPPORTING DOCUMENTS	

Figure 3.1   Strategic Business Plan Table of Contents

3.3
The Executive Summary

The first part of a business plan is, in fact, the last one to be written as it contains a short and precise summary of the essential sections of the plan and a conclusion on the business concept and the business plan.

The conclusion should contain the risks connected with the project and suggestions regarding financing, including financial needs.

The summary and conclusion should not extend beyond one or two pages.

This is the first – **and for many external readers the last** – part of the business plan they read!   Make it the best you can; you have only one chance to capture the reader.

3.4
Company Profile and Mission Statement

The section of the company profile and mission statement consists of:

The Business Concept,

The Company Profile, and

The Mission Statement

The Business Concept

A description of the company's background and idea is a significant part of the business plan, as this is the core material. Therefore clarity and precision in your description are especially important.

The idea usually springs from either a new need in the market niche of the business concept in question or from the introduction of a new product or technology. Describe the background of the idea and how it originated. Also cover the overall backgrounds of project participants, their experience and competence, answering the implicit question, "Why is this group of people competent to operate in this space?"

The business idea should be further described and explained, and arguments should be provided as to why customers would choose this product/service rather than existing products on the market, if any. This is achieved by describing the properties of the idea, along with its advantages and benefits for customers.

Company Profile

The Company Profile is a summary of key information on the company being established. It usually provides details on which line of business the company is in and which geographical areas it will be covering. It also covers the product area, including quality and price levels, and which functions will be handled internally and externally.

It is very important that the project participants describe the company's general objectives and specific measurable goals, such as sales, profits and market share, *etc*. Typically these items are listed in bullet form in this section, then expanded upon in later sections.

The following areas are usually described in the Company Profile section:

- What line of business is the company in?

- What product areas will the company be selling in?

- Which geographical areas will the company be covering?

- Which functions will be taken care of by the company itself?

- Which functions will be assigned to other companies?

- What quality and price levels will the company operate on? and

- What general objectives does the company have?

Mission Statement

The Mission Statement is a short, concise description of exactly what the company will be doing, which needs it will be covering in the market, for which target groups, how it will be doing so now and in the future, and, finally, how the company is differentiated from its competitors.

You can also say that the Mission Statement addresses the following:

- Which needs will the company satisfy?

- What market exists with these needs?

- How will the company differentiate its offering? and

- Why will it be successful in doing so?

Some companies separate this area into two parts, a mission and a vision, the latter also sometimes referred to as the "guiding star." In this separation, the mission portion basically states where the company currently is, while the vision states where it wants to go — hence the "guiding star" image. The reason why the term "mission" is used throughout this book is that some countries do not use the "vision" term in this context, as is, for example, usually the case in the USA, where only the Mission Statement is used. But how you choose to do it is entirely up to you.

The Mission Statement should, of course, be revised if or whenever the company changes its course or business area. If the company's business fundamentals — usually a more thorough description of needs, competencies and competition — have been defined by project participants before the business plan is developed, the Mission Statement can usually be developed fairly quickly and precisely.

The Business Fundamentals are often compared to the company's Mission Statement, but the former are, in our opinion, a more thorough description of needs, competencies and the competitive situation. Consequently, the Business Fundamentals must draw the limits of the business area and point out how the company can develop in the long term. A short and precise description of the Business Fundamentals thus accompanies the company's Mission Statement.

The Business Fundamentals consist of the following three main areas:

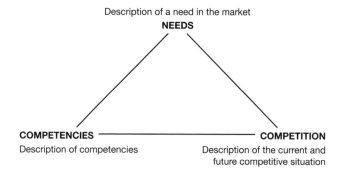

Figure 3.2   The Competition Triangle

Needs

You will have to describe which needs you are planning to cover, for whom, and how you are planning on doing it.

Competencies

Special competencies should be described, including competencies the team will be using to realize the project. It is, of course, important that the competencies match those required by the market.

Competition

This is where the current and future competitive situation of the market is described.

The purpose of defining the company's Mission Statement is to easily communicate the company's business principles and give everyone, both internally and externally, a common understanding of the company's fundamental functions – what it will actually be doing. The statement is also used to outline the company's areas of interest, *e.g.*, what it will and will not be dealing with. If you step outside these boundaries later on, the statement will have to be modified!

3.5
Company Overview

The Company Overview consists of:

> The legal business description,

> The organizational structure,

> The Board of Directors,

> The management team,

> Key personnel, and

> Strategic alliances.

Legal Business Description[37]

The legal business description usually spans four areas, one of which is the company's legal name and any registered secondary names. A company's legal name is the name registered by the authorities. The addresses of the company and any branch offices are then written. Finally, the company type must be stated, *e.g.*, whether it is a one-man company, a limited liability company or a public limited liability company. The net capital should be stated here, though it should also appear in the balance sheet in the Financial Plan section.

To sum up, the legal business description consists of the following areas:

Company name,

Business location(s),

Legal form of business, and

Current net capital.

If the company is subject to any kind of governmental regulations, these should be described, along with a statement on whether or not they have been fulfilled. Make it absolutely clear which approvals have been obtained and which are still pending, and state when approvals are expected.

Organizational Structure

This sub-section has two main areas: the internal organization and the external organization. The latter describes existing and planned strategic alliances that are material enough to warrant inclusion in the Strategic Business Plan.

The internal organization is described using an organization chart that shows the major departments and their management. Usually, one of three different chart types is used: the linear, the functional, or the matrix organization:

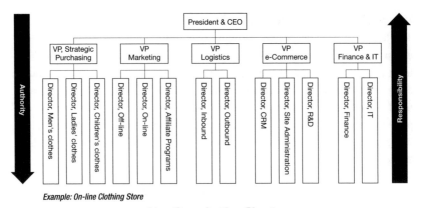

Example: On-line Clothing Store

Line Organization Chart

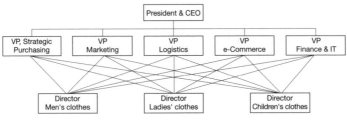

Example: On-line Clothing Store

Functional Organization Chart

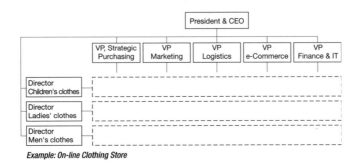

Example: On-line Clothing Store

Matrix Organization Chart

Figure 3.3   Sample Organization Charts

The degree of detail included in the "org chart" at this point depends on how far you have gotten in assembling the complete management team. Do not go overboard defining an organizational structure to a high level of detail since, realistically, the org chart serves only specific purposes at this point: showing external readers of your business plan that you have thought through the issues of how to structure the organization – and forcing you to do the thinking, and showing your team's strengths and the remaining gaps to be filled. It is acceptable if certain management positions are listed as "to be filled" or filled in an "acting" capacity, as long as these areas are clearly identified and a plan is in place to hire permanent staff.

External organization: if you already have or expect to enter into strategic alliances in the future, these should be listed along with an explanation of what the scopes of the alliances are/will be and why you have decided on them.

Companies create alliances for different reasons. Here are just a few examples:

Outsourcing of all non-strategic business processes in order to be able to focus exclusively on the strategic issues – this is a characteristic trend of the new economy. Even business processes such as logistics, production and marketing are often outsourced in companies of the new economy.

Strategic alliances with a third party company concerning distribution and/or sales of your products/services via their distribution networks and/or sales channels. The advantage is that you can get started quickly, without having to build a network of your own from scratch. The disadvantage is, of course, that you cannot control your distribution networks or sales channels.

Nike (sportswear), for example, has outsourced everything -- production, distribution, marketing and design -- not within its core competence. What they do take care of is brand management. Nike does not see itself as a mere sportswear producer, more as a sports company.

The section on external alliances thus contains a description of your strategic alliance partners, such as the following:

- Third-party supplier partners,

- Other strategic partners.

We will not go any further into this section but, as a final remark, mention that a newly started company should definitely consider making strategic alliances in areas not connected to its core business.

Board of Directors

We strongly recommend, in both newly established and existing companies, that you assemble a strong Board of Directors that can aid in decision-making in the complex startup and growth phases, as well as follow up on the strategy and the planned budgets.

Having a strong Board of Directors conveys a serious image to potential investors. The main objective, however, is that the board should act as a sparring partner for management; a board consisting entirely of attorneys and accountants would thus make a less desirable choice due to the lack of specific business skills.[38]

This section should contain not only the names and standard personal data of the internal board members (members of management), but also those of the chairman of the board, the deputy chairman of the board, and other members. Their qualifications relevant to this company should be described, indicating why they have been chosen. You should also state the responsibilities and obligations of each board member.

You may also want to attach their individual resumes (CV's) as an appendix to the business plan (Supporting Documents).

The Board of Directors' section consists of the following areas:

- Names of the Board of Directors,

- Background and qualifications of the Board of Directors, and

- Responsibilities of the Board of Directors.

Management Team

This section of the business plan is one of the most important when attracting potential investors. It must show that the management team is competent, within the areas of the business and within their assigned functions, and complete, or — in the case of an incomplete team, it must show the plan to complete the team. The management team is, after all, half or more of the company's executive team. This makes it essential to explain why this particular management is unique, both as individuals and as a team.

Start this section with a short overview of the management as a team, particularly if the team or parts of the team have worked together before. In addition, discuss areas of the team that are light or not filled in yet and present the plan for completion.

Present the team members hierarchically,[39] for example:

- CEO, President or Managing Director

- COO

- CFO

- CIO

- CTO

VPs or Directors for:

- Marketing

- Sales

- Finance

- Production

- R&D (Research and Development)

- Operations

Describe each team member's background and qualifications, concentrating on whatever is relevant to their jobs and responsibilities. Present a job description with areas of responsibility for each member of the management, making it clear exactly who is in charge of what.

Include the management team members' resumes (CVs) with the business plan in the supporting documents section. Make sure you use the same layout, so the reader can quickly gain insight into individual profiles. Resumes (CVs) should as a minimum contain:

- Personal data,

- Job experience,

- Education.

The Management Team section consists of the following areas:

- General discussion of the management team,

- Names and positions of the management team,

- Background and qualifications of the management team,

- Responsibilities of the management team.

Key Personnel

Here you can use the same model and method as in the section on the Management Team, although you should probably keep it a little shorter.

The definition of key personnel is essential employees or positions just below management with a strategic importance to the company, such as the following:

- Marketing manager,

- Sales manager,

- Finance manager,

- Production manager,

- R&D manager,

- Operations manager.

Strategic Alliances

If you already have or expect to enter into strategic alliances in the future, these should be listed along with an explanation of what the scope of each alliance is and why you have decided on it. The Organizational Structure section above contains a description of the material strategic alliances from the organizational perspective. Use this section to describe in as much detail as relevant the particular selections of strategic partners and the process that led to the selections.

3.6
Market Description

This section contains:

> Market Definition,
>
> Customer Profiles,
>
> Competition,
>
> Company Positioning,
>
> Risk.

Market Definition

This topic is one of the more interesting but also more difficult parts of the business plan. Defining the market can mean a lot of things, but in the context of a Strategic Business Plan it means quantifying the market and identifying the external forces that may impact it.

Quantifying the Market

This important task lets you gain insight into the market potential and find out how big a market share the company can expect to gain. These are the first real numbers the reader will see in the Strategic Business Plan, and they had better be believable and backed up. Always think of the heckler in the back of the room who asks, "Says who?," all the time; have a good answer for him/her.

Markets are usually quantified in either units or money (or in some cases both), depending on price variations in the market. If a market is characterized by large variations in prices, it will be quantified in money. Be clear in your description as to what kind of money you are working in, constant or current, *i.e.*, whether you have included projected inflation in the calculations. You can use either, but be consistent.

A simple example will show what we are talking about:[40]

Total Market Value	$1,000,000
Expected Market Share	10%
Price per Unit	$10
Market Share – Turnover	$100,000
Variable Cost	$55,000
Fixed Cost	$20,000
Financial Cost	$15,000
Profit – before tax	$10,000

Note that only the top three rows have relevance for the market analysis: how big is the market, what market share can the company gain, and what price will the market bear. The rest of it, though of obvious relevance to the business as a whole, belongs in other areas of the Strategic Business Plan.

How do you determine these three numbers? If the market is a generally acknowledged, large market, you can typically find values for it – and sometimes for the acceptable unit costs as well – in surveys and analyses conducted by consultants and research groups such as McKinsey, Accenture, PricewaterhouseCoopers, Gartner Group, Ernst & Young, PA Consulting Group, Jupiter Communications, Forrester Research, Dun & Bradstreet, *etc.*

For smaller, more specialized markets, trade organizations, governmental departments, or Chambers of Commerce may provide answers.

You will have to determine which market share you expect to be able to obtain. This will typically be based on a marketing plan; see below.

External Forces
Any factors outside of your line of business – *e.g.*, the labor market, environmental issues, political relations or the national economy — that could influence the demand for your company's products/services (threats and possibilities) should also be included in the market description.

A technique called PESTE analysis is often used to conduct an analysis of the external forces, both current and future. These are forces that the company cannot control but which, in some way or another, affect the company directly or indirectly. The analysis covers the following external forces:

- **Political forces**

- **Economic forces**

- **Social forces**

- **Technological forces**

- **Environmental forces**

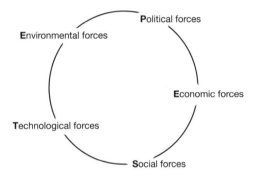

Figure 3.4   The PESTE Model

Customer Profiles

In this section you describe the profiles – and thus the implied buying behavior — of your target customer groups. The target groups should already be somewhat clear from the Company Profile and Mission Statement – defining the customers from the markets and business model. In this section we describe the customer profile first. This helps the general understanding, aids in the marketing plan, and will be useful in sizing the market.

Customer profiles can take many forms: "single males, twenty to thirty-four years old, with little or no college education," "second home owners," "the metal bending industry," *etc.*

The profiles are generally from one of two markets: the business-to-consumer (B2C) market or the business-to-business (B2B) market.

Naturally, individual markets exhibit varying buying behaviors. Buying behavior is the searching and deciding process and the factors connected with the purchase and subsequent use of the product. Again, the definition of the buying behavior aids in creating the marketing plan.

Business-to-Consumer market
Customer profiles in the B2C space will typically have demographic components, including social parameters. In addition, they should include a description of the type of buying behavior expected.

The decision process in the business-to-consumer market, impulse-buying excepted, usually consists of the following steps:

> Recognition of a need
>
> Searching for information
>
> Evaluation of alternatives
>
> Purchase
>
> Evaluation of the purchase.

Buying behavior in the business-to-consumer market can be categorized into the following types:

Routine response behavior

> These are routine purchases that are mostly inexpensive and have a short searching and deciding process. Example: a pound of flour.

Limited decision-making

> These are more unusual purchases with a longer but still modest searching and deciding process. Examples: a wristwatch, a single massage session.

Extensive decision-making

> These are one-off purchases with high to very high price tags and a long searching and deciding process. Examples, in ascending order of time involved: a membership in a fitness club, a car, a house.

Impulse buying.

> This is a spur-of-the-moment, impulsive purchase that has no
> searching and deciding process. Examples: a magazine, a bouquet
> of flowers.

The closer your proposed buying behavior fits the types above, the easier it
will be to justify the customer profiles and buying behavior. If the behavior
does not fit the norm – for example, if your product is an impulse product
with a high price – your demographics should reflect this — multi-million-
aires?

Business-to-Business market
There are currently lots of arguments as to which kind of business models are
viable in the B2B space. It is wise to stay out of this in your business plan
and describe the customer profile as straightforwardly as possible. The following points should be covered:

- Category of business: corporate, institutional, governmental

- Type of business, which industry

- Size of business

- Where the product or service fits in the processes of the target businesses

- Distribution method: direct, channels, catalogs, *etc.*

Be aware of buying behavior specific to the B2B space:

- Buying is often done via tenders, Requests for Quotation, or Requests for
  Proposals.

- Companies of a certain size maintain Approved Vendor Lists from which
  they purchase, sometimes with fewer approvals needed for repeat buying.

- Buying – and settling – via the Web is growing.

- Some Web Exchanges are still around, including exchanges set up by large
  corporations for their own buying.

- Maintaining large MRO – Maintenance, Repair, and Operations – catalogs on the Web is complex.

- Determining price for a given purchase is also complex; negotiated prices and quantity pricing makes it likely that two purchases may have two different unit prices.

Competition

This section contains a competitor analysis, which usually includes the following elements:

- Identification of direct competitors.

- A description of the three to five largest and most critical competitors.

    o What are their strategies?
    o What are their strengths and weaknesses?
    o What are their competitive advantages and unique selling points?
    o What are their values, external and internal?
    o What resources do they have at their disposal?
    o What are their market shares?
    o How serious competition are they?

- A forecast of where the competitors and the market are generally heading.

You need to perform this analysis on the companies that you – and your audience – will consider your close competitors. Be careful with the argument one hears sometimes: "We are unique, we have no competitors." Common feedback to that statement is one of two responses, either one dangerous: "You do not know your market," or "If you have no competitors, is there a market at all?"

When you perform the competitive analysis, research the following:

- Product/service selection,

- Prices and discount structure,

- Conditions on delivery,

- Marketing mix,

- Number of customers,

- Customer relations and loyalty,

- Other specifications.

Information on your competitors can be gathered from their own Web sites, their white papers, the Web in general, trade papers, periodicals, financia filings, *etc.* If you can, make a map of the market positions.

It can be quite difficult for a newly started company to gain a full understanding of the competitive situation, though thorough data collection will usually result in a relatively clear overview.

As we said in Chapter Two, traditional companies analyze competition matters through the use of Michael Porter's 5-forces model[41] that outlines five types of competition forces:

- *Industry competitors – rivalry among existing products/firms in geographically defined areas*

- *Threat of new entrants*

- *Bargaining power of buyers*

- *Threat of substitute products or services*

- *Bargaining power of supplier*

Many strategists of the "new" economy have criticized this model, as it is meant for businesses of the old economy where competition conditions were/are different. However, it has proved very useful with the addition of two more "forces" for today's e-Business situation: obsolescence, typically of digital technology, and globalization – driven by key features of the Internet.[42]

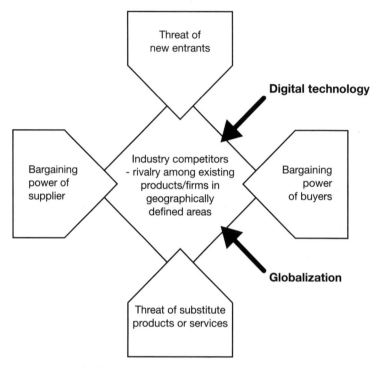

Figure 3.5   Competitive Forces

Obsolescence of digital technology

The power of digital technology and the speed of evolution of the next "killer app" have multiple impacts: a competitor can come out of nowhere with a new technology and make your products obsolete – think, for example, of the growth of optical networking components — and the generations of existing technology are so short in length that constant product evolution is required.

Globalization

The Internet is global, which in effect means that your company can no longer be considered a local, national or international player, rather a global one – or at least it has the option to become that in a much greater sense than earlier. You may also encounter new and unforeseen competition that was not possible earlier on. The geographical barrier to entry has been lowered dramatically.

In many markets there is a conscious attempt by the dominating companies to regulate the level of competition along with the amount of influence of the customer – think, for example, of the high fashion brands. With globalization it has become extremely difficult for these companies to maintain their control, as the Internet has put the power in the hands of the consumers. This also means that companies now need to think entirely differently; their niches in the market can be threatened overnight by newly-started competitors on the other side of the globe.

You should further analyze and evaluate your primary competitors' marketing strategies, both present and future forms. Analyzing and evaluating their strengths and weaknesses will allow you to guard your company against their strengths and at the same time apply pressure to their weak spots.

Lastly, the company should conduct an analysis of general competitive forces, including types of competitive structures, competitive tools, and methods for monitoring competitive behavior.

Company Positioning

This section of your Strategic Business Plan has, up to now, told the reader about the market, the customers, and the competition. It is now high time to help the reader understand why (s)he is reading all of this, *i.e.*, why this proposed company is the answer. This section is not meant to be the complete answer — much is yet to come — but it should put the stake in the ground. A good way of doing that is to use what is called a SWOT analysis – Strengths, Weaknesses, Opportunities, and Threats — an extremely powerful tool to analyze a company's internal and external situation.

Let us first take a look at how to use it. The SWOT analysis can be divided into two steps:

First, identify the company's strengths so you may develop them later on, as well as identify its weaknesses with the intention of creating a plan for remediation:

Strengths. What are your strengths (competitive advantages)?

Weaknesses. What are your weaknesses?

Next, identify the company's opportunities in order to take advantage of them. At the same time identify any threats it may be facing so you are ready to deal with them:

Opportunities. What opportunities do you have (marketwise)?

Threats. What threats are you facing in the market?

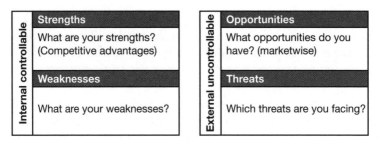

Figure 3.6   The SWOT Model

It is important to take your time with the SWOT analysis, as it is fundamental for stating your objectives, strategies, strategic activities and goals later on. Creating a good SWOT analysis usually starts with a general brainstorm session that identifies the appropriate areas. They are then expanded upon.

Risk

We live in a world full of risk, and starting a company is no exception. This section is dedicated to specifying the appropriate risk factors concerning your company. Be consistent and thorough in enumerating and discussing the risk factors, but do not go overboard. Nobody expected a company presenting on September 10th, 2001, to foresee a serious recession hitting the airlines.

You should examine the market risk factors and the appropriate external forces that have appeared during your market analysis with emphasis on the following:

- Market sizing, growth and/or change

- Customers, changes in target groups

- Changes in competition

You should also describe your expense structure in relation to supply and demand and account for your sensitivity towards ups and downs in the market.

Attempt, as well as you can, to rank the risks both in terms of occurrence and in terms of potential impact. This will illustrate what should be perceived as high-risk factors in the company and, therefore, what to focus on in future strategic efforts and company management.

3.7
Objectives, Strategies, Strategic Activities and Goals

This section of the Strategic Business Plan is the first one dealing with "how." Up until this section, most of the description has been of "what" the business will do. Now you will develop actionable activities leading to quantifiable goals using the Strategy Breakdown – SBD – method.

The SBD method works as follows: first the Mission Statement and the market and competitive environment are used to identify opportunities for and threats to the company. The **opportunities** and **threats** identified allow for definition of the company's **objectives** — broad statements of the company's ambitions in a given period.

Based on the set of objectives, **strategies** are developed that will help achieve these objectives. The strategies are then implemented through **strategic activities**, specific activities aimed at putting the strategies into practice. The strategic activities will allow for definition of concrete operational **goals** that are quantifiable and set within a timeframe. Monitoring these goals will show the company's progress in executing the strategic activities. Further breakdown of the strategic activities and goals is used to develop the Operational Plan.

The SBD model requires that connections be established from individual opportunities and threats throughout the system towards concrete goals to ensure that strategic actions are taken on *all* opportunities and threats and none are bypassed. We will elaborate on this throughout the chapter and provide a full example to further understanding. The idea is illustrated in the following figure:

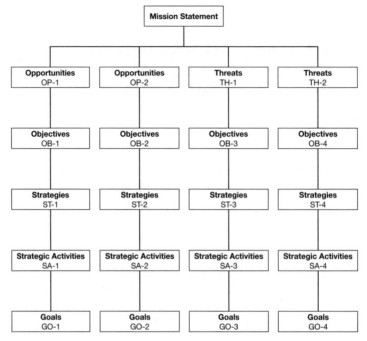

Figure 3.7 Strategic Breakdown Analysis

We will examine a case in this section in order to demonstrate the method in question. The basis will be a fictive company with the following profile:

- The company is created by two students and is a first mover on the market within its business area.

- It promotes (sells/buys) used textbooks to students at institutions of higher education (B2C market).

- It is only represented in Denmark, though expansion is desired.

- The company has a small number of employees and is newly-started.

- The company's Website is in its first phase/version and needs improvements and new services.

- The company had problems with funding in the initial phases, but is pulling through for now.

- So far, the company has produced a minor profit.

Before we go any further, let us define the company's mission. Remember to include the following in a mission statement:

- What the company will be doing,

- Who the target group is,

- Which needs the company will be covering,

- How it is differentiated from its competitors,

- How the company will be covering these needs now and in the future.

The company's mission statement would go something like this:

We are virtual brokers (buyers/sellers) of second hand textbooks for students at institutions of higher education in the B2C market. We aim to become the leading virtual second hand textbook broker in Scandinavia via an offensive expansion supported by the best services on the market within our business area.

Objectives

The main idea is to identify a number of objectives based on previously defined opportunities and threats.

Note the difference between an objective and a goal: objectives are more descriptive/non-operational (broad statements), whereas goals are more concrete/operational (specific statements) and are in fact the realizations of the objectives. An example of a strategic objective could be to focus on increasing market share; the strategic goal could be to increase sales 20%.

Objectives are thus broad, non-specific statements that describe a desired general situation some time ahead in the period of the business plan. As mentioned earlier, they are brought about by analysis of the opportunities and threats previously defined in the business plan. We recommend that a number of objectives be assembled, based merely on the opportunities and threats without taking chronology and overlaps, *i.e.*, repetition, into account. Also be aware that one opportunity or threat can easily have several objectives connected to it and, in turn, that one objective can be connected to several opportunities and threats.

Once you have defined all your objectives, it is important to check for over-laps and make sure that all opportunities and threats are connected to one or more objectives, as well as verify that all connections from the opportunities and threats are correctly joined.

It is important that the objectives be realistic for the period ahead, both in financials and in time/resources/capability relations. The objectives in question should also be strategic, which means they can be considered key drivers in the period of the business plan in question.

Let us now define objectives for our fictive case-study company with the following opportunities and threats (simplified):

Opportunities:
OP-1: Niche area, also first mover = leading position.

OP-2: European expansion = growth.

Threats:
TH-1: The concept and Website are relatively unknown.

TH-2: Funding problems.

From the above, we can derive the following **Objectives**:

OB-1: To become the leading virtual dealer of second hand textbooks for students at institutions of higher education.

(Connected to OP-1 and TH-1).

OB-2: To improve the cash-flow situation for future growth.

(Connected to TH-2).

OB-3: To introduce the concept in Scandinavia.

(Connected to OP-2).

Once the objectives have been fashioned, we can move on to the construction of the strategies. We should, however, take our time at this point, as this will be the foundation for our further strategic work, including work on specific strategies, strategic activities and goals.

Strategies

Strategies are broad statements on how you expect to achieve your objectives. Each strategy must be connected, at minimum, to one objective.

It is a good idea to have a brainstorming session in which you think up a number of strategies based on your objectives. Later on you can give them proper structure, clean out overlaps, *etc.*

Let us return to our example: we have now defined the current opportunities and threats relevant to the business, along with objectives that will take advantage of the opportunities and reduce the threats, thereby turning both to our advantage. If all goes well, we should see the current opportunities and threats under the strengths section of our next business plan. This will prove whether or not our current business plan has been a success.

We can define the following **Strategies** to make sure we achieve our objectives:

ST-1: To market the company and concept in a focused and cost-effective manner.

(Connected to OB-1 and OB-3).

ST-2: To become the preferred choice for the target group when buying or selling textbooks.

(Connected to OB-1 and OB-3).

ST-3: To find a financial partner to support future growth.

(Connected to OB-2).

ST-4: To establish a virtual presence in Sweden and Norway with a Website suited to those markets.

(Connected to OB-3).

We have now defined the strategies that will make sure our objectives are fulfilled. We can connect each strategy to one or more objectives, and link each objective to one or more opportunities and threats. Now move on to defining strategic activities:

Strategic Activities

Strategic activities are specific activities that can be quantified in relation to both cost and time. Their purpose is to implement and execute the strategies you have created, making sure all activities are linked to one or more strategies. Strategic activities are the bond between the strategic and the operational plan.

Again, a brainstorming session in which you define a number of strategic activities based on your strategies will help, followed up by a process of structuring, removing overlaps, *etc*.

Let us return to our case and define some strategic activities with the intention of implementing the strategies previously described.

The following **Strategic Activities** will make sure our intents are fulfilled:

SA-1: Digital mass-communication campaigns aimed at the target groups in Denmark, Sweden and Norway.

(Connected to ST-1, ST-2 and ST-4).

SA-2: Establishment of affiliate programs with institutes of higher education in Denmark, Sweden and Norway.

(Connected to ST-1, ST-2 and ST-4).

SA-3: Improvement of the buying/selling process on the Website.

(Connected to ST-2).

SA-4: Completion of the business plan for the next three years and, subsequently, beginning of negotiations with banks and venture capitalists.

(Connected to ST-3).

SA-5: Development of Websites adapted for Sweden and Norway, respectively.

(Connected to ST-4).

We have now laid out a number of strategic activities that will be the means of fulfilling our strategies. All strategic activities are connected to one or more strategies. Let us therefore move on to the last area: defining goals.

Goals

The reason for having goals is to be able to make sure strategic activities are being carried out according to plan and to monitor them during execution. Goals are also the glue that binds the strategic and the operational plans together.

Goals must be quantitative and operate within a specific timeframe. This means that each goal must have a quantifiable measurement, such as money, and a timeframe for its execution. If a goal is qualitative, it must be quantified enough so it can be measured objectively.

In our case, the final step would be to define a number of **Goals** to measure whether the execution of our strategic activities is going according to plan.

GO-1: Execution of the digital mass-communication campaigns in Q-4 with a total budget of $20,000 in Denmark, Sweden and Norway.

(Connected to SA-1).

GO-2: Establishment of an affiliate program with one new institute of education each month in each country, in Sweden and Norway starting from the 1st of October.

(Connected to SA-2).

GO-3: Usability test of the Website must be complete by the 1st of February. The usability result and new interface must be implemented on the 1st of May.

(Connected to SA-3).

GO-4: The business plan must be finished by the 1st of January, after which negotiations with banks and venture capitalists must be started. A financial partner and a deposit of at least $150,000 must be secured by the 1st of June.

(Connected to SA-4).

GO-5: The Websites adapted for Sweden and Norway must be completed and marketed by the 1st of October.

(Connected to SA-5).

The total structure of the example will thus look like following figure:

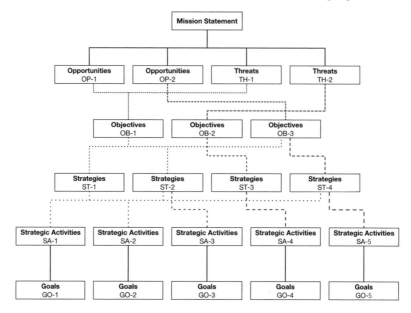

Figure 3.8   SBD Example

As you can see, we have successfully broken our objectives down via a number of strategies and strategic activities to observable goals. In reality though, we would need a lot more strategies, strategic activities and goals to gain the objectives defined in the case. We would have even more objectives than those mentioned. But, by keeping the example as simple as possible, we hope to make the method (SBD) more comprehensible.

The strategic activities and goals are the bond between the business plan (the strategic plan) and the operational plan, including the marketing plan. They will be broken down further in their respective plans. The strategic activities and goals dealing with the marketing side of the company are developed further in the strategic marketing plan later in the business plan, *e.g.*, SA-1, SA-2, GO-1 and GO-2 in our example. They would probably be broken down (simplified) as follows in the operational plan:

Operational Activities

OA-1: Internet banner campaign on "Free Mail Portals" (such as Hotmail.com) targeted at students currently undergoing higher education in Denmark, Sweden and Norway.

(Connected to SA-1).

OA-2: Establish an affiliate program with the institutes of higher education, in which an icon is placed on their Websites in exchange for a commission for each active (buying/selling) customer referred from their Website.

(Connected to SA-2).

Operational Goals

GO-1: Execute the banner campaign at "Free Mail Portals" (such as Hotmail.com) in Q-4 with a total budget of $20,000. Ads will be distributed at a ratio of 50/25/25 to Denmark, Sweden and Norway, respectively.

(Connected to OA-1).

GO-2: Establish an affiliate program with one new institute of education each month, in each country, in Sweden and Norway starting from the 1st of October.

(Connected to OA-2).

Be aware that you will often have to modify your mission statement during this process, as new elements will emerge that can affect it. Also, you are not working on fulfilling just your strategic goals; you have financial goals as well. We shall discuss those in the Financial Plan section.

3.8
Resources

This section of the Strategic Business Plan consists of a discussion of:

> People,
> Facilities, and
> Equipment.

People

Now we are ready to estimate how many employees you will need in order to execute the strategy and the business plan and to consider average wages for all employee categories. Salary expenses in most companies are the largest financial burden. We recommend that you create a chart from figures that represent the salary allocations of different departments and employee classes, such as:

- Marketing

- Sales

- Finance

- Production

- R&D

- Operations

If your company relies heavily on employees with special capabilities, it would be a good idea to describe how and with which type you expect to run the company, though this is more than one would normally expect of a business plan. If you are up to it, by all means include this part, but make sure it does not take up too much space.

Facilities

The Strategic Business Plan would normally not include a lot of discussion about facilities, other than as a financial entry. If there are any specific facility needs, e.g., a complex facility infrastructure, they should be listed. Otherwise, a short discussion of space needs and location will suffice.

Equipment

Draw up a list of fixed assets and operating assets for the equipment. They can be anything from office furniture to production equipment. Again, not much detail is required. If the company does its own production, the resources it uses must be described along with how they are being allocated. The general process of production should also be analyzed and described.

It is, of course, important that there is a connection between the predefined sales goals and the company's production capacity, as production weighs heavily when setting the goals in the first place.

The description of the company's production should, at minimum, contain a process description of the production, a list of equipment required for production, and a production calculation for individual products. The Financial Plan section must, obviously, include the appropriate calculations for production as well.

3.9
Marketing Strategy

The aim of marketing is to make selling superfluous. The aim is to know and to understand the customer so well that the product or service fits him/her and sells itself.

— Peter Drucker

The marketing concept holds that the key to achieving organizational goals lies in determining the needs and wants of target markets and delivering the desired satisfaction more efficiently and effectively than the competition.

— Philip Kotler, the guy with the four Ps[43]

This section lays out the Marketing Strategy for your business. The sub-sections will likely include:

> Overall market strategy,
>
> Competitive position,
>
> Product/Brand,
>
> Channels,
>
> Pricing, and
>
> Customer communication and interaction.

The section must leave the reader with the understanding that you have a clear, believable and thorough plan for the strategy that you will use to capture the market you are describing. To help you be crisp in your writing, we shall be somewhat long-winded here.

Marketing is the kind of topic about which, "gurus," sometimes "du jour," write massive tomes. They can be useful, but you may not have time to read them while you are writing your business plan. If you have read them, or know somebody who has, skip the rest of this section except for the bolded introduction to each sub-section. If you have not read them, consider the following sub-sections our approach to giving you enough background to write a first version of the section. In either case, expect some intense brainstorming with your team and with outside help if appropriate.

Overall Marketing Strategy

In this section you will lay out the overall marketing strategy, to be expanded in the following sub-sections. Keep it clear, crisp, and based on the earlier discussion in sections 3 and 4 of the Strategic Business Plan.

Definition of marketing

Marketing is a term that spans several different disciplines. It has several definitions, but we believe that ideas already mentioned above – when brought together — describe the concept of marketing pretty well. The following areas are thus essential:

- Understanding the company's customers and their needs and desires,

- Maximizing customer satisfaction as a benefit to both company and customer,

- Identifying marketing opportunities, including maximization and optimization,

- Targeting the right customers, including advertising,

- Optimizing the utilization of the company's marketing resources.

Emphasizing the above will result in increased market share and a head start in competition, which in turn should increase the profitability of the company. We shall focus on the marketing concept itself and, above all, on how to develop and implement a marketing strategy.

The company's marketing environment affects the company and its customers. Based on this fact, the company has to set a marketing strategy, which is implemented using the set marketing mix — the product/brand, channels, pricing, customer communication and interaction.

Before you start developing the marketing strategy and initiating the marketing activities, it is important to understand the concept itself:

The main philosophy behind marketing is that a company, via coordinated activities, must develop products/services that meet its customers' requirements, thereby allowing the company to achieve its objectives and goals through maximizing customer satisfaction.

Customer satisfaction — the main objective of the marketing concept — is all about having a customer-centered process as opposed to a product-centered one. The idea is to always listen to your customers and thereby develop the company's products/services based on their needs and desires, without forgetting, of course, the company's own objectives.

You may think that all this goes without saying, but in reality a lot of companies eventually forget to listen to their customers and start developing products/services that are not adapted to the target group. There are a lot of examples of this; take, for instance, VCR (Video Cassette Recorder) manufacturers, and in general a lot of other technology developers.

VCRs usually feature a vast range of functions and options that, in reality, hardly anyone uses, and the functions that are more commonly used are often obscured by the myriad of useless (or not used) ones. This demonstrates that the producers of these VCRs have a far more product-centered process than a market-centered one. In addition, their marketing efforts are usually focused on fancy product features instead of the needs the VCRs in question fill for their target group. The manufacturers seem more interested in their own technology than in their customers. They need to change to a more market-centered approach in order to meet their companies' overall objectives.

Implementing the marketing concept in practice usually requires — apart from a change-oriented management — that the company invest in electronic systems for customer communication and interaction, including CRM – Customer Relationship Management.

"Marketing concept" is not just a new term for "marketing," but rather a management philosophy of how the company can coordinate all general activities with a more market-oriented approach. With this in mind, marketing becomes an integral part of strategic planning and is rooted firmly in every part of the organization. The VP/director of marketing is part of the company's management, and marketing is considered a strategic hotspot in the company. If you are a market-oriented entrepreneur, this will come as no surprise to you, though many product-oriented entrepreneurs seem to overlook this.

Marketing strategy

Marketing strategy is all about designing a strategic plan for each market and product portfolio the company wishes to target and developing different types of competitive advantages.

When developing its marketing strategy, the company must first define its general marketing objectives based on the overall strategy in section 4, after which it can proceed and the planning process can begin.

Product portfolio analysis

Many companies use the "product portfolio analysis" developed by Boston Consulting Group for developing and defining the company's marketing strategy for the portfolio in question. This generic model operates with four different categories of products:

- Stars: These are market-dominating products with great potential for growth.
- Cash cow: These are also market-dominating products, but belong to a market with little or no growth.
- Dogs: These are products with a smaller share of a market exhibiting little or no growth.
- Problem children: These are products with a small market share in a market with high growth.

Relative Market Share

		High	Low
Market Growth	**High**	**STARS** These are market-dominating products with great potential for growth	**PROBLEM CHILDREN** These are products with a small market share in a market with high growth
	Low	**CASH COWS** These are also market-dominating products, but belong to a market with little or no growth	**DOGS** These are products with a smaller share of a market exhibiting little or no growth

Figure 3.9 The Product Portfolio

Following this, you would normally create a "Market Attractiveness-Business Position Model." This is a generic two-dimensional matrix with the individual products/SBUs drawn in according to the product categories above. This allows you to identify which products/SBUs are worth promoting and which products/SBUs should be assigned lower priority or completely removed from the portfolio.

The so-called A-B-C classification method is also used for marketing purposes. It involves classifying product groups, products, and customers by their profitability for the company (A = High / B = Average / C = Low). Having done that, you can create an "ABC Contribution Chart" of the product groups, products, and customers in order to gain a better overview of the company's portfolio and how profitability relates to it.

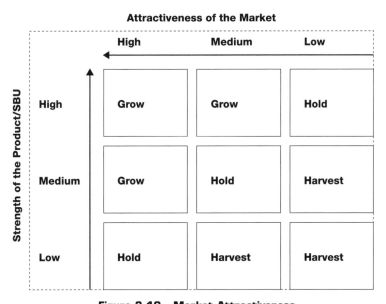

Figure 3.10   Market Attractiveness

When the time comes to define the company's general marketing growth strategy, one of the following generic strategies is typically used:

- Market penetration: This strategy aims to increase sales of existing products in existing markets.

- Market development: The idea here is to increase sales by pushing existing products into new markets.

- Product development: This strategy aims to increase sales by improving existing products or developing new products for existing markets.

- Diversification: Increasing sales by introducing new products to new markets.

Competitive Marketing Strategy Building Blocks
The traditional structure in a market has four different types of generic competitive strategy profiles:

- Market leader
  The product with the largest market share. Strategic focus is on growing the category.

- Market challenger
  The product is second, third or fourth in the category but wants to have a lion's share. Focus is on out-performing the market leader in the most important customer selection criteria (price, design, quality, imagery, *etc.*).

- Market follower
  The product is a copy-cat product which has not incurred the development or marketing investment costs of the leading products. Strategic focus is on making a good product as cheaply as possible and distributing it as widely as possible.

- Market niches
  The product is unique within a small sub-segment of the market/category. Strategic focus is on staying ahead in the niche and penetration of the rest of the niche with the product.

Strategy alternatives
Peter Drucker[44] has described a number of generic entrepreneurial competition strategies based on Michael Porter's three generic competitive strategies — differentiation, focus and overall cost leadership.[45] We shall explain each of Drucker's strategies to aid you in finding a suitable one for your business concept.

Firstest with the Mostest Strategy
The "firstest with the mostest" strategy is an overall leadership strategy aimed at putting a company in a leading position in the market. So far, we have often seen this strategy utilized in the new economy and, in general, by many

technology companies. This strategy is probably the riskiest of them all as it allows no room for mistakes but, of course, it also has the best pay-off.

To gain success this way, you probably need a new and innovative product/-service or a new market, which could be the virtual market.

Creative Imitation Strategy

The "creative imitation" strategy is a strategy of differentiation aimed at copying existing products/services while at the same time making them more market- and/or customer-friendly, *i.e.*, picking up potential the originator did not notice. Or, as Peter Drucker puts it, "Hit them where they aren't."

The advantage of this strategy is that you can learn from the mistakes/omissions of the innovator, while at the same time focusing 100% on your market and customers.

Entrepreneurial Judo Strategy

The "entrepreneurial judo" strategy is also a strategy involving differentiation, this time making use of companies' habitual thinking and lack of perception of market signals. A good example of this is, in fact, the virtual market; many established companies overlooked its possibilities and therefore started too late. Amazon.com is probably the best example of a newly-founded company that took the whole of its market niche by surprise and at the same time was capable of utilizing and holding its head start.

Drucker points out five common traits that open up, for an entrepreneur, the possibility of attacking the market leader:

- Companies that do not recognize and/or accept new technology and knowledge or do not observe the signals of the market.

- Companies that rest on their market position.

- Companies that are strictly product-oriented, overlooking market- and customer relations.

- Companies that raise prices because of their dominating position in the market.

- Companies that maximize instead of optimize.

This strategy is often used when established companies ignore new technology or knowledge, or when they simply sit back because of their dominant market position. The strategy is also used in markets where the structure is frequently changing — this includes the virtual market.

The entrepreneurial judo strategy is fixed on a leading market position and is always market- and customer-driven (not product- and technology-driven).

Tollgate Strategy

The "tollgate" strategy is a focus strategy with the purpose of achieving a market monopoly. It requires that the market can only sustain one provider, making it unattractive for others to attempt to compete. At the same time, the product or service offered must have a very vital function, one that cannot be easily copied.

It is quite rare to see this strategy in action, and the growth potential is quickly depleted for companies using it.

Specialty Skill Strategy

The "specialty skill" strategy is also a focus strategy with the purpose of specialization within a certain area. The prerequisite of this strategy is to have a special technical competence and a new area of growth in which to utilize your unique competence. It is also important to establish your business rather quickly, creating a market position and head-start over your competitors.

This strategy is far more common than the tollgate, but requires that you identify a new area of growth and, of course, that you have the required technical skills.

Specialty Market Strategy

The "specialty market" strategy is also a focus strategy aimed at specializing within a specific area, but this time with a market-minded angle, *e.g.*, you would use your market competence to find a new area of growth.

The difference between the Specialty Skill Strategy and Specialty Market Strategy is that the first is built around a specific technical competence, whereas the second is based on a specific competence and knowledge of the market.

Competitive Position

This section will contain your description of your competitive position as it relates to the market in which you want to compete, the segments into

which you want to enter, and your competitive positioning in these segments. You may already have segmented the market earlier, as well as defined your target segments; in that case concentrate on the market positioning in this section.

Segmentation

Before a company can decide which market to target and position itself in, it must divide the market into segments. If the market has already been analyzed earlier in the business plan, an actual segmentation can be performed straight away.

The market in question must, for the segmentation to be at all relevant or, for there to be a market at all:

- Be in need of the company's products/services.

- Have the opportunity to buy the company's products/services.

There are two general methods of identifying a company's target markets, one of which is the segmenting method. In it, the company divides the entire market into several more consistent sub-markets, thus developing a marketing mix for each individual segment. The other method is known as the total market or undifferentiated market method. This involves viewing the entire market as the company's target market, so that only one marketing mix is developed.

There are two different types of markets, namely the homogeneous and the non-homogeneous. The homogeneous market consists of consumers with similar requirements, whereas the non-homogeneous market consists of consumers with different requirements. The idea of segmenting is to divide the total non-homogeneous market into smaller segments with similar needs and requirements, making the segments themselves more homogeneous.

There are certain requirements that must be met by the market before it is possible to effectively segment it:

- The market must be identifiable and measurable,

- The market must be of at least a certain size,

- The market must be accessible,

- The market should be relatively stable.

Segmenting your customers in a B2C market is usually based on a subset of the following variables:

- Geographical variables:

    o Regions,

    o Countries,

    o Cities,

    o Degrees of urbanization;

- Demographic variables:

    o Sex,

    o Age,

    o Size of family,

    o The family's location,

    o Stage of life,

    o Education,

    o Religion,

    o Occupation,

    o Income;

- Consumer variables:

    o User/non-user,

    o New customer/repeat business,

- ○ Frequency of use,

- ○ Extent of use,

- ○ Usage history,

- ○ Knowledge and interest,

- ○ Loyalty;

- • Psychographics/lifestyle:

  - ○ Standards,

  - ○ Opinions,

  - ○ Values,

  - ○ Lifestyle.

Remember that there is usually a connection between behavior and demographic variables. The behavior of an individual is closely connected to his or her social and financial status. This means that by identifying the parallels between behavior and demographic variables you can trace behavior and buying preferences back to variables such as gender, age, income, education and occupation. Subsequently, you can "reach" your target group and also use this information for estimating the size of a market, as demographic variables are usually obtainable from public statistics.

Traditional segmenting of a B2B market will use demographic variables such as business, size of company, geographical location, *etc.*

After the market is appropriately segmented, it is time to quantify the demand of each segment. If there are any public statistics or market reports available, you may as well use them. If not, the project participants will have to conduct their own surveys or hire an opinion-research institute to do this for them. In either case, you should include information on how much uncertainty is connected with the numbers in the market report, a factor that depends on both the method and size of the survey.

It is very important that the figures in the market report are not too uncertain, *i.e.*, "make sense." If necessary, retain a professional service to define and segment the market as part of your overall market research.

Targeting

Once the market segments have been identified and defined, it is time for the company to develop a targeting strategy, stating which segments will be targeted, and when. The idea is to decide which segments the company wants to target and in what order, thereby giving some segments higher priority in the company's sales and marketing efforts.

There are generally two targeting strategies:

- Concentration strategy, based on a single segment that is the center of all the company's marketing activities;

- Multi-segment strategy, in which the company's marketing efforts are directed at two or more segments.

There is no doubt that the multi-segment strategy in most cases is the most effective in the long run, though you will probably want to phase in the effort, starting with one or a few segments. You should consider the following factors before choosing a strategy:

- The company's marketing resources and financial situation,

- The competitive situation,

- Size of the market,

- Your company's market share,

- Market behavior and consistency.

The complete set of factors will depend on your actual product or service.

Positioning

Positioning is the process of creating an image for a product or a company as a whole within the target group. Positioning a company as a whole is usually done by defining its overall marketing mix.

Before you start the positioning process, it is important to first obtain a general view of the current situation and to forecast as much future behavior as is necessary for your marketing.

For the current situation, you analyze/evaluate the current market(s) as well as the environment of the company, as described earlier in the chapter.

Forecasting the future, however, is slightly more complicated! The goal is to create a realistic view of what to expect.

Forecasting will give you certain advantages:

- The ability to identify possible tendencies in the market that could affect your business and to identify new markets, products, and services and, above all, new ways of fulfilling your customers' needs;

- Better feeling for the market, giving you the ability to act quicker;

- Better control of your strategic direction and positioning.

In analyzing the future, the so-called "Delphi" method is sometimes used. This involves a panel with the relevant competence and knowledge answering a series of written questions. After the questioning, the results are given back to the members of the panel along with a revised questionnaire. The purpose is usually to analyze the effects of introducing a new product or service under given circumstances. Members of the panel are usually employees, customers and suppliers.

Another frequently used and effective method is scenario planning. In this context, it is a method of identifying the possible future situation in the internal and external business environment, including factors such as potentials and threats. Scenario planning gives you a much better general view and forces you to think hard about and thereby understand any possible changes, including how to place them in the correct context.

Remember that the process of future forecasting is, by definition, dynamic. A forecast must be regularly updated. This is particularly relevant in the new economy, which is characterized by change and seemingly inconsistent behavior in the market.

You would usually analyze and define your company's added values and potentials in order to optimize through the value chain, which step-by-step describes the processes of the company, thus giving you the opportunity to optimize individual steps in relation to your competition – either by differentiation, focus, or overall cost leadership – the three positioning strategies defined by Porter.[46] By thinking a little unconventionally and differently, it is often possible to create good positioning compared to that of your competition.

In Porter's first strategy, differentiation, the objective is to add value to create an advantage over your competition, *e.g.*, to have a number of added values that benefit your customers and encourage them to do business with you instead of your competition. Customers are not really buying products or services, but benefits. But remember that different people have different ideas of value, and the same offer will be interpreted differently from person to person. This is part of why we work with segmenting, so we can target different values to different groups of customers, corresponding to their perceptions of value.

A focus strategy is about focusing on a particular customer group or segment, whereas an overall cost leadership strategy is to create an advantage in competition by implementing cost effectiveness, for example, by way of more effective use of capacity, effective production, effective logistics, and lower payments. You can, of course, combine the strategies.

You can analyze your choice of a general positioning strategy using the "competition triangle" (company, customers and competition). It contains the following questions:

- Does the market show signs of preference?

- Which segments exist in the market?

- How is your competition servicing the existing segments?

- How strong is their financial competition capacity?

If, for example, the market does not show any signs of preference, there is no point in adding excess value to the products or services you offer your customers, as they will hardly notice any difference. The preferred strategy would therefore usually involve overall cost leadership based on cost efficiency and optimizing business processes.

Another important positioning question you should ask is why your customers should even want to do business with you. This is usually identified through the company's Unique Selling Points (USP), where you can note the aspects that differentiate you from your competition. The requirement for a USP is the ability to offer unique advantages in individual areas — advantages that none of your competitors can match offhand or use in their marketing. USPs are usually connected to a company's products or services, but can also be generally linked to a company. An added value can also be defined as a USP, as long as the value is unique and not offered by any of your competitors. USPs are usually used in a company's marketing and are a way into your positioning strategies.

The tactical tool for positioning a company is its product mix, which is what we shall take a look at next.

Product/Brand

In this section you will describe your strategy for your brand and your products. This will include describing how you are going to manage the lifecycle of the products you have identified and how you are going to create the brand and brand awareness in your target markets. There was much discussion about how to create brands in the dot.com go-go days. Be careful setting expectations in your plan as to when you will have created a meaningful brand. The dot.com era showed us that a solid brand takes time to create and, even if you get lucky and create brand awareness in a hurry, it will not save you if the rest of your plan does not hold together – remember webvan.com, etoys.com, pets.com?

The glory days of the dot.com – 1999 and 2000 – brought us much discussion of "The Brand" and how quickly you could create one. Unquestionably there is money in a brand; *Business Week's* annual listing of valuable brands shows that:

The World's 10 Most Valuable Brands

RANK	BRAND	2001 BRAND VALUE ($BILLIONS)
1	COCA-COLA	68.9
2	MICROSOFT	65.1
3	IBM	52.8
4	GE	42.4
5	NOKIA	35.0
6	INTEL	34.7
7	DISNEY	32.6
8	FORD	30.1
9	McDONALD'S	25.3
10	AT&T	22.8

Source: Business Week Online, August 6, 2001
Data: Interbrand, Citigroup

Figure 3.11   Brand Values

It also shows, however, that valuable brands are not young upstarts. Do not expect to create a world-class brand in no time flat, and do expect to be questioned about your plans for brand creation.

Your market research will have shown you how your company capabilities fit with the needs of the chosen market segments. This section will show the resulting product mix that will satisfy the needs and desires set forth.

Remember the four stages of a product lifecycle, ignoring product enhancement for the moment:

- Introduction stage: the product is introduced to the market;

- Growth stage: the product grows until it reaches the maturity stage;

- Maturity stage: the product is now mature and does not grow any longer;

- Decline stage: the final stage of the product's life cycle where sales start to drop significantly.

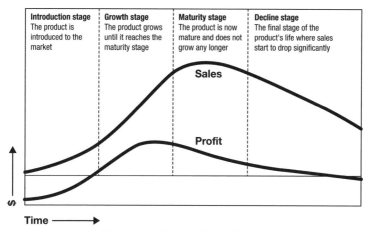

Introduction stage	Growth stage	Maturity stage	Decline stage
The product is introduced to the market	The product grows until it reaches the maturity stage	The product is now mature and does not grow any longer	The final stage of the product's life where sales start to drop significantly

Sales

Profit

$

Time ⟶

Figure 3.12   Product Life Cycle

Your plan should establish a product/brand mix, *i.e.*, a group of products/ brands that the company wishes to offer to the market, including depth and width of the product assortment.

A large part of the brand creation and product awareness will be based on Customer Communication and Interaction. We discuss those topics further in a separate section below. For now, let us briefly introduce the concept of **e-Services**: how you can utilize the net to create new services, at the same time increase the efficiency of the company's existing services (if any), and in general improve penetration and awareness.

Electronic service (e-Service) is an area that really allows a company to position itself and create long-lasting and deep brand awareness and competitive advantages. In order to do this, the company must define e-Service as a strategic competition parameter, and implement e-Service in its strategy. This is where "e" meets the new economy, where the fallout from the "e"-Revolution has permanently changed what is normal. The successful entrepreneur will integrate use of the Web tightly into the business model, not only for financial reasons but, even more, for connecting ever closer with prospects and customers.

Subsequently, all the processes and the organization of the company may need to be totally redefined, which calls for effective change management. (Remember our earlier warning about Strategic Business Plans evolving during their development?) This process is very difficult and time-consuming for an existing company, but will create long-lasting competitive advantages. It is much easier to implement for a newly-started business, as there are no outdated processes or existing employees to worry about. So keep in mind that e-Service should, from the beginning, be defined as an area of strategic importance that should be implemented in the strategy and throughout all business processes and the value chain.

Channels
In this section you will describe:

- **Which sales channels you are going to employ, by product;**

- **What the breakdown of revenue will be by channel, both current and future;**

- **The timing of bringing additional channels into the mix.**

Make sure that you consider the changes to the channels brought on by the Web — exchanges, outsourcing part of the functioning of a channel, dis-intermediation, *etc*. Additionally, discuss the e-Services aspects of your channel strategy.

It is unlikely your business will be able to handle all the channels you would like to employ right from the beginning. You will need to choose in what order you will bring channels on line and what the end result will be, by product and by revenue.

Conventional channels are, in B2C:

- Producer – Agents – Wholesalers – Retailers – Consumers

- Producer – Wholesalers – Retailers – Consumers

- Producer – Retailers – Consumers

- Producer – Consumers

And in B2B:

- Producer – Agents – Distributors – Buyers

- Producer – Agents – Buyers

- Producer – Distributors – Buyers

- Producer – Buyers

The Web has added additional channel types, such as exchanges, both public and private. Outsourcing part of a channel – for example, outside fulfillment and returns handling with the producer maintaining the marketing Web presence — is a separate channel type.

It is critical in any channel strategy that the handling of the customer data be well defined: how is it captured, what is captured, who owns it, who stores it, what is its availability, and how is it mined. Your discussion of channels should include answers to the complete e-Services spectrum: how you are using the Web to find, sell to, and retain your customers.

Pricing

In this section you will describe pricing philosophy and policies for your business. Remember that "nobody pays retail" any more — if they ever did — and that the Web has brought us comparative shopping with a vengeance. In the B2B space, negotiated prices and various exchange implementations have made pricing of a specific order for a specific customer on a specific date a complex undertaking.

Pricing is key to your business success. Price your product or service wrongly, and the inevitable follows: no business.

One of the first decisions you will have to make is whether you will compete on price. If so, you have to study the competition very carefully so you know how your price and feature set compare. The Web has drastically changed the meaning of competing on price. Your competition may be many miles, but only one mouse click, away, and a comparison shopping Website may find more competition than you knew existed.

If you are not going to compete on price, you either have no competition – as we discussed above, a dangerous assumption in a business plan – or you have found some distinguishing factor that makes it unnecessary for you to compete on price. You can expect to be challenged on those findings; make sure the market research backs you up appropriately.

The old saying "nobody pays retail" is truer than ever, both in B2C and B2B. Pricing in the B2B space is quite often based on negotiated prices based on volume or other factors. Although this is not pricing *per se*, it is quite possible, and relevant for your pricing engine, that your B2B agreement may cover selling, say, pencils at specific prices, while prohibiting you from selling, say, desk lamps to this particular corporate customer, since another vendor has that agreement. Exchanges and various kinds of auctions are also having an impact. Everything did not turn into reverse auctions, as once forecast, but a private auction with a small set of invited suppliers requires different and novel pricing mechanisms.

The ability to collect data on your customers and then process it intelligently gives you new opportunities in terms of customer and occasion-specific pricing.

So, before you set your pricing policy, know your competitors, your market, and your customers and know your answer to the request for a discount.

Customer Communication and Interaction

In this section you will describe how you are going to get prospects, how you are going to convert them to customers, and how you are going to keep them as repeat customers through appropriate sales and marketing efforts, through ongoing customer communications, and through CRM. Create and present this plan for each of your customer segments. You will likely deal with the following for each segment:

- **Advertising**

- **Direct Marketing**

- **Marketing Communications**

- **Customer Relationship Management**

Customer communication and interaction deal with the activities related to broadcasting company and product/brand information to the correct segment(s). The aim is to communicate the desired messages to selected segments, thereby increasing product awareness, creating brand preference and, subsequently, also sales.

When initiating promotional activities it is important to understand what type of people you are dealing with. Consider the following types when introducing a new product:[47]

- Innovators,

- Early adopters,

- Early majority,

- Late majority.

With any type, however, the goal is – using the right tools and messages for the particular segment – to guide them along the KAB hierarchy used in studies of advertising efficiency: "K" for knowledge (the prospect becomes aware of the product), "A" for affective (the prospect develops an interest and/or preference for the product), and "B" for behavioral (the customer intends to buy or creates a habit of buying).

The following areas are usually found in a company's customer communication and interaction mix:

- Marketing communications, including public relations,

- Direct marketing,

- Advertising,

- Sales promotions,

- Sponsorship/Event making,

- Customer Relationship Management and e-Service.

Direct Marketing
Direct marketing became an immensely popular marketing tool in the 90's – which is no coincidence, since the Web added a very efficient channel for Direct marketing.

Direct marketing includes:

- Mass-communications,

- Direct marketing targeted at segments,

- Direct marketing targeted at individuals,

- 1-to-1 dialogue, communication and mutual value increase.

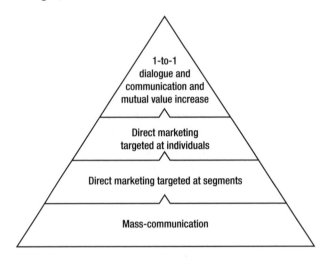

Figure 3.13 The Direct Marketing Process

Direct marketing can be divided into segment targeting and individual targeting. The latter requires that the company has already built a functional and effective Direct marketing database, that it has a good understanding of its customers, and that it has the necessary processes implemented. Needless to say, this method – individual targeting — is significantly superior to segment targeting.

Regardless of targeting style, Direct marketing can be split into different types, of which the following are the most widely used:

- Direct (e)Mail: A method in which the company sends a letter or e-mail directly to the customer.

- Direct Response Advertisement: A method in which the customer is urged, via the marketing activity, to contact the company, for example by telephone, coupon or letter.

- Door-to-Door Marketing: For example, distribution of a brochure by mail to all segment addresses.

- Telemarketing: Outbound marketing calls from a call center, either stand-alone or supporting one or more of the other methods.

The purpose of Direct marketing is to individualize and target any marketing activities at individuals/segments. Direct marketing is also about getting more loyal customers and building up a database for this purpose.

Marketing Communications

e-Marketing communication is revolutionizing marketing. In fact, there are arguments stating that conventional marketing will disappear and customer connectivity through the Web will become the principal foundation for a company's efforts in the future. We are moving away from mass communications to individualized communication by focusing on differences instead of similarities.[48]

What makes the net such a unique medium for a company's marketing activities is the possibility of two-way communication and the possibility of effectively differentiating and individualizing marketing campaigns. There is no doubt that a targeted, differentiated, and/or individualized effort has a more profound impact than mass marketing – not to mention the fact that it is more cost-effective. But you will need an extensive knowledge of your target groups and an effective CRM strategy and coordination in order to conduct an e-Marketing campaign of this type.

Another advantage of using the net as a marketing communication medium is that you can far more efficiently and precisely measure the success of the e-Marketing effort afterwards. The reason for this is, of course, that the Internet is electronic, meaning that everything in theory can be measured.

It is important to use e-Marketing in the correct strategic sense, *e.g.*, by utilizing the best qualities of the net – response-oriented marketing and general two-way communication. Response-oriented marketing allows the customer to react to the advertisement via the same media. Always make sure to assess all e-Marketing activities so you can determine the success rate for individual ones.

There are a lot of possibilities and methods of e-Marketing communication on the net, including the following — all of them widespread, some more effective than others. We call it the e-Business marketing communication mix:

1. Website name

2. Search engine/Portal registration

3. Affiliate programs

4. Partner/alliance co-communication

5. On-line advertising: banners and pop-ups

6. Sponsorships and events

7. e-Mail

8. Micro sites

9. Information placement

The following describes each:

Website name

The actual name of the site must be easy to remember and spell. A good name, especially for marketers who do not have a large mass communication budget, says something about the Website content or Website owner and is, of course, an integral part of the overall branding effort. A good, simple, meaningful name can make or break the business idea, but certainly cannot carry the business in the face of fundamental problems – think of pets.com and etoys.com. Conversely, a name can be good without necessarily being meaningful – think of Amazon.com and Yahoo.com, both easy to remember.

Simple is better in this case. If you are planning an international rollout, now or in the future, make sure your name has no negative connotations in the countries where you plan to do business.[49]

Search engine registration

Search engine registration is the most cost-effective form of e-Marketing among those listed here. Registering your Website with a search engine is usually free, and the effects can be quite noticeable. Having a professional company take care of such registrations and their maintenance is recommended, as this will ensure your company a good ranking on the major search engines.

There are many search engines on the net, such as:

- Google.com

- Yahoo.com

- AltaVista.com

- Lycos.com

- Excite.com

- Hotbot.com

- Infoseek.com

- WebCrawler.com

- WhatuSeek.com

New search engines appear constantly, so it is good to have the company working for you keep up on new ones. Search engine registration alone is not enough to cover all your e-Marketing needs, but it is a good and effective part of your company's e-Marketing mix.

Banner advertising
Banner advertising is probably the most common form of marketing on the net and, according to our experience, the least effective considering the invest-ment involved – the contact price is simply still too high, compared to tradi-tional media. The click-through rate is usually somewhere around 0.5% - 1.5%, which is really not much.

There are several types of banner ads, such as:

- Static banner ads (first-generation banner ads): merely a static image in an advertising column.

- Animated banner ads (first and second generation banner ads): One type of banner ad contains several images displayed as an animation (giving the effect of motion) – these are first-generation animated banners. Flash banner ads, which allow for more effective and complicated animations, have since entered the scene – these are second-generation animated ban-ner ads.

- Rich text (HTML/JAVA) banner ads (second generation banner ads): These are probably the most effective of the ads mentioned, as the banner itself is like a small Website. Rich text banners provide the following advantages:

  - The user can search directly from the banner.

  - The user can make choices via the banner.

  - The user can place an order or purchase directly via the banner.

Pop-up Advertising
A more recent advertising method on Websites is the pop-up ad, which appears in a separate window and is itself a small Website. Pop-up ads do not have the size limitations of banner advertising, and they seem to be growing in popularity, maybe only among advertisers however.

Affiliate programs
Affiliate programs (also known as associate programs) are probably the least common and yet the most effective form of marketing and selling on the net, compared to the other methods explained here.

Amazon.com was one of the first companies to implement this type of marketing, and today it has several hundred thousand participants in their Amazon Associates Program. This move has no doubt been of vital importance to Amazon.com's fast and efficient success on the net.

The basic concept of an affiliate program is to pay other companies for sending a paying customer to your Website. There are many different types of affiliate deals, but the two most common are to reward a certain percentage of the sale or to reward a fixed amount per referred customer who actually makes a purchase.

Affiliate programs are incredibly cost-effective, owing to the fact that you only pay for the marketing effort when a customer actually buys something.

Partner/alliance communication
This type of cooperation is a traffic swap setup, in which two (or more) companies include a link/door to one partner's Website free of charge in exchange for the same service from the other partner.

This is virtually a no-cost traffic generator, but raises a number of issues, not the least being control of the buyer. Once a buyer clicks through, for example, is the original site still visible and easy to return to?

Sponsorships
There is no actual difference between sponsorships on the net and traditional sponsorships.

Sponsorships are in many cases more effective than banner advertising as the notices are usually placed in a fixed spot on the Website and become a natural part of it. They may not appear to be advertisements.

The cost per exposure is usually lower in a sponsorship than in ordinary banner ads.

e-Mail marketing
e-Mail marketing is very widespread on the net, due to its cost effectiveness. It has two types:

- Mass e-Mail marketing, in which the company sends out a large number of e-Mails without any previous relationship with the receivers. Some direct marketing agencies have their e-Mail databases categorized according to the most common segmenting categories — geographic variables, demographic variables, consumer variables, and sometimes also psychographics/lifestyles.

- Individualized e-Mail marketing, in which the company sends a number of marketing e-Mails to a list of known and hand-picked recipients.

The problem with mass e-Mail marketing is that in many cases Internet users do not bother to read this type of e-Mail. Mass e-Mail marketing is known negatively as "spam;" certain mail servers will not forward or deliver mail from addresses thought to be spam-mail generators, and filters exist to prevent its delivery.

Permission e-Mail marketing — for example, in the form of daily or weekly newsletters — is a way of using e-Mail without the spam connotation. By requiring sign-up and sometimes a positive response to a follow-up e-Mail, the sender gains permission from the recipient to send information. As time passes, the permission can be expanded to allow the company to send even more material.

Microsites

Microsites are often used to market single products by creating small Websites designed exclusively for the products in question. In some cases, they are placed within a separate domain name, in other cases, under the domain name of another company or the company's own.

A microsite is thus a small Website that is separated from a company's main Website and in most cases used for campaign purposes for one or a few products, for example, a movie.

Information placement

This type of marketing communication is also known as "content advertising." It is communication by content, that is, by having content valuable to the recipient. It could be an innovative game that is made available to other Websites free of charge as part of their content, or it could be any other content which your company owns, which is used free of charge or for a payment by another site.

As a final remark, we would like to mention that it is not always the most popular and common types of e-Marketing that are the most effective. Try using less conventional e-Marketing methods. Amazon.com did – and just look where it got them!

CRM and e-Service

It would not make sense to end a section about Customer Communication and Interaction without mentioning the opportunities inherent in a well–designed Customer Relationship Management system. The Web gives you, the business owner, an incredible opportunity to get close to your customer and to make decisions based on your knowledge for the benefit of your business and your customer. Regardless of whether your business is B2C or B2B, your system should include the buying history of the customer and an interaction log showing every interaction you have had with the customer, and you should use this for recommendations, alerts, special offers, *etc*.

Generalizing somewhat, the point is that new technology offers opportunities for additional service – remember the days prior to Automated Teller Machines when you actually had to worry about whether your bank branch would be open? – and customers adapt amazingly quickly and come to expect the improved level of service. A successful business will offer not only the e-Services that customers have come to accept but will up the ante, offering more.

In the discussion below, we assume that a business offers all applicable traditional services common to its particular industry. We shall then classify e-Services as follows:

- e-Service related to the company's products. This type of e-Service is connected to the company's core services, *i.e.*, the services that are fully associated with the company's products such as manuals, product support, *etc.*

- e-Service related to the company's service. This type of e-Service is connected to the company's supplementary services, *i.e.*, all the added values that help create a positive business environment and customer relationship. An example is the services offered for product pickup or return.

- e-Service related to the company as a whole. This type of e-Service is connected to the company's general service from initial contact to the end of the deal, which should give the prospect/customer a positive experience and loyalty to the company. Examples here include an Investor Relations button and industry news on the Web site.

We shall ignore the last – it is reasonably well understood and implemented – and concentrate on e-Services relating to product and service.

Another way of looking at e-Service presents it as a hierarchy with an increasing level of sophistication of service:

- **The Documentation Level**. At this level, which is anonymous, the business offers product information online, including manuals, product glossies, Frequently Asked Questions for installation and trouble-shooting, and appropriate contact information for dealers and/or repair locations.

- **The Basic Commerce Level.** At this level the business offers basic commerce, *i.e.*, selling of product, handling returns, customer service for tracking, *etc.* This can be offered directly from the business or outsourced.

- **The Enhanced Commerce Level.** At this level the business offers value-added services in the buying process: for example, a buying history, purchasing suggestions, a configurator for selling complex products, *etc.* Again, this can be in-house or outsourced.

- **The Cooperative Services Level.** At this level the interaction becomes pro-active on the part of the business – with appropriate permission from the buyer – and the business will inform the customer of possible expiration/depletion of consumables, will inform him/her of environmental/governmental regulations that might impact the customer's infrastructure, will design additional services/products in cooperation with the customer, *etc.*

Although the Cooperative Services Level is sort of the "Holy Grail," few Web sites have progressed past the Basic Commerce Level. Once you are there, the customer is committed.

Outsourcing e-Services

As mentioned above, it is possible to outsource e-Services, but is this a sensible thing to do? It depends on the company in question, but the following advantages can be gained in many cases:

- The company will not have any start-up costs for this technology.

- The company will in many cases have the option to upgrade the service later on, assuming the provider has the capacity.

- The company will be able to act faster and implement new services.

- The company will be aware of all expenses for individual services, as might not be the case if the company were to offer all services independently. (It is often difficult for a company to figure out the cost of individual services, as there are usually many factors in play.)

- The company can utilize the provider's specialization and competence in the area in question.

- The company can quickly give up a certain service without causing any friction or further implications for its own organization.

- The company may easily differentiate its services.

- The company can focus on its core areas.

The disadvantage of outsourcing e-Services compared to keeping them in-house is, of course, lack of control. Strategic e-Services should not, as a general rule, be outsourced unless material advantages can be achieved. The same is even more true for core services.

An alternative to outsourcing is partnering, in order to optimize the service and achieve an effect of synergy.

Should e-Services be free?
Or, to put it differently, does one size fit all? Usually not. The Web has been characterized as the place where information, at least, must be free since otherwise you would go elsewhere to get it. That is, albeit slowly, becoming less and less true.

You need to separate e-Services into standard e-Services, *i.e.*, the services that all customers get, and optional/extra e-Services that can be purchased by all customers or offered free to premium customers. Additionally, you should identify possible delivery vehicles for the e-Services. A premium service may be free to all customers when it is offered by e-Mail only, for example, but only free to premium customers when offered online with a human operator.

You can position your company well by differentiating and individualizing e-Services for your customers, and you might be looking at significant savings, as your company will then not be offering free services to customers who do not need them or who are not profitable enough to you.

The net offers a unique opportunity to automate your company's service processes and thereby create large savings related to your company's service offerings. By automating your service processes and making them accessible via the net you can achieve:

- Operational savings,

- Self-service for applicable services,

- A higher degree of customer loyalty.

Be careful, however, that you live up to your Service Level Agreement, whether stated or implied. A customer does not stay loyal if e-Mails go unanswered or if implementation help on the Web is unintelligible.

A lot of companies focus solely on the core services related to their products. The problem, as already mentioned, is that this type of approach often does not position a company well in the long run. Of course, these core services should be offered, but be aware that, on their own, they will not create lasting competitive advantages – in most cases, just short-term advantages.

We have noticed the following five general problems with the services of companies, including product-related services, services related to the company's service offerings, and services related to the company in general:

- The company does not understand the need for service mix and other value-creating needs of the individual customer or segment.

- The company does not differentiate and/or individualize its services for individual customers or segments, but offers the same services to all.

- The company focuses on and adds new services only to the company's core services (product related).

- The company develops/creates new services that have no actual value or importance to customers.

- The company has too many standard service offers that do not justify their own cost or have no actual value or weight to a customer choosing his supplier.

You should have as many standard services as the market segment requires and a lot of optional/extra services that can be differentiated and individualized for your customers. In many cases you will actually be able to charge your customers for your extra services. You will not, of course, be able to differentiate or individualize services for your customers until you have a certain degree of knowledge about them. Because of this, services are often first customized on the segment level and later individualized to specific customers.

Implementing an e-Service strategy is a difficult and time-consuming process, especially for an existing company. The company should ask itself the following questions:

- Can we afford to offer the same services to all customers in the future?

- How can we optimize the level of service for our most profitable customers and decrease the level for less profitable customers?

- How can we utilize e-Services to offer our customers better value?

- Which e-Services help create loyal customers?

We shall once again use Amazon.com as an example, as it has really put e-Services to good strategic use, giving the company both large savings and greater customer loyalty. Among other things, Amazon.com uses automated e-Mail agents that answer questions and enquiries from customers without the need for human intervention, but still in a personalized manner. What the customer experiences is incredibly fast and efficient customer service.

So remember: e-Services should be an integral part of any business strategy, as they present an area where a company can really position itself and thereby create long-lasting advantages over its competition.

3.10
Financial Plan

This is where "the rubber meets the road!" This section includes the financials for the business, *i.e.*, what an investor or banker will look at to decide whether this is a worthwhile opportunity, once he/she has decided that you are believable in terms of opportunity, team, and market size. It is very important that this section is presented in a form that is acceptable to the audience, meaning that — at least as far as the presentation goes — you may have more than one version of it. It is also important that the presentation be in accordance with the appropriate accounting standards for the country in which you incorporate – or do business – and with the background of your audience.[50]

Another issue for this section is how much to present here and how much to move to the Supporting Documents section. Obviously, this is not a question of hiding information but of pleasing various audiences. The expectations may vary from only including the Operating Statement in this section to including everything. The description below will include all you could possibly think to include in this section. Choose what you want, then move the rest to the Supporting Documents section.

The complete section is quite extensive so it requires a lot of time and work. The financial plan shows the expected financial effect of the business plan. Its primary purpose is to define the expected future income and, at the same time, lay out the capital requirements of the business plan. It is also a crucial management tool.

A complete set of financial plans will include:

- Assumptions

- Financial statements

- Capital requirements

- Exit and payback strategies.

Assumptions

The first thing to do is to list the assumptions on which you will base your financial statements. Assumptions will include general assumptions, such as:

- Future inflation rate to calculate present values

- Tax rates, including depreciation allowances

- Cost of money for loan financing

And specific assumptions for your business:

- Market share growth

- Unit pricing – or overall sales

- Cost of goods sold (manufacturing costs), broken down as well as possible

- Sales, General and Administrative costs – SG&A.

These assumptions are the foundation on which you build your financial statements. Weak foundations, weak building!

Take your time with this section and, when you have finished the financial plans, review your assumptions. Chances are you will want to make a few additions.

Financial Statements

The financial statements consist of five parts:

- Revenue projections

- Income statement

- Balance sheet

- Cash flow statement

- Break-even analysis.

In general, revenue projections display your variable income sources (sales) and expenses (cost of sales). The income statement contains information on the revenues and expenses involved in running the company. The balance sheet displays the effect of the plans on the company's assets and liabilities and also the development of the net capital. The liability part also shows the composition of the company's financing, including self- and external financing. The cash flow statement shows the company's capital requirements, *i.e.*, how much capital will have to be injected into the company in order to establish and run it. Finally, the break-even analysis shows when the business will start turning a profit.

This section is not a textbook in Financial or Management Accounting. We are working under the assumption that you already know, or know someone who knows, how to put together an operating statement, balance sheet, cash flow statement and break-even analysis. We shall only examine the figures we consider essential for individual statements in the business plan.

The statements we use as examples below include key figures only and not detailed numbers, which incidentally should – or rather, must — be included.

Revenue Projections

Revenue projections first show how much money you expect to get in the door – called turnover, sales, or revenue – prior to any deductions. The revenue projections are based on the assumptions of market size and growth, and on the expected unit sale price. They will typically be done separately for each different product or service. You may do a monthly or quarterly projection for the first year; for the second year onwards, yearly will probably suffice in this section, with backup in the Supporting Documents section.

It is useful to create multiple scenarios – best case, worst case, and expected sales — for a possible sensitivity analysis later.

For example, let us imagine an Internet store with 10,000 initial customers/members, a monthly member growth of 10%, and an average expenditure per member per month of $20.00. The first year revenue projection would then look like:

Member Growth:	10% per month											
Member Expenditure:	20 per month											
Month	1	2	3	4	5	6	7	8	9	10	11	12
Members	10,000	11,000	12,100	13,310	14,641	16,106	17,716	19,487	21,436	23,579	25,937	28,531
Total Revenue	$200,000	$220,000	$242,000	$266,200	$292,820	$322,102	$354,312	$389,743	$428,718	$471,590	$518,748	$570,623

Revenue Year 1: $4,276,857

In this example, the scenarios could be based on either a change in growth of the number of members or a change in the average expenditure per member – for example, to include an initial membership fee, followed by later monthly purchases. We shall choose to vary the growth in number of members, with a worst case growth of 5% per month and a best case of 15% per month. The worst case looks like:

Member Growth:	5% per month											
Member Expenditure:	20 per month											
Month	1	2	3	4	5	6	7	8	9	10	11	12
Members	10,000	10,500	11,025	11,576	12,155	12,763	13,401	14,071	14,775	15,513	16,289	17,103
Total Revenue	$200,000	$210,000	$220,500	$231,525	$243,101	$255,256	$268,019	$281,420	$295,491	$310,266	$325,779	$342,068

Revenue Year 1: $3,183,425

And the best case:

Member Growth:	15% per month											
Member Expenditure:	20 per month											
Month	1	2	3	4	5	6	7	8	9	10	11	12
Members	10,000	11,500	13,225	15,209	17,490	20,114	23,131	26,600	30,590	35,179	40,456	46,524
Total Revenue	$200,000	$230,000	$264,500	$304,175	$349,801	$402,271	$462,612	$532,004	$611,805	$703,575	$809,112	$930,478

Revenue Year 1: $5,800,333

The next step is to derive the Gross Profit numbers using Cost of Goods Sold numbers based on your assumptions. For example, assume that Cost of Goods Sold is 70% of the Revenue number.

The following layout is often used, assuming in this case three products. (The figures do not relate to the preceding example.)

	Product category A	Product category B	Product category C	Total
Sales	$50,000	$100,000	$75,000	$225,000
Cost of Sales (70%)	$35,000	$70,000	$52,500	$157,500
Gross Profit	$15,000	$30,000	$22,500	$67,500

It is very important to make revenue projections and to define clearly the assumptions that underlie the projections. This illustrates that the figures provided are not merely wild guesses but well-considered calculations.

Remember that a newly started company has no history, making it difficult for a venture capitalist to evaluate whether the figures are realistic unless you clearly state the assumptions.

Income Statement

The Income Statement is a financial statement that takes you from Sales to Net Income, typically on a yearly basis:[51]

Income Statement	YEAR 1	YEAR 2	YEAR 3	TOTAL
Sales	200,000	250,000	300,000	750,000
- Cost of Goods Sold	140,000	175,000	210,000	525,000
Gross Profit	60,000	75,000	90,000	225,000
- Selling and General Administrative – SG&A	45,000	50,000	60,000	155,000
Operating Profit	15,000	25,000	30,000	70,000
- Other Revenues and Expenses	5,000	5,000	5,000	15,000
Net Profit Pre-Tax	10,000	20,000	25,000	55,000
- Taxes on Earnings (assume 34%)	3,400	6,800	8,500	18,700
Net Income	6,600	13,200	16,500	36,300

The income statement as shown belongs in the Strategic Business Plan for a couple of reasons: it shows the overall result to be expected – if the assumptions are correct — and it is a required financial statement in the annual reporting for a public corporation.

Other than for those reasons, the Income Statement is not a very useful operational tool. Expanded and with appropriate re-ordering of the items, however, it becomes a very useful tool for planning and execution. You will expand on it as part of your operational planning, and you should include the Operational Plans in your supporting documentation.

The following three ratios should be calculated and included. They will help your audience do a consistency check of your financials.

Gross Profit Margin = Gross Profit divided by Sales

Example for Year 1 above: 60,000/200,000, or   30%

Operating Profit Margin = Operating Profit divided by Sales

Example for Year 1 above: 15,000/200,000, or   7.5%

Net Profit Margin (also called ROS – Return on Sales) = Net Profit pre-tax divided by Sales

Example for Year 1 above: 10,000/200,000, or   5%

Balance Sheet

The balance sheet is a statement of financial position for the company at a particular time, typically at the end of the corporate fiscal year. A progression of balance sheets for the years being projected for the company will show the growth of capital in the company, as shown in the example below:

Balance Sheet	YEAR 0	YEAR 1	YEAR 2	YEAR 3
Assets				
Current Assets				
Cash	10,000	5,909	15,350	22,300
Accounts Receivable	0	25,000	31,250	37,500
Inventory	0	20,000	25,000	30,000
Total Current Assets	10,000	50,909	71,600	89,800
Other Assets				
Plant, Property, and Equipment, less Depreciation	0	55,000	50,000	45,000
Intangibles, less Amortization	0	0	10,000	9,500
Other Assets	0	0	0	0
Total Other Assets	0	55,000	60,000	54,500
Total Assets	10,000	105,909	131,600	144,300
Liabilities				
Current Liabilities				
Accounts Payable	0	20,909	25,000	30,000
Income Tax Payable	0	3,400	6,800	8,500
Total Current Liabilities	0	24,309	31,800	38,500
Non-Current Liabilities				
Long-Term Debt	0	25,000	20,000	10,000
Deferred Income Taxes	0	0	0	0
Total Non-Current Liabilities	0	25,000	20,000	10,000
Total Liabilities	0	49,309	51,800	48,500
Shareholders' Equity				
Capital Stock	10,000	10,000	10,000	10,000
Additional Paid-in Capital	0	25,000	25,000	25,000
Retained Earnings	0	21,600	44,800	60,800
Total Shareholders' Equity	10,000	56,600	79,800	95,800
Total Liabilities and Shareholders Equity	10,000	105,909	131,600	144,300

Certain ratios are calculated based on amounts from the Income Statement and the Balance Sheet. They are used to further analyze the financial information. These ratios include:

Days Receivables   365*Accounts Receivables/Annual Sales

Days Payables   365*Accounts Payable/Total Costs

Inventory Turns   Cost of Sales/Inventory

Current Ratio   Current Assets/Current Liabilities

Debt Ratio   Total Liabilities/Total Assets

Return on Assets   Net Income/Total Assets

Return on Equity   Net Income/Total Equity

Using the values from the examples above, we get:[52]

	Year 1			Year 2			Year 3		
Days Receivables	365*25,000/200,000	46		365*31,200/250,000	46		365*37,500/300,000	46	
Days Payable	365*20,909/140,000	55		365*25,000/175,000	52		365*30,000/210,000	52	
Inventory turns	140,000/20,000	7		175,000/25,000	7		210,000/30,000	7	
Current Ratio	48,409/24,309	1.99		67,450/31,800	2.12		84,000/38,500	2.18	
Debt Ratio	49,309/103,409	0.48		51,800/127,450	0.41		48,500/138,500	0.35	
Return on Assets	6,600/103,409	6%		13,200/127,450	10%		16,500/138,500	12%	
Return on Equity	6,600/54,100	12%		13,200/75,650	17%		16,500/90,000	18%	

We shall not venture further into "financial engineering;" many sources exist for further study.[53]

Cash Flow Statement

A Cash Flow Statement, which shows you where cash comes from and where it goes, is a very important tool for managing a business. As you can imagine, there are few things more essential in a business than knowing how much cash you have. Having a Cash Flow Statement as one of your financial statements in the Strategic Business Plan is important too. Since it can be hard to predict the actual figures in the cash flow statement, you will need to make some assumptions about accounts receivables, inventory, capital equipment, accounts payable, *etc.* with regard to the operating statement.

There can be two types of cash flow statements in the business plan, one that states the direct and one that states the indirect cash flow. However, the direct cash flow statement is in practice very difficult to do. We will therefore only show you the indirect cash flow statement on an annual basis. But remember also to make it on a monthly basis if possible!

You should include the fully specified cash flow statements under Supporting Documents of the business plan.

The following show a sample Cash Flow Statement:

Cash Flow Statement	Year 1	Year 2	Year 3
Cash at Beginning of Year	10,000	5,909	15,350
+ Net Income After Tax	6,600	13,200	16,500
+ Taxes	3,400	6,800	8,500
+ Depreciations	5,000	5,000	5,000
+/- Changes in Value of Accounts Payable	20,909	4,091	5,000
+/- Changes in Value of Accounts Receivable	-25,000	-6,250	-6,250
+/- Changes in Inventories	-20,000	-5,000	-5,000
Cash Flow from Operations	-9,091	17,841	23,750
- Investment in Capital Equipment	-55,000	0	0
Cash Flow from Investments	-55,000	0	0
+ Cash Deposit Shareholders at a Premium	15,000	0	0
+ Cash Deposit Venture Capital at a Premium	20,000	0	0
+ Increase in Long-term Loans	25,000	0	0
- Repayment Long-Term Debt	0	-5,000	-10,000
Cash Flow from Financing	60,000	-5,000	-10,000
Cash Flow prior to Tax Payment	-4,091	12,841	13,750
- Taxes Paid	0	-3,400	-6,800
Net Cash Flow	-4,091	9,441	6,950
Cash at End of Year	5,909	15,350	22,300

Our last comment on this subject is on the topic of managing your company's liquidity/cash flow, an extremely important area. A company can easily produce a steady profit, making everything seem all right. But if, for example, the payment terms for your customers are too long, you could end up in a situation where you are unable to pay your own bills, making the company insolvent despite the fact that it is producing a profit. So, always keep a close eye on your cash flow!

Break-Even Analysis

The last financial statement is the aptly-named break-even analysis that states when your business is expected to break even, *i.e.*, when it will begin to turn a profit so you can pay a dividend, *etc*. If you are working with an existing, profitable company, you should skip this step. However, when making a large investment, it is a good idea to make a break-even analysis so you can calculate when the investment will break even.

The example used above is not applicable for a break-even analysis since it assumes making money from day one. A better example for this purpose is:

Suppose you are making widgets that cost you $10 each to manufacture; you sell them for $15 each. Your fixed costs are $60,000 per year, and you expect to sell 600 widgets the first month with sales growing 10% per month. When will you break even?[54]

As shown in the table below, break-even is in month eleven.

Month	1	2	3	4	5	6	7	8	9	10	11	12	13
Widgets Sold	600	660	726	799	878	966	1063	1169	1286	1415	1556	1712	1883
Gross Margin	3000	3300	3630	3993	4392	4832	5315	5846	6431	7074	7781	8559	9415
Fixed Costs	5000	5000	5000	5000	5000	5000	5000	5000	5000	5000	5000	5000	5000
Cumulative Net Profit (Loss)	-2000	-3700	-5070	-6077	-6685	-6853	-6538	-5692	-4262	-2188	594	4153	8568

Capital Requirements

Once you have created your revenue projections, an operating statement, a balance sheet, a cash flow statement and a break-even analysis, you will be able to deduce how much capital you will need to be able to execute your business plan. Once you have reached this figure, it is, of course, important to give a brief explanation of how you did it. You can do this by stating investments you will be making, along with necessary liquidity/cash flow in the period.

In this part you should describe the division of your capital requirements, *i.e.*, how much will be financed by yourself and how much will be needed from external funding/capital.

The following table shows an example of a breakdown for a capital requirement of $70,000:

Total Cash Available	$10,000
Cash deposit from existing shareholders at a premium	$15,000
Bank loans by existing stockholders with personal liability	$25,000
Cash deposit from venture capitalist at a premium	$20,000
Total capital required	$70,000

Which financing method you choose depends on availability and personal choice. Loans are typically only granted with appropriate security, which may not be available in a start-up – unless you count equity in your house and/or your pension account! On the other hand, while a loan has to be paid back at specific time intervals, you do not give up equity when you take a loan.

Shareholders, whether friends or Venture Capitalists, expect equity in return for investments. The amount of equity – control – you have to give up will depend on many factors, not the least being your ability to convince your audience about your business.

The timing of your business growth will also have an impact on the type of financing you can consider. The growth of your business may be such that you cannot afford to service loans in the first periods.

Exit and Payback Strategies
The final topic is exit and payback strategies. Exit strategy is all about finding out when your investors can capitalize their investments and how much they can expect to earn from them. Payback strategy shows when you can expect to be able to repay any loans your company has taken. You determine one or both by taking a closer look at your cash flow statement and your break-even analyses.

Remember that this section of the business plan is quite crucial for your financial situation, as your financial partners will ultimately use it to make up their minds and estimate whether or not your project is an attractive option for their investment or loan.

3.11
Supporting Documents

The last section of the business plan is Supporting Documents, *i.e.*, all the attachments that document or verify the contents and conclusions in your business plan. It will include CVs of Board members, management and key personnel; financial statements; and market research material, including the marketing plan. The marketing plan, which is covered later in this book, demonstrates how you expect to execute your marketing strategy.

Do not expect your readers, or presentation audience, to be overly interested in your supporting documents. In the best of all worlds, you state your case so succinctly in the body of the Strategic Business Plan that no one even looks at the supporting documents. In reality, however, the supporting documents are there to support arguments, statements, and facts in the Strategic Business Plan that, for some reason or another, are not "bought" immediately by your audience. That does not mean they are not right; it may just mean that the audience is coming at them slightly differently than you.

Supporting documents need not be as succinct as the main body. They cannot be, since they will include a lot of detail. You should, nevertheless, try to make them as clear and logically consistent as you can. Think of supporting documents as the skins of an onion: you don't expose the audience to everything at once, you present it logically, layer by layer, with more information at each layer.

We are going to spend the rest of this section discussing the market analysis and research that lead up to the marketing plan.

Market Analysis
Market analysis is usually used in a company to reduce uncertainty in decision-making. In most cases, the goal is to predict the future behavior of, for example, the company's customers or competition. Part of the analysis involves identifying predictors of behavior. Some examples are:

1. Planned behavior

    a. Is the behavior intentional?

2. Previous behavior

    a. What behavior have you observed in the past?

3. Demographical variables

    a. Gender

    b. Age

    c. Income

    d. Education

    e. Occupation

    f. Other

4. Information requirements

    a. What information do you have on the area in question that is presumably defining for behavior?

5. Attitudes

    a. Which attitudes exist on the area in question?

6. Motives

    a. What are the motives for the behavior?

Market analysis itself is a vast topic, and there are quite a few methods for dealing with it. That is why we shall only take a general look at it, especially the following areas:

- Market research

- The explorative analysis

- Descriptive and causal analyses

- Secondary data

- Primary data.

Market Research

Market research is an efficient tool for validating areas of the business plan, for example, defining the market, developing customer profiles, defining competition, *etc*. It is typically done by professionals in the field.

In general, there are two approaches to market research:

- Quantitative research: research that allows you to quantify the market statistically,

- Qualitative research: all other types of research.

A market analysis will produce information on the company's environment, thereby acquiring a serious decision-making foundation for activities the company wishes to initiate. It is an extremely important tool for working out the company's business plan since, without it, decisions would be based on assumptions created by the authors of the Strategic Business Plan, assumptions that in many cases would be guesses.

The process of conducting a market analysis usually begins with the creation of a problem statement, in which the problem you wish to solve or analyze is clearly defined. This may sound trivial, but a vague or poorly-worded problem statement can/will in most cases result in an incorrect or at least incomplete market analysis.

The next step is to define your information requirements, which involves deciding how extensive you want the market analysis to be. Then you select your preferred data sources, collection methods, and form of contact and produce questionnaires. If you are dealing with a representative analysis, a sampling plan must also be prepared.

When you have completed the above, the data collection process can begin. Gathering and analyzing the data leads to the final market analysis report, presenting the results as shown in figure 3.14.

1. Problem statement
Theme Assumptions Questions

2. Defining information requirements
Listed item by item Descriptive

3. Choosing data sources
Secondary data Primary data

4. Selecting collection method
Explorative analyses - extensive strategy (wide analysis strategy) Descriptive analyses and causal analyses - Intensive strategy (narrow and deep analysis strategy)

5. Method of contact and questionnaires
Internet based (Web and e-mail) questionnaires Mail distributed questionnaires Personal interviews Telephone interviews Mall intercept

6. Sampling plan
Conscious picking Random picking

7. The data collection process

8. Data analysis

9. Conclusions and recommendations

Figure 3.14   Market Analysis Table of Contents

Be careful with statistical sampling plans: they need to be representative of the areas which you want to sample, which means in turn that they must sample within your business area and sample enough people for the data to be representative.

The Explorative Analysis
An explorative analysis is conducted without a concrete, predefined purpose, and is thus, in most cases, merely based on a specific theme-oriented problem statement. The purpose of the analysis is not to find answers to specific questions, but to seek out relevant questions to pose in a subsequent market analysis. An explorative analysis is therefore to be seen as a sketchy, initial analysis with the purpose of creating a basis for one or more subsequent analyses.

For an entrepreneur, first conducting an explorative analysis to gain a better foundation for later analyses is standard procedure. It gives the entrepreneur a hint of whether or not the business concept is strong enough and has the right strategic direction.

Descriptive and Causal Analyses

Descriptive and causal analyses are, in contrast to explorative analyses, conducted with a clearly defined research purpose, and are therefore based on a set problem statement that consists of either a number of questions or hypotheses or both. The analysis can then be planned in detail, based on the structure of the problem statement.

The basic concept of a descriptive analysis is to describe a certain situation, whereas a causal analysis is meant to determine the cause(s) behind it.

Conducting a descriptive or causal market analysis in continuation of an explorative market analysis is a logical step for the entrepreneur, as it provides both a serious and well-documented platform for adding the final touches to the business concept and business plan and, to a certain extent, validates the business concept and business plan.

Secondary Data

Secondary data is, *per* definition, data that has not been produced specifically to solve the problem at hand. There are generally two types of secondary data, internal and external.

Internal secondary data consists of information/data present in the company, whereas external data originates in the company's external environment as standard analyses/data.

Internal secondary data

Internal secondary data are data present within the company.

The most important sources of information for most companies are the ERP (Enterprise Resource Planning) system and the CRM (Customer Relationship Management) system. You should be aware, however, that useful data may also be found outside of these two systems. Therefore it is important to seek out *all* the company's information sources, both electronic and manual, before the market analysis is initiated.

At the same time, it is extremely important that you fully understand the information/data — for example, from the company's ERP — that is used in the analysis, as the analysis might otherwise lead to incorrect conclusions. It is also essential to gain insight into and understand the company's accounting principles and methods.

External secondary data

External secondary data are found in the company's external environment as standard analyses/data. They can be derived from many different sources, such as:

- Public statistical offices that continually produce standard analyses on different areas of public interest;

- Private analysis institutes, for example, Jupiter Communications (www.jup.com) and Forrester Research (www.forrester.com), that produce market analyses on different areas that are usually available for purchase, on an annual subscription or *ad-hoc* basis.

Furthermore, most countries offer public and non-public publications with different types of standard analyses, for example:

- Media data

- Media index

- Media information

- Market information

- Standard market analyses

- Public records of registered companies.

The above does not cover all information sources — it merely offers a few examples for your inspiration.

In general, secondary data is the most widely used, as primary data is far more expensive and takes longer to produce.

Primary Data

Primary data is produced specifically with the intention of solving a given problem. There are generally two methods of harvesting primary data: structured and unstructured data collection.

Structured data collection involves an interview that is based on a number of guidelines and contains only fixed answers, *e.g.*, "yes" or "no."

Unstructured data collection, on the other hand, happens when guidelines have not been set in advance, making it possible to conduct a more thorough interview, *i.e.*, allowing open answers and not just "yes" or "no." Unstructured data collection is very expensive to carry out, requires a lot of time to complete, and requires a highly qualified interviewer, usually a psychologist. It is difficult to produce statistically representative data this way, as the time factor is almost always a problem.

Here are some of the most recognized and most widely-used methods for collecting unstructured primary data (usually collected via personal interviews and mall intercepts):

- Depth interviews

- Focus groups

- Observation

- Role-playing.

In contrast, structured primary data is usually collected with set questionnaires, typically using the following methods of communication:

- Internet-based (Web and e-Mail) questionnaires

- Questionnaires distributed by mail

- Telephone interviews.

...And Next...

This chapter showed you how to write a Strategic Business Plan, taking you from idea to plan. Read on for the next step, Raising Capital.

Chapter 4
Raising Capital

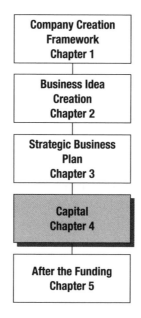

```
┌─────────────────────┐
│   Company Creation   │
│     Framework        │
│     Chapter 1        │
└─────────────────────┘
           │
┌─────────────────────┐
│    Business Idea     │
│      Creation        │
│     Chapter 2        │
└─────────────────────┘
           │
┌─────────────────────┐
│  Strategic Business  │
│        Plan          │
│     Chapter 3        │
└─────────────────────┘
           │
┌─────────────────────┐
│      Capital         │
│     Chapter 4        │
└─────────────────────┘
           │
┌─────────────────────┐
│  After the Funding   │
│     Chapter 5        │
└─────────────────────┘
```

In this chapter we shall take a look at raising capital: what your options are in terms of classes of financing, what you need at different phases, how to estimate your needs, what venture capital is all about and, finally, how to make a persuasive presentation to sell your business idea to the financial community. The venture capital world is going through a lot of changes currently, as it does from time to time, so the description here will be more general than specific to 2002.

4.1
Types and Sources of Capital

Capital management generally consists of three disciplines: managing investments, securing financing, and controlling resources. Capital management is therefore about acquiring capital, but also about allocating and conserving as well. We shall concentrate on the acquisition aspects.

Acquiring capital is by far the start-up's first and greatest headache because — in contrast to product development, market analysis, recruiting, *etc.* — it is not something the entrepreneur can do himself. It involves outsiders and getting money from other people who want hard facts about why they should give the money to you, the entrepreneur. It is one of the areas where outside expertise can make a real difference.

For external financing, the principle of risk taking is often what distinguishes capital suppliers.

Low risk capital — like bank loans with solid security in, *e.g.*, real estate — has a low upside potential; a bank can only charge a competitive interest rate on a loan, generating a relative low but safe ROI. It is highly unlikely that such an investment will not generate the estimated ROI. The most risk-averse investors, typically traditional, conservative banks, are satisfied with a lower return on their investment or loan (interest rate) but demand a high level of certainty of cash-flow, either through their evaluation of a business concept's short-term cash generating abilities or guarantees based on real estate or other tangible, sellable equity. On house loans, banks typically expect to have an estimated payback of well above 99 % of their investments, either in cash or sellable equity.

High risk investments — like investment in precious metals or venture capital investments in companies — are considered to have a high upside potential, generating high ROI. But there is a real chance such investments will not yield the hoped-for ROI and, in fact, will be lost. Thus most risk-seeking investors like venture capitalists are looking for extraordinarily large returns on investments in exchange for taking calculated higher risks. Out of a large number of investments in companies, venture capitalists typically expect only a few to make it big but rely on their experience – hope? — that when an investment makes it big, it makes it very big.

4.2
Three Classes of Financing

In this section we shall provide an overview of three classes of financing: short-, medium- and long-term. Note that many of these require that you already have been funded – have credit – through, for example, venture capital funding.

First, let's get the shortest term financing of all out of the way: your credit cards, your retirement fund, personal lines of credit, your house, *etc*. Successful companies have been financed by maxing out credit cards or through personal loans, but, on balance, you'd better have a good backup plan.

Short-Term Financing

Short-term financing is repaid or renegotiated within three years, usually within one year. The most used within this financing category are the following:

Bank credit line — Overdraft

Probably the most popular form of short-term financing on the capital market, allowing the company to draw up to a certain amount from their account. The terms of this deal are usually renegotiated each year. It is flexible, as the company itself can perform the transactions, withdrawals and repayments.

If you can get it, *i.e.*, if your credit or security is good enough, it may be quite cheap and fast to get, but usually with a low credit limit.

Bank loan

This is also quite a popular type of financing, but not nearly as flexible as the credit line. A bank loan works by first setting the amount of the loan and then repaying it over a certain period of time with a fixed monthly payment.

Trade credit

This is another type of short-term financing that gives the company credit with its suppliers, meaning that it can use its capital for other purposes in this period. In many cases, any trade discounts will disappear when dealing with a longer credit period.

Factoring

Yet another type of short-term financing, in which the company makes a deal with a factoring company that bills the company's customers, at the same time taking over the debtor risk. The factoring company usually pays the company within a short time of billing the customer. The disadvantage of factoring as a form of financing is that it is usually quite expensive, although this downside is usually eliminated by the transference of the debtor risk and administration – especially for small and medium-sized companies.

Medium-Term Financing

Medium-term financing is paid back or renegotiated within four to ten years. Popular types are:

Term loan

This is probably the most popular type of medium-term financing. It is essentially a longer term loan with a relatively low interest rate and a fixed repayment plan. The repayment terms are, in many cases, extremely flexible.

Leasing

This type of financing has become extremely widespread over the last fifteen years. The basic concept is to have a leasing company buy all of a company's assets and lease them to the company over a fixed period of time. The advantage of leasing, apart from the financial benefit, lies in the tax benefits associated with leasing, although these may vary according to the country your company is registered in. There are generally two types of leasing:

Financial leasing

This is a non-cancelable contract in which the company pays a set amount each month or each quarter, thereby paying back the full value of the assets including depreciation, interest and profit to the leasing company during the leasing period. The company can/must then purchase the assets from the leasing company at an agreed price, usually via the last leasing payment. The company must take care of maintenance and insurance of the assets during the leasing period. The period usually spans three to five years but can also be longer, depending on the asset.

Operating leasing

In contrast, this is a contract that can be cancelled during the leasing period — usually with come some financial compensation. It is also paid monthly or quarterly, although the full value of the assets is not paid through the leasing payments, which means that the company cannot purchase the assets later on or, at least, that it will have to pay the full market price. In operating leasing, as opposed to financial leasing, the maintenance and insurance of the asset are included. This type of leasing is particularly popular for investments in IT technology. The leasing period usually spans one to three years but can in some cases be longer, once again depending on the asset in question.

Long-Term Financing

Long-term financing is basically equity capital and long-term loans, whether direct loans, lines of credit, or commercial paper, where repayment spans more than ten years. In planning for the future of a start-up, the most popular type of long-term financing is an Initial Public Offering (IPO), *i.e.*, making shares in the company publicly available to the market as investment objects, thereby raising additional capital.

An IPO, also called "going public," is thus categorized as long-term financing on the capital market. Most companies carry out an IPO to gain capital for further expansion or to fully or in part repay the initial investors of the company, thereby reducing their risks. If a company wishes to buy out other companies, it is also considerably easier for a "public company" as it can offer vendors shares instead of cash.

The following are some of the advantages of an IPO:

- The company gains easier and more extensive access to the capital market, thus considerably easing access to funds.

- Larger investment companies in the capital market primarily – and sometimes exclusively — invest in companies on the stock market.

- Investors in the company can trade the stock on the open market.

- The company achieves a considerably higher valuation compared to a "private" company.

- The company can offer its employees share option schemes.

- The company achieves a recognized market value.

Of course, there are also certain disadvantages to an IPO, such as the following:

- The incidental costs are usually quite high.

- There are minimum requirements for a company's capital basis, though these differ from one stock exchange to the next. For example, the KVX (Københavns Fondsbørs Vækstmarked) – the Copenhagen Stock Exchange Growth Market — requires a market value of DKK 300 million or more, and the Nasdaq SmallCap Market requires a capitalization of US$ 50m for an initial listing.[55]

- The company must implement complex reporting systems and financial routines in the company that meet the stock exchange's demands.

- The company loses some control compared to a "private company."

- The company becomes vulnerable to take-over by unfriendly buyers when its stock is bought and sold on the "free" market.

A company can have multiple classes of stock, each with different voting rights and par values; examples are Ordinary Shares and Preferred Shares. Ordinary shares (also known as equity shares) are in general the voting and controlling shares, whereas preferred shares are non-voting shares and have a prior right to dividends before ordinary shares.

There are alternative stock exchanges especially intended for smaller and medium-sized growth companies that do not fulfill the capital requirements and other high demands set forth by regular stock exchanges. An example would be the Frankfurt Neuer Markt. Some of the advantages of this type of stock exchange are:

- Registration is cheaper and faster.

- The alternative exchanges require a lower capital basis.

- Trading records are in most cases not required.

- The level of information required is significantly lower than on the traditional exchanges.

Benefits of Going Public
Going public is a big effort which risks taking the eyes of senior management off running the company and focuses them instead on the steps required in the IPO process. The steps include the writing of a prospectus offering the company's stock for sale, change-over of internal systems to support the requirements of a public company, and interactions with prospective investors and stock analysts.

But going public can provide the capital needed to develop new technologies and products, fuel future growth, fund acquisitions, and provide investor liquidity. In addition, a company that goes public may gain publicity and prestige, improving its potential for attracting new business as well as potential acquisition candidates.

Because an IPO will increase the net worth of a company, going public not only enables the organization to obtain capital or borrowings on more favorable terms but also increases management's future financing alternatives. It may allow them to undertake a merger or an acquisition more easily — not only because they have access to the capital but also because they have solidified relationships with investment bankers, accountants, and attorneys.

Owners usually experience a psychological boost and sense of financial achievement. Company principals may be able to eliminate current and future personal guarantees to lenders, landlords and suppliers. Stock and stock options can be used to lure and retain key personnel. Options have also become a significant part of management and officer compensation, in other words, incentives to increase shareholder value.

Disclosure requirements, which essentially put your company on display, help to garner publicity for your organization. Going public, as a result, may enable your company to expand its relationships. The so-called direct offering of securities via the Internet has recently become popular. Some of the more successful and better-publicized offerings have been approached less like a traditional IPO and more like a new-product launch.

Challenges of Going Public

Entrepreneurs may find it difficult to transition from running a private company to operating in a fishbowl. Decision-making becomes more difficult because of accountability to shareholders. There are new considerations when launching new products or expanding into new areas, such as how the market will react.

Public ownership of your company brings a great deal of responsibility. You, as the owner, now have a boss too: the board of directors. They will carefully monitor everything you do. If they determine that you are not performing well for the company's shareholders, they can remove you from your position. In addition, you must now share company gain with all public owners. This is the return shareholders expect when investing in your company.

4.3
Capital Needs Estimation

Before going after capital, you should analyze your needs, especially the current financial requirements of the company. Your financial requirements are not fixed amounts of money; rather they are ranges of numbers between best and worst-case scenarios for both costs and cash flow. In other words, you are trying to identify a spot on a continuum.

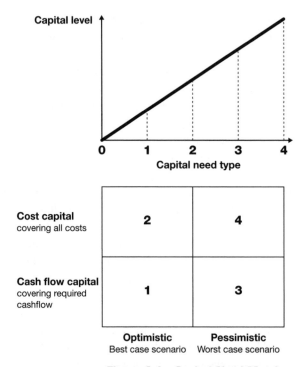

Figure 4.1   Capital Need Matrix

Based on the ranges, choose an estimate that seems to fit.

The first startup capital-need analysis should, optimally, cover all costs expected in the period that this book covers, in both worst- and best-case scenarios. A typical cost structure of a startup company includes Salaries, Rent, Other Expenses, and Capital Expenditures. This is obviously quite simplified and each of these categories will have a – possibly large – set of underlying assumptions:

Salaries	The assumptions include the size of the staff, their salary categories, when the staff is hired, and what amount of capital expenditure and expenses will be required to support personnel in different categories.
Rent	How much space you are going to need when, both for staff offices/cubicles and for required production facilities.
Other Expenses	You will want to create the relevant cost categories for your business, for example, Sales and Marketing

expenses not covered by salary, *e.g.*, trade show expenses and sales and marketing collateral expenses; T&E — travel and entertainment — expenses; Communications expenses — phones; Purchased Materials — materials which you cannot capitalize; and, of course, Miscellaneous — expenses which are specific to your business.

Capital Expenditures Assuming you are capitalizing certain expenditures,[56] you will want to estimate the requirements. Depending on the tax situation in the area where you are starting your business, you may want to — or have to — capitalize equipment and/or other expenses.

In addition, you will want to predict the revenues for the period for which you are calculating the capital need.

The figure shows a cash flow analysis for one year using these categories. This is, of course, a simplified version of the Cash Flow Statement we discussed in Chapter 3 and is solely for internal use. What it tells you is how much capital you are going to need and when. In this example — with all the amounts being arbitrary — you can see that your Beginning Cash will only support you through month two, so additional financing is required.

Cash Flow Forecast (in $000's)	Month 1	Month 2	Month 3	Month 4	Month 5	Month 6	Month 7	Month 8	Month 9	Month 10	Month 11	Month 12
Revenue	1.00	1.50	2.00	3.00	4.00	5.00	6.00	7.00	7.00	8.00	10.00	12.00
Total Salaries	2.00	2.00	2.00	3.00	3.00	4.00	3.00	3.00	4.00	4.00	4.00	4.00
Total Rent	0.20	0.20	0.20	0.30	0.30	0.33	0.33	0.33	0.34	0.40	0.40	0.40
All Other Expenses, including for example:	3.00	3.00	3.00	3.00	3.00	3.00	3.00	3.00	3.00	3.00	4.00	4.00
Sales and Marketing Expense												
T & E Expense												
Communications												
Purchased Materials												
Miscellaneous												
Total Expenses	5.20	5.20	5.20	6.30	6.30	7.33	6.33	6.33	7.34	7.40	8.40	8.40
EBITDA	(4.20)	(3.70)	(3.20)	(3.30)	(2.30)	(2.33)	(0.33)	0.67	(0.34)	0.60	1.60	3.60
Change in Accounts Receivable	(1.00)	(0.50)	(0.50)	(1.00)	(1.00)	(1.00)	(1.00)	(1.00)	0.00	(1.00)	(2.00)	(2.00)
Change in All Other Exp	3.00	0.00	0.00	0.00	0.00	0.00	0.00	0.00	0.00	0.00	1.00	0.00
Capital Expenditures	(0.10)	(0.10)	(0.10)	(0.25)	(0.10)	(0.10)	(0.10)	(0.10)	(0.10)	(0.10)	(0.20)	(0.20)
Net Cash Adjustments	1.90	(0.60)	(0.60)	(1.25)	(1.10)	(1.10)	(1.10)	(1.10)	(0.10)	(1.10)	(1.20)	(2.20)
Net Cash Usage	(2.30)	(4.30)	(3.80)	(4.55)	(3.40)	(3.43)	(1.43)	(0.43)	(0.44)	(0.50)	0.40	1.40
Cash - Beginning	10.00	7.70	3.40	(0.40)	(4.95)	(8.35)	(11.78)	(13.21)	(13.64)	(14.08)	(14.58)	(14.18)
Funding - Investments	0.00	0.00	0.00	0.00	0.00	0.00	0.00	0.00	0.00	0.00	0.00	0.00
Cash - Ending	7.70	3.40	(0.40)	(4.95)	(8.35)	(11.78)	(13.21)	(13.64)	(14.08)	(14.58)	(14.18)	(12.78)

Figure 4.2   Cost Estimate Structure

In addition, the start-up company must outline its expected long- and short-term financial requirements. This is done by creating cash-flow forecasts/analyses based on the following elements, also in best- and worst-case scenarios:

- Operating activities

- Investing activities

- Financing

- Taxes payable

- Returns on investments and servicing of finance.

The annual increases or decreases in the company's cash-flow/liquidity should emerge from the above. The total estimated need can be considered the threshold startup capital need.

If we have not said it enough above or at least inferred it, let us repeat: get help both with the determination of the capital needs and the process of looking for financing. Unless you are a very unusual entrepreneur, your strengths will not be in those areas.

4.4
Typical Capital Need Phases

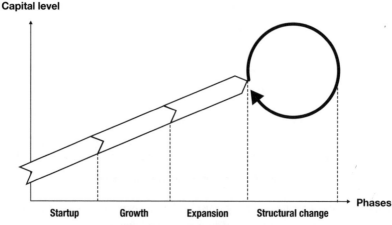

Figure 4.3 Capital Need Phases

Even though the focus of this book is on the start-up phase, a new company can expect to go through at least four phases in which it requires capital. All the types of capital acquisition have specific situational benefits and requirements in a given phase:

i. Start-up

    1. Venture capital

    2. Loan capital

    3. Grants and subsidies

    4. Personal capital

ii. Growth

    1. Venture capital

    2. Equity capital

    3. Loan capital

    4. Grants and subsidies

    5. Merger

iii. Expansion

    1. Equity finance

    2. Loan capital

    3. Merger

    4. Acquisition

    5. Spin-offs of company activities into stand-alone operations

    6. Going public

iv. Structural change/diffusion

    1. Management buy-out

    2. Management buy-in

    3. Creditor write-off

    4. Spin-offs

    5. Merger

    6. Acquisition

    7. Sell-out

The forms of financing used to manage structural changes/diffusions are many. One of them is the management buy-*out,* which involves a company's management and/or employees' buying part of or all of the company from its existing owners. A management buy-*in* involves an outsider's buying his/her way in, in order to change the management/handling of the company. Write-offs are deals with creditors in which a certain amount of debt is written off in order to avoid a bankruptcy, when the creditors would be even less likely to get their money back. A spin-off is separating a part of the company's activities into a stand-alone operation. Sell-out is selling a portion of the company's ownership/equity — a significant minority share, a majority share, or the whole company.

4.5
Venture Capital

Venture capital (VC) is at-risk money invested by investment professionals in fast-growing companies that have the potential to be significant economic leaders in their markets. Professional investors provide the capital required at important stages of a company's development in exchange for a commensurate equity stake in the company.

The concept of venture capital – capital invested in high-risk undertakings with the hope of high returns – has existed as long as there has been capital to invest – one could argue that Columbus was venture-capital funded, as was the Dutch East India Company. Formalized as we know it, however, the concept is a relatively new phenomenon, dating from just after World War II. One of the early successful investments by a venture capitalist was Digital Equipment Corporation (DEC),[57] funded by the American Research and Development Corporation, the first private venture capital firm founded in 1946 by General George Doriot. That first investment, by the way, was US$ 70,000. for which ARD got 70% of the company! But, then again, Ken Olsen got a mentor:

The General was patient then, too. He also had a lot of simple rules for running a business which are always helpful to keep in mind. Most of his ideas he didn't present in a way you had to accept. He presented them in a way which, after it was done, you thought [you had thought] of them youself. Or if you didn't accept them, there was no hassle. There are a few exceptions. He said you never want a lawyer on your board, you never want a banker on your board. These are black and white and you'd have to definitely go against the General to pick either one of them. He was always there as a mentor and for help.[58]

The venture capital and private equity area has grown tremendously since then, as the following table shows:[59]

Private Equity and Venture Capital Investment
US B$

	1998	1999	2000
The World	83	136	177
USA	56	99	126

It has gone through a painful adjustment process in 2001:[60]

Venture Capital Invested in US
US B$

1999		2000		2001
First 9 months	12 Months	First 9 months	12 months	First 9 months
27	47	73	90	25

As you can see, 2001 has not been an easy year for companies seeking venture capital; the run rate for investments is about one-third of the run rate in 2000.

Investment Process of Professional Venture Capitalists

It is important to realize that "The Venture Capital Industry" is not one industry. There are many subsets of the industry, categorized by preferred investment space – which industries a given VC invests in – or by preferred investment stage – which stage of a company the VC prefers to invest in. Also be aware that, at least in the dot.com bubble days, roughly 1999 and 2000, the combination of industry analysts, financial analysts, VCs, and "irrational exuberance" created a climate of fashionable investment targeting in which choosing the right buzzwords in one's presentation was very important.

Venture capital firms invest in many ways – private placements, VC fund investing, *etc.*, but one of the typical ones is the use of a venture capital fund in which investors – institutional investors such as big universities, pension funds, or high-net-worth individuals with appropriate funds to invest (funds which can be put at risk) – pool money in a specific fund which is managed by a venture capital company. This fund will have a planned duration and will invest according to a specific investment strategy – industry, stage, *etc.* – with the goal that the fund's overall performance should provide a return in the target range. The following figure shows a possible timeline for a venture capital fund:[61]

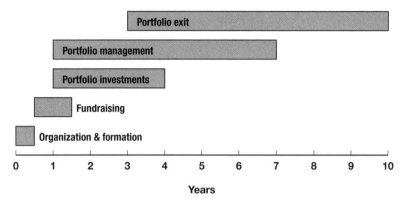

Figure 4.4   Venture Capital Fund Timeline

The "stages" of investment which you will see mentioned in VC firms' literature refer to the stages of a start-up company. There are many different words for the same things, but typically you will see something like:

- Seed, or Angel: very early investing, maybe even in the proof of concept phase;

- Round 1, round 2, *etc.*, or , equivalently, Series A, series B, *etc.*: investment at specific points in the growth of a start-up, for example: round 1 for building the prototype, round 2 for building product and starting the marketing, round 3 for setting up a sales force, *etc.*

- Mezzanine, or restart: financing for a corporate restructuring or sometimes for going public.

Obviously, how much you raise in a round and how many rounds you require depend on the needs of the corporation and its overall financial management: money costs different amounts at different times in the growth of a start-up.

We shall not go into details in the financial management area but it is worthwhile for you, the entrepreneur, to have done calculations like the one below:

If I am just starting out and my company is valued at five million US$, I will need to give up at least 20% of the company to raise one million US$. If, eighteen months later, my product is on track, the company is in a hot niche, and the valuation has risen to fifty million US$, I will need to give up – at least but on the order of — an additional 2% to raise one million US$. The point of this very simplified example is that "when" and "how much" have great impact on the funding of a company.

Sources of Venture Capital

There are many different kinds of venture capital companies, and you need to look around to find the groups with which you feel the most comfortable. This also means feeling comfortable with the personality of the firm — you are going to be spending a lot of time with the company that finally invests in you. The following is one list of different kinds of venture firms; there are more:[62]

- Private management firms

- Public management firms

- Small business investment companies

- Financial institution venture groups

- Corporate venture groups

- Family venture groups

- Minority-focused venture capital firms

- Venture leasing firms

Since the options are many, it is important for you to seek professional advice regarding raising capital. We shall give an overview of three additional areas to conclude our description: angels, venture leasing, and incubators.

Angel Investing

Angel investing involves smaller amounts of funding, typically going to early stages and typically done under somewhat different rules than straight venture capital. The archetypical angel is a local high-net-worth individual with at-risk capital and an interest in early stage funding. The term "DDF" – doctors, dentists, family and friends — has been used for this kind of investor. Now the term "angel investing" is also used to describe a venture fund investment target.

The benefits of angel investing can be that the investors are local, at least in the case of the original definition, that they may be able to offer business advice as needed, and that they may be more flexible in the terms and conditions and in the execution.

Possible drawbacks of angel investing can be that the investors are local and may be able to offer too much business advice!

Venture Leasing, or "Can I Pay You in Options?"

Venture leasing is asset-backed venture capital for start-up and early-stage companies. It provides financing, for example, for equipment, in return for equipment lease payments and some form of equity in the company. Typically, this kind of financing is only available following regular VC financing.

With venture leasing, entrepreneurs can finance equipment and free up capital — to expand their companies and increase shareholder value – to spend on things such as employees, marketing, research and development, and the like.

The concept of using some kind of equity – or promise of equity — as payment was taken quite far during the dot.com era, at least in San Francisco. Requests for options as part of real estate lease payments were not unheard of.

The reality of this is that the sharing of risk and reward – which equity really is – is an appropriate means of commercial exchange, but the risks and rewards should be understood in the perspective of the overall market and of GAAP.

Incubators

The incubator concept has been somewhat discredited since the dot.com era, but it represents a point on the continuum of different venture capital funding schemes. At its best, the incubator model takes a number of early-stage companies and co-locates them, offering shared services – IT, accounting, *etc.* – and mentoring in return for equity and/or payment. The success of the incubator model comes down to – yet again – the appropriateness of the business models of the individual incubatees.

Venture Capital Issues

Raising capital is a lengthy and hard process. It can be quite difficult for a newly-established company to raise enough capital to cover the needs of its start-up and growth phases. This problem can, of course, have many explanations – for example:

• The company is in a high-risk line of business;

- The management has no experience with the capital market and financing in general;

- Interest rates are too high;

- Demand for venture capital is much higher than the supply, due to market conditions.

Entrepreneurs have raised a number of objections against venture capital:

- It is too expensive;

- It is unnecessary if you can just bootstrap your operation;

- It takes too long and is too much of a hassle;

- Too much money in the wrong hands can be worse than too little;

- Some venture capitalists never really take the time to understand the business and yet intervene in critical decisions.

The reality is, of course, that the worst time to raise money is when you need it. There is no easy way to undo the potential imbalance between a company in need of capital and the VC firm that has the capital.

The best advice — which we shall reinforce in the section on how to make a presentation — is to phrase your play to the VC as a "win win" (mutually beneficial), *i.e.*, do your homework, talk their language, and satisfy the requirements that the particular financing need requires. Once you do have their commitment, good venture capitalists will be there to help you, and the situation will become "us," instead of "us versus them."

A Final Word on Venture Capital

The following is a quote from an interview on vcapital.com about the venture capital process. The speaker is Sanford Morganstein, who started a voice-response technology company:[63]

We were successful, I believe, because we satisfied most of the classic, text-book criteria that the venture investor seeks. ... We had a good management team ... we also had a strong, independent board consisting of outsiders ... and we had a new product that had already demonstrated success in the market. ... At the time we went to raise money, we were a very small company that was managed as professionally as a much larger firm. Our success relied on our ability to convince investors of this fact.

There are people arguing that the smaller amount of venture capital available after 2000 does not represent a precipitous decline that will be made up but a return to normalcy. Reality is probably somewhere in between, but minding the fundamentals when starting a company will never go out of style with venture capitalists.

4.6
The Capital Raising Process for Start-ups

For start-ups, a comprehensive capital-raising strategy is essential to target, solicit, and raise the required capital for the initial phase, subsequent growth, and other phases. We recommend that the effort be split into at least two parts:

1. Start-up capital acquisition

2. Growth capital acquisition

Start-up capital needs to be secured as soon as the business idea and the strategic business plan are made. It is virtually impossible to persuade external capital providers to provide any start-up capital before that point. Start-up capital is needed to finance the creation of the company, the hiring and salaries of the key people/management, and the out-of-pocket costs needed to pay for setting up and taking the company to market, a period of usually one to two years.

You will want to have a deal for growth capital signed by the time the company has been set up, has become operational, and has entered the market. By then start-up capital will have begun to run low. Raising growth capital is included in this book because it is a major activity that has to begin at the same time as the securing of start-up capital. The efforts have to be concurrent because growth capital usually takes much longer to secure. With luck, the participants in the start-up round will help and/or participate in the later rounds.

Securing start-up or seed capital is usually a smaller endeavor than securing it for the growth phase.

A strong capital-raising strategy for both smaller investments in the start-up phase and larger investments in the growth phase entails a number of steps:

- Creating the foundations for a business

- Developing a Strategic Business Plan

- Identifying and getting to prospective investors

- Selling the deal

- Creating and managing contingencies

Figure 4.5   Capital acquisition process

We covered some of these areas in Chapter Three, so we shall quote from it at times in the discussion below.

Creating the Foundations for Your Business

To present a credible investment opportunity to prospective investors you must have a business plan that defines what you are going to do, what the competition is, and how you are going to make money. But remember that investors do not invest only in a business idea; they also invest in a team. In fact, it is not unusual to see a statement like *"I would invest in just about any-thing XX wanted to do"* in biographical sketches of successful entrepreneurs.

Investing is very much a "people" business based on trust in a team. For start-up investing you need an initial core team; it need not cover all func-tions, but all its members must have the drive to want to succeed. For later stages the team should be growing at an appropriate rate, filling out all the "C" roles and the senior management. Present the team clearly to prospective investors and select one of the senior team members – the CEO is ideal – to make the pitches.

Developing a Strategic Business Plan

The Strategic Business Plan is a key communication tool when interacting with prospective investors. As we said in Chapter 3:

Please note that the points can be listed in the business plan in whatever order seems most logical and comprehensible to the recipient/reader. In fact, it is usually a good idea to find out whether the groups to whom you are going to present this have any particular idiosyncrasies regarding presentation. If so, format at least the presentation that way, and, if necessary, reformat it for the next audience.

In other words, make sure that both the Strategic Business Plan and the specific presentation to a set of investors are formatted to their expectations.

The Strategic Business Plan will typically appear in several forms during the capital-raising period:

- The standard version as described in Chapter 3, complete with appendices

- A – or perhaps many – presentation form for presentation to a prospective investor

- A short overview presentation that you can use as a "teaser," for example, in an e-Mail to a prospect.

You should remake the latter two for every investor based on your knowledge of the person(s).

Due Diligence

One way to critique your Strategic Business Plan is to look at it through the eyes of investors. Professional investors usually have a proprietary due diligence list of things they need to know about a company in order for their own company to make a decision on investment, just like their counterparts involved in mergers and acquisitions. Due diligence lists vary greatly, and it is unlikely that potential investors will give you a sample. However, a screening version of a "soft" due diligence list can help make sure that all relevant information has been included. See figure 4.6 for an example:

FINANCIAL CAPITAL	Revenue streams Cost structure EBIT Equity development Cash flow Working capital Contracts (Personnel, suppliers, customers) Pipeline (sales forecasting)
STRUCTURAL CAPITAL	Technology platform Culture (Comparative) Market strategy Quality assurance process Methodology Board Shareholders Accounting and reporting system
MARKET CAPITAL	Business idea/positioning in the market Added value and growth potential Customer orientation (Product driven or customer driven) Market Geography Segments Size Players Customers Type Size Price/Pricing Sales process Partners
HUMAN CAPITAL	CEO/Founder Management/key personnel (Vision/Leadership) Overall business ability (Contractual) Personnel situation Number/competence Recruitment/potential Development Entrepreneurship Products & Services Customers Business model Motivation/Spirit Network

Figure 4.6   Sample Due Diligence Checklist

Identifying and Getting to Prospective Investors

You will typically have to work hard to get your first meeting, since a large number – some VCs would say most – of the business ideas actually presented to VCs are received through the "network."

But before you even try to get in contact with a specific prospect, learn as much as you can about the different VCs around — what their strengthes and weaknesses are, what areas they invest in, and so forth. Some of this information you can find on the Web, but your best source will be contacts. The more, the better.

Once you have found some investor prospects, use your network to find somebody who knows somebody and is willing to put in a word for you. (VCs receive thousands of business ideas; those without some kind of personal endorsement usually end up in the trash.)

Selling the Deal

In the first serious meeting with potential capital suppliers, your presentation is often the pivotal point for success or failure. It gives the first impression of your business idea and company setup and — because most investors are short of time — you will not have a second chance.

Realistically, you typically have five – yes, five – minutes or less to capture their attention and, say, twenty minutes overall to make your pitch.

If the first meeting goes well and the impression you have made is favorable, you have passed the first hurdle to a commitment. Likewise, if the first meeting for some reason does not go well, there is almost a 100% chance that you will not get funded by this group. The first professional and personal impression you make in a serious meeting about your business idea is that important.

A good persuasive presentation has not one purpose but three. Of course it has to persuade the audience – the VCs - to take the desired action (*i.e.*, supply the capital), but before that can happen, two other purposes have to be met. First, the presentation has to make the audience believe that the presenter understands the investment purpose/problem of the audience. Secondly, the presentation has to put across the most logical solution to the investment purpose/problem – as suggested and defined by the presenter, of course.

Therefore, a good presentation is not just a normal "sales pitch" with an outline of your business plan and a lot of good arguments for why your business is worth investing in. A more sophisticated approach persuades the audience that you are solving their problem, *i.e.*, helping them get their VC fund invested successfully.

Creating and Managing Contingencies

You may not get funded! Whether this results from your idea's being hard to sell, the overall market situation or some other reason, you may not get funded through the professional venture capital community.

It behooves you as the founder of the company to develop contingency plans, whether for alternative funding sources or for how to wind up the business. Not very nice thoughts, but you are better off planning when you are not under the gun.

4.7
Persuasive Capital Acquisition Presentations

The presentations you make in your quest for capital may very well be the most important presentations you will ever make in your career. Because of that, we shall spend the rest of this chapter discussing how to make a persuasive presentation. We call the presentation under discussion here "persuasive" to make a distinction between it and other kinds of presentations, such as informational or entertaining ones. Not that this kind of presentation is not supposed to be informative and at least partially entertaining, but first of all it must persuade, *i.e.*, "sell the product," in this case your business idea.

Before we go further, let us place the presentation in a more general context:[64]

Presentation context
A persuasive presentation takes place in a specific situation, with specific people, about a specific topic, such as a business idea. Every specific situation has its own rules of persuasion, and success is relative to the context in which the presentation is given. Some presentations have a large audience where interaction is controlled and limited; in others just a few participate, making the presentations more like interactive discussions. The particular styles of the presenters vary, and, of course, there are other factors which are virtually impossible to include in a general model. There may be factors at work in the specific situation which are impossible to alter on a short-term basis, thus potentially limiting the success of the effort.

As we have already said, the first serious meeting with potential investors is often pivotal. You have just a few minutes to get your audience's attention and perhaps fifteen minutes more to complete your initial pitch. If all goes well, you've passed one hurdle; if not, you're unlikely to be funded by this particular group.

Lobbying before or after the meetings can have a significant impact, so by all means do what you can to promote your idea, your company and yourself. In fact, you will typically have to lobby in order to get your first meeting, since a large number – some VCs would say most – of the business ideas actually presented to VCs are initially received through the "network." Use your own network to find somebody who knows somebody and who is willing to put in a word for you.

The focus below is on the presentation itself, not on what you do in terms of lobbying beforehand nor on "how you fry the fish once you have it in your net", that is, how you capitalize on the changed points of view of your listeners after the presentation is over.

The one overriding rule of successful presentations is:

Know Your Audience

This is an easy statement to make, but it covers a lot. It means trying to get as much knowledge as you can about the group you are going to present to and, equally importantly, about the "tribe" to which they belong. This may seem like a strange noun to use in a description, but remember that all groups – VCs among them – have certain distinct beliefs and ways of thinking and acting. You would not pitch to a French VC the same way you would one from California, for example, nor would you pitch to an early investor the same way you would to a middle or late stage investor. Equally importantly, although slightly catty, you should not pitch to any VC using yesterday's buzz-words. So make sure you gather as much information as you can beforehand.

The Process of Persuasion
To change something in the minds of other people – to persuade — on the basis of a presentation is a process:

1. The presenter identifies communication goals in terms of the wanted changes in knowledge, attitudes and/or actions of the audience. In this case: I want the audience to invest in my idea

2. The presenter prepares the messages

3. The presenter delivers the messages

4. The audience hears the persuasive messages (with or without interaction/questions)

5. The messages impact audience attitudes. The attitude impact is reflected in three types of changes:

   5.1 Cognitive changes (knowledge: what is heard, seen, experienced). In this case: I saw a detailed and professional presentation about selling XXX to YYY.

   5.2 Affective changes (attitudes: what is felt, liked, hated, deducted, actively understood, concluded). In this case: I believe selling XXX to YYY is something my company should invest in.

   5.3 Behavioral changes (actions: what is actually done or not done physically). In this case: I am going to champion this investment opportunity within my group.

6. Persuasive success is evaluated based on whether the change of audience attitudes goal behind the persuasive message is reached. In this case: they invest.

One scholar[65] calls persuasion the "true rhetorical situation," "a mode of altering reality through the meditation of thoughts and action." Using argumentation and persuasion is only relevant when there is doubt in the minds of your listeners, or when the listeners does not think or act as you want them to. If you do not aim at an actual change or action in some sense, you are not planning to persuade, just to inform or maintain the current beliefs and commitments. For example, when you later do a monthly presentation to investors, assuming everything is going the way you wanted, you will not be trying to persuade, you will be simply trying to maintain the belief that, "I did right when I championed this investment."

Your audience will digest your presentation input with three filters that relate to cognitive, affective and behavioral changes. The investors will ask themselves three questions before they will consider any action/change you try to push on them:

• What's new? – New knowledge

• So what? – Relevance for listeners (attitudes)

- Do what? – Possible actions

First, they will ask what is new about this business proposal. "What's new" relates to understanding your business idea and why this might be different from other investment opportunities.

Secondly, they will become critical and ask what this has to do with them. "So what" relates to how the business idea becomes relevant for, and could benefit, the investors' portfolio of investments.

Finally, the investors will want to understand what, how and when they must act in order to secure a possible investment. "Do what" relates to what kind of action they are expected to take and when.

The goal of a persuasive presentation is to impact the behavior of the listeners, but people can only act on what they know about and feel positive about in relation to the action. So, when talking about changing behavior and getting "a signature on a big check," you have to be aware that first you must change or reinforce the listener's attitude and beliefs in the desired direction before you can expect him/her to take action on what you say. (S)he has to "learn" or be convinced by your presentation that your business is worth investing in.

To master this form of the "persuasion" process, more appropriately called the "teaching" or "coaching" process, you have to be aware of some factors which influence the responsiveness of your listeners:

1. Members of the audience differ in their ability to respond

2. They differ in their readiness to respond

3. They differ in their motivation to respond

4. Reinforcement is helpful in establishing the desired response

5. In learning, active participation is better than passive listening

6. Meaningful responses are accepted more easily than meaningless ones

People differ significantly in the way they remember a presentation.[66] The **visually oriented** think and remember in pictures, gestures, visual elements and illustrations; they "see" what you are talking about. The **auditive** pay close attention to how and what you are saying, the wording and the sound, and they read between the lines of what you are saying; they "hear" what you are saying. The **kinesthetic** form "gut" feelings about you and your business proposal and listen with their hearts; they "feel" that they understand what you are saying. Good presenters cater to all three types of audiences in order to cover all bases. They use visuals to illustrate the important points, they plan their delivery carefully with pauses, examples, *etc.*, and they go out of their way to talk to the hearts of people, not just their minds.

As we said earlier, a good capital acquisition presentation is not a normal "sales pitch" with an outline of your business plan and a lot of good arguments for why your business is worth investing in. A truly sophisticated approach persuades the audience that you are solving their problem, *i.e.*, helping them get their VC fund invested successfully. It implies that you not only understand their dilemma but can tell them what to do about it.

Presentation methodology

There are different ways of planning your presentation. Let us first split them up into "psychological models," called **Pathos** and **Ethos**, and "logical models," called **Logos**.

The psychological **Pathos** models are strong when dealing with emotions and feelings; they are non-rational and feelings oriented. The psychological **Ethos** models have to do with audience perception of your credibility, believability, your "name" in the business, your charisma or, in one word, your image. Things like prejudice and expectations play major roles in these models. The logical **Logos** approach is rational and message-oriented, and is normally used when dealing with persuading someone to make a sound and professional business decision. Feelings and emotions are important to everyone, and many people are easily persuaded by a charismatic speaker with an admired image, but rational, message-oriented arguments are the normal keys to persuading business professionals.

Of the logical presentation models, there are some which are structured chronologically, geographically, *etc.* and some which focus on needs and problem-solving. Of the latter, you probably recognize one or more of these models of preparation:

- *Ask yourself who, what, how, when, why, where*

- *Define purpose, analyze target group, research subject, make outline, prepare manuscript, prepare visual aids, rehearse, present*

- *Opening, middle, closing, questions*

We propose you use a new strategic rhetorical model[67] which, in our experience, is the most detailed and most effective model. It takes you through thirteen steps to prepare a presentation. The steps are listed below; we expand on them in the following sections.

Presentation Strategy:

1. The brainstorming session

2. Create the information outline

Content Preparation:

3. Create the introduction

4. Evaluate the information presentation

5. Review the presentation arguments

6. Create the presentation outline

7. Create the presentation conclusion

Presentation Form:

8. Create notes and visual aids

9. Fashion the presentation delivery

Quality Enhancement:

10. Rehearsal

11. Quality control

12. Review question and answer session

13. The on-site preparation.

Presentation Strategy Development

The first part of the methodology helps you collect your thoughts and ideas for your presentation and capture and structure them into a format, a comprehensive and logical basis for developing your persuasive presentation. This section consists of two parts:

> 1. The brainstorming session
>
> 2. Create the information outline.

Step 1 – The Brainstorming Session.

You have just received word that you have been asked to make a presentation at a meeting next week. Landing the client/investor could mean immediate funding. Ideas are racing through your mind. How do you harness them? Easy! — you do some free brainstorming, with pen in hand. Brainstorming will generate unique ideas and thoughts on which your whole presentation can be built. These ideas will be modified, expanded, rearranged, changed, blown up, rephrased, *etc.* during the preparatory work based on relevance and persuasiveness, but they they will remain the basis of your presentation.

To begin with, ask yourself the following questions in order to come to grips with what you have to do. Draw out your thoughts in a Mind Map (see below).

1. Do I know exactly what I want? What is it?

2. Do I really believe in my case? Why?

3. Have I got all the facts that support my case, and have I checked that they are actually correct?

4. What are the strongest arguments for my case?

5. What are the benefits for my listeners? Can they see them too?

6. Why must the present situation be changed? And who should change it?

7. What is the client's problem or need? Is it out in the open, or are they not aware of it yet?

8. Who else is affected? And so what?

9. What are the arguments against my plan? Coming from whom?

10. What are the alternatives to my plan? And who are my competitors?

11. Do my benefits clearly outweigh counter-arguments and alternative courses of action?

12. To whom am I presenting my plan? Have I done any lobbying? Do I need to?

13. Do I know who my probable allies and opponents are?

14. Should I prepare handouts of any complicated figures? Is anything confidential?

15. Have I discussed the financial and economic sides with the experts?

16. It was a good idea when I first thought of it. Is it still a good idea? From the listeners' points of view too?

17. Do I have time enough, and can I prepare a really effective presentation?

18. How can I emphasize the benefits they — the clients/investors — will gain? Nothing induces agreement faster than self-interest — the other person's, that is.

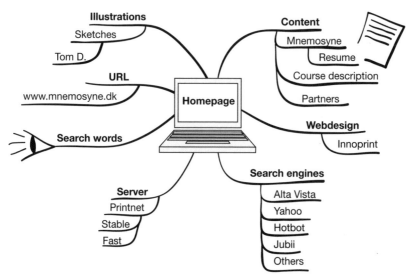

Figure 4.7   Example of Mind Map

Step 2 – Create the Information Outline

Once you are finished brainstorming, write the initial information outline:

1. Main idea

Write a brief explanation of what the listener should invest in — your business and business idea — max, one page. Although this is very basic, you would be surprised at the number of presenters who fail to write it down on a single piece of paper. This is not a management summary but a summary of your business plan for the investor that caters to his/her specific point of view.

2. Insights about the listeners

Many people are more concerned about *what* they have to say than to *whom* they are saying it. It should be the other way around: always remember that different people have different concerns. "Angels" are in the market to help people, venture capitalists are in the market for high pay-off opportunities, and conservative banks are in the market for "secure" profits. This variance will not affect your core idea, but it will affect how you present the idea to your listener. Note the investor's professional affiliations, religion, gender, societal background, income, car ownership — anything else you can discover. If you know absolutely nothing about your listener, talk with someone who does. If all else fails, make assumptions. What sort of professional is he/she? Have you talked to this type of professional before? If yes, list your educated assumptions about a person in that profession.

3. Action step you would like your listener to take

Write it down. What do you want your listener to do — take your idea to top management? come back with questions? accept your idea today and sign a preliminary contract? Whatever the action step may be, make sure that it's realistic. Will your listener be willing and authorized to take that step? If not, think of another action step. Make sure that the listener expects the same of the presentation as you do. Secondly, pinpoint *when* you want your listener to take the action step. This is vitally important. Should he/she discuss it with his/her manager today or next month? If you do not specify when the listener should take action, he/she may never take it. If that happens, your presentation will have been a waste of your time and the other person's.

4. Look back at the idea outlined under point 1 and examine all the benefits for your listener

Make sure the benefits you list are really benefits to your listener. Ask yourself, "Why is that a benefit?" If the answer would satisfy your listener, it's valid. On the other hand, if your listener would respond with "So what?," it's not a benefit.

There are usually three major strategic concerns for an investor that you must address: the first is what market are you in — what is the actual market or industry?, what is the value of it now?, is it on the way up or down?, is there a market?, *etc.* The second is who are your customers — how many?, where?, what size?, a list of prioritized customers, pipeline, *etc.* The third concern is how you plan to make money — what is the business model?, what are the expected cash-flows, costs, and necessary investments?, what will be the ROI?

Beyond the strategic considerations, be aware of the more tactical/operational concerns of your would-be investors. If your listener tends to be extremely busy, show how investing in your company will make her/his job easier. If he/she's concerned about investment in your specific sector or country, use examples of successful companies there which made it big. If he/she is concerned about spending too much time in front of the computer, provide all the documentation needed for processing the investment evaluation speedily.

5. Write down the main benefit your listener will derive from your idea.
This benefit becomes your listener's objective in taking the recommended action steps. For example, if he/she seriously considers investing in your business, he/she will be able to sell the stock in the company in one year's time for ten times the current value. Keep your listener in mind when describing the objective!

6. Write down 3-4 questions, objections, or concerns your listener may have about your idea.
This can be where you drive the persuasion home. Even if you only come up with one or two questions, you show your skills and thus come across as someone concerned for the welfare of your audience and not just out for yourself. So consider well what reasonable objections or questions the audience might have: list them carefully and, if possible, prioritize them in terms of relevance and importance. Put yourself in the investor's shoes and ask yourself the most relevant questions when someone wants you to invest in their scheme. Then you will know what the investor is looking for in your presentation. Remember that you must objectively discuss other options, even though you hold the opinion that investing in your company is the best choice.

7. Answer those questions with persuasive reasoning.
There are quite a few ways of going about answering questions with persuasive reasoning. Here are some:

You can reason by making an **analogy**, where the parallel example shares characteristics relevant to the claim you make and does not have differences that would destroy the analogy. You can reason from a **generalization**, where you make a specific example or two support your claim. You can reason from the use of **signs**, in which certain current circumstances can be used to predict the success of your proposition. You can reason based on **cause**, where you argue that certain circumstances will necessarily cause your success. You can reason by **authority**, meaning establishing someone as an expert and quoting him/her. You can argue out of **relativity,** *e.g.*, outline the choices and identify a choice between two situations in which your proposition is the better. You can argue from **classification**, where you argue your propositions as belonging to a class of – obviously – successful undertakings. You can argue from **opposites**, where one radical difference suggests another difference between two things or situations. And you can make downside (or natural) **threat** arguments, in which you use the competitive situation, other outside forces, and factors out of control of the audience to prove that your listener has to invest in your business or risk getting further behind.

You can use these five strong and almost foolproof approaches to build reasonable answering strategies in a business presentation:

1. Statistics
If at all possible, use statistics that are not your own. Attribution to an outside source makes statistics more believable.

2. Facts.
Remember the saying, "One man's fact is another man's fiction." A fact is anything that your listener accepts as fact. (This underscores the importance of knowing your listener.) When using facts, make sure you use relevant facts, ones that do not contradict other facts known by your audience, without undue explanation as to why this fact is more cogent than some other one.

3. Experience.
Draw on the experience of your listener or that of an expert. Do not be afraid to use your own experience as a guide occasionally. Remember, you're an expert in your field and your listener will value your experience too.

4. Analogy.
Keep the analogy simple and make sure that your listener can relate to it.

Do not cite an analogy about traveling in Spain, for example, if your listener has never left his/her home country.

5. **Expert testimony**.
Be sure that the expert is indeed an expert in the opinion of your listener.

8. Provide a quick summary

Your summary should restate the listener's problem, your solution, and the benefits to your listener. Never introduce new information in your summary; you'll confuse the listener and yourself. If possible use other words for the same things. This will increase the correct understanding of the issues involved.

9. Ask for action from your listener

Tell the listener specifically what he/she must do to achieve the benefits of your idea. Keep the action simple and realistic.

Are you ready? You have now thought through your presentation, what you want to say. You have organized your thoughts and you know whether you need more information to strengthen the content of your presentation. Have you done all this in writing? If not, go back and do it. And are you ready to present it? This is exactly where most presenters go wrong: they charge forward with the presentation because they "feel" ready. But, for you, making your presentation really stand out requires more planning. What do you do? Well, you have to rethink your presentation, based not on how you yourself think it through, that is, not on your information outline, but on what will make the greatest impact on your listener. To do this, you have to plan how to open, how and in what order to present the content, how to close, how to deliver your presentation and what language to use.

Content Preparation

With the presentation strategy in place, the next step is to prepare the actual content of the presentation that you are to give. The content preparation elements are:

1. Create the introduction

2. Evaluate the information presentation

3. Review the presentation arguments

4. Create the presentation outline

5. Create the presentation conclusion.

Step 3 – Create the Introduction
The introduction is how you open your presentation and how you get the attention of the audience.

The audience must be made confident that the speaker knows what he is doing. They must find his first thoughts intensely interesting. This rules out the usual dreary openings, for instance, where the speaker talks about him/herself and his/her worries as a speaker. Your opening is intended to attract the interest and attention of the audience so that they want to listen to what comes next, pure and simple. If the audience does not know you, do not despair. In general, an audience does not think poorly of you even if you are completely unfamiliar. As a matter of fact, scholars[68] have documented that unknown presenters are rather positively perceived.

However, remember that you need to build trust with your listeners as soon as possible; you need to show them you understand their situation and issues. A good opening in a short presentation (15-20 min.) will tie into this objective immediately, while a longer presentation (45+ min.) gives you time to take a more circular road and start off much more off-beat.

For the introduction consider the **P3 opening technique** which usually works well:

Part 1:   You make any vivid, unexpected, off-beat, truly-interesting opening remark you like, always, of course, keeping your audience in mind. (For ideas, see below.)

Part 2:   You skillfully link part 1 to your subject, making clear exactly what your subject is and why you are presenting it your audience.

Part 3:   You involve the audience in both your opening remarks and your subject.

There are hundreds of ways to open. Below are some possible approaches:

The question opening
The intention is to make the audience think. The question should be carefully chosen, and the more dramatic and unusual it is, the better:

Have you ever tried playing football in plimsolls (sneakers) on rubble?

Have you ever seen the inside of a Spanish prison?

If I were to ask you your dearest wish, what would you answer?

If you use a more rhetorical question like "Do you know what kids fear the most?," remember to answer the question and do not let the audience hang, unless that is your explicit purpose.

The factual opening

The intention is to gain the attention of the audience and to appeal to their intelligence.

A man's expectation of life may be roughly calculated as being one third of the number of years between his present age and 80.

Every year 11,167 men and women die from bronchitis. This is an average figure of ....

The humorous opening

To capture the audience's attention quickly by using the entertainment factor in a speech:

A French farmer's widow had her husband's ashes put into an old egg-timer made out of glass. "For," as she said, "he never did a day's work for me when he was alive, so I am going to make sure he works now he is dead."

The shock opening

To gain the attention of a potentially apathetic audience:

We lost DKK 1,000,000 worth of orders last week. We could lose even more this week. During this presentation, I would like to show you what I think we can do about it.

The mind-reading opening

To get the attention of a potentially skeptical audience:

If I were sitting where you are sitting, without possessing the knowledge of the facts which I possess, I would feel just as skeptical as I am sure you do. But let me try to put this case to you from a different angle ....

The personal opening

To demonstrate the speaker's own involvement in the subject:

When I was selling to supermarkets ....

The story opening
Telling a story or an anecdote, maybe even based on your own experience, which relates to your theme in some way will put you in friendly if not intimate contact with your audience. Audiences loves self-disclosure where they can see the real person behind the mask. This is sometimes nicknamed "Getting in bed with the audience," but it usually has a very positive impact in a business presentation.

A problem opening
In order to underline the importance of what you are going to approach:

I have just talked to your largest retail customer, and he says that this month's sales of your product is expected to be less than half of last month's, so obviously you have a big problem on your hands.

A demonstration opening
In order to focus the audience's eyes and attention on you: (The example below can be used to illustrate the effectiveness of intelligent cheating.)

Ask someone to think of a number between 1 and 60. Make him/her write it down or say it to the one sitting next to him/her without your hearing or seeing the number. List the following 6 lines of numbers, and ask him/her to tell you in which lines the number is found:

> *A:* 1-3-5-7-9-11-13-15-17-19-21-23-25-27-29-31-33-35-37-39-
> 41-43-45-47-49-51-53-55-57-59
>
> *B:* 2-3-6-7-10-11-14-15-18-19-22-23-26-27-30-31-34-35-38-
> 39-42-43-46-47-50-51-54-55-58-59
>
> *C:* 4-5-6-7-12-13-14-15-20-21-22-23-28-29-30-31-36-37-38-
> 39-44-45-46-47-52-53-54-55-60
>
> *D:* 8-9-10-11-12-13-14-15-24-25-26-27-28-29-30-31-40-41-42-
> 43-44-45-46-47-56-57-58-59
>
> *E:* 16-17-18-19-20-21-22-23-24-25-26-27-28-29-30-31-48-49-
> 50-51-52-53-54-55-56-57-58-59-60

F: 32-33-34-35-36-37-38-39-40-41-42-43-44-45-46-47-48-49-
*   50-51-52-53-54-55-56-57-58-59-60*

By adding up the first number in each of the picked lines, you will know what number (s)he has picked.[69]

In order to make it even more effective, you can even make this exercise more interactive and interesting by telling the audience that you want to play a little game with them, and next asking if there is someone in the audience who is willing to put money on the fact that you cannot guess the number, just from knowing which rows the number is in. Remember to tell them that it has to be a number between 1-60, without commas, fractions or the like. This variety of exercise usually goes especially well with sales-oriented personnel.

When you have chosen your opening statement, try to put it into the P3 opening format if at all possible by linking the opening to your topic. Make sure that you tell them **what** the presentation subject is and **why** you are giving the presentation, and then involve the audience in the presentation. This makes the opening relevant and opens the minds of your audience. Guard against any anti-climax following your introduction; that is, do not create such high expectations in the opening that you cannot fulfill them in your presentation.

Step 4 – Evaluate the Information Presentation

If you deliver the curtain-raising introduction to your presentation skillfully, you will, at best, have captured the interest of your listeners, aroused their curiosity and sense of anticipation, and prepared them for your main message. At a minimum, you will have made it clear that you feel you have something significant to say. It is important that the main body of your presentation should live up to expectations, particularly since it represents the whole reason for the talk. This is where the real substance is communicated.

Take a look at your information outline. These are the major points you have to think about now:

1. Recall the purpose of the presentation and the specific results you want to achieve.

2. In the light of 1, decide what the main points are that you want to put across. Identify and list them very clearly.

3. Arrange your list in a logical progressive sequence so that your listeners' understanding will advance step-by-step easily.

4. Think about each of the main points and decide how you are going to describe each in the most effective, graphic, punchy way. Write this down.

5. Check that what you have written really conveys your meaning and con-
   tributes to the results you want. If you are not satisfied, do it again.

6. Plan to support description or intention with chapter and verse as far as
   possible but not with masses of statistics or long quotations from other
   sources. Have any complex or detailed sources you use close at hand in
   case questions are asked afterwards and your answers require substantia-
   tion.

7. Plan to finish the main body with a statement which reminds your listeners of the message: "What I have described to you is ..." or some expression with the same effect.

Step 5 – Review the Presentation Arguments
Next, it is time to look at the argumentation in your information outline, in
your notes from above.

To ensure good argumentation, you have to consider how a typical strong
argument is built up. For a minute, think of yourself as a professional management consultant who is asked to make a brief statement to a group of US
gamblers about to place bets on European Soccer. Consider these two statements:

1. *Milan will at least get into the Champions' League finals this year because I know I am always right about European soccer.*

2. *Milan has the strongest and best-balanced combination of offensive and
   defensive players in the professional Champions' League today, while all
   its chief rivals, like Paris SG, Real Madrid, Ajax, are relatively weak in
   either the offensive or the defensive game.*

   *Past records in the field of professional soccer indicate that only a team
   that is really strong in both offense and defense can be expected to win the
   Champions' League.*
   *So presumably, unless Milan is plagued by injuries or the other teams do
   some quick and costly talent buying or there is a general upset of the
   record, Milan is a sure bet in this year's Champions' Leagues final.*

Even though both statements are short, it is obvious which one is the more persuasive. In order to document why, we use a rhetorical analysis of the statement based on a simple building-block model.[70]

There are six basic building blocks of a full argument: **Grounds** are facts, statistics, observations, or anything the listener will accept at face value. **Warrants** are general rules about how to generalize from the grounds to the Claim. **Backings** are further support to prove the validity of warrants. The **Claim** is the aim and goal of the persuasion attempt. A **Qualifier** is a model presumption in essence, a type of likelihood or certainty of the claim's being true, which is often possible to relate to a percentage of certainty that the claim is true. A **Rebuttal** is the "exception that confirms the rule," that is, in which conditions the claim is not valid. A full argument can be described like this:

Given grounds (G), we may appeal to warrants (W), which rest on backing (B) to justify that the claim (C) or, at any rate the qualifier (Q), is correct, in the absence of some specific rebuttal or disqualification (R).

A statement can be called an argument if it includes at least **a claim, a ground and a warrant.** If any of these three is not present, a statement is not, technically-speaking, an argument but just a general statement.

Now look at how a strong logic statement is created:

Ground (G): *Milan has the strongest and best balanced combination of offensive and defensive players in the professional Champions' League today, while all its chief rivals (Paris SG, Real Madrid, Ajax) are relatively weak in either the offensive or defensive game.*

Backing (B): *Past records of form in the field of professional soccer indicate that*

Warrant (W): *only a team that is really strong in both offense and defense can really be tipped for victory of the Champions' League.*

Qualifier (Q): *So presumably,*

Rebuttal (R): *unless Milan is plagued by injuries or the other teams do some quick and costly talent buying or there is a general upset of the form record,*

Claim (C):   *Milan is a sure bet in this year's Champions' Leagues final.*

By comparison, look at how a weak statement is build up:

Ground (G):

Backing (B):   *I know I am always right about European soccer*

Warrant (W):

Qualifier (Q):   (it's a fact)

Rebuttal (R):

Claim (C):   *Milan will at least get into the Champions' League finals this year.*

The weak statement above can easily be criticized for not having any grounds, a most questionable backing, no explicit warrant, and an absolute implicit qualifier with no rebuttal. These reasons show why the first statement is weak and questionable; in fact, it cannot be called an argument at all. What makes the second argument stronger is the presence of all the building blocks.

You can use this model to test your own arguments. The two arguments most critical to your presentation are the overall claim that the investor should invest in your business, and the sub-claim that your idea/solution is better than the alternative solutions.

Use building blocks and sub-arguments. It is not a matter of life and death in what order you use the different building blocks. Use a format which you are comfortable with. Try to strengthen every argument you make by making sure you have thought about all the building blocks, that you have enough of them, especially enough grounds, and that you have sound arguments (called sub-arguments) for each of the building blocks used. Sub-arguments relate especially to the grounds used, but have to be considered for all building blocks.

An argument can be weakened by questioning of the soundness or strength of one or more of its building blocks. If you fail to have reasonable building blocks, or if you have not thought about them and thus overlooked them in your build-up, your argument will be open to direct criticism. Even if all the blocks are there, the argument might not be strong enough to survive scrutiny if the building blocks themselves are not plausible, or if there are no plausible connections between them. But this doesn't happen that often.

Remember that the listener does not have a lot of time to make his/her mental analysis of your arguments, even though he/she might be very perceptive of fallacies in logic. Be careful not to explicitly include all the building blocks in all your arguments all the time. It is mandatory for you to state grounds and claims, but the rest of the building blocks can be omitted sometimes, especially if you do not want to bring up a problem area.

If you spell everything out, your run the risk of boring your listener or, worse yet, irritating the person by implying that you consider him/her a fool or a bit ignorant. When you prepare your arguments, however, always try to identify all building blocks so you can omit out of choice and not out of carelessness.

If you analyze your arguments with the building block format, you can discover where you will have problems and questions from the audience before you give your presentation. So diagram your arguments and use the diagrams to improve your argumentation. Do not expect to build your arguments perfectly the first time around. Make reasonable questions – the ones to which you know you have strong answers — part of your presentation, and then answer them with persuasive arguments including all the relevant building blocks.

Trains of arguments persuade. Be aware of the possibility of making "trains" of arguments. This means that one argument acts as the grounds for a new argument, which acts as grounds for the next argument, and so on. This is the way to make trains of arguments support your final claim. If your idea is hard for the listener to swallow, then take the best ground in your main argument and build a full argument that sustains that specific ground, turning it into a claim. In this way you can chain arguments together and build a stronger case for your ultimate claim or goal.

A proven technique to approach a train of arguments is to imagine a train with four carriages. The first carriage is used to agree on the given situation, based on establishing the facts of the events/situation. The second carries the claim of what the consequences (problems) of the situation are. The third carriage contains what should be done about the problem. And the fourth has what the listener should do specifically to help solve the problem.

Step 6 – Create the Presentation Outline
Next you create the outline of the presentation. This outline of content is the one you will use for the presentation itself. Please note the difference in lay-out between the "Information outline" and the "Presentation outline." The former captures your thoughts and ideas rationally and logically, while the latter organizes them for the maximum benefit of your listeners, who will then be persuaded more easily. The presentation outline should include:

1. **Result**   The main benefit, the objective, the result the listener derives from your idea, why you give the presentation in the first place.

2. **Obstacle**   The problem keeping the listener from reaching the objective.

3. **Idea**   What you are addressing in the first place.

4. **Benefits**   Remember, these are benefits to the listener derived from your idea, the most important advantage or benefit of which is the same as the objective, the result.

5. **Q & A**   Possible questions in your listener's mind and their appropriate answers based on "proofs" like statistics, experience, facts or experts that support your idea.

6. **Resume**   Restate the listener's obstacle, your idea, and the benefits and results to the listener.

7. **Action**   What specifically must your listener do to obtain those benefits, and when must he/she take the action step(s).

Write the presentation outline like a script, something you can say naturally. Make sure that you write it using words for speaking, not words for reading. It should be outlined based on words you want to say — ones that comes out of your mouth, not just out of your brain. Words for reading allow one's eye and mind to do the work. The reader decides the speed at which the words come at him, and he/she can decide to go back and reread or to stop for a while. This you cannot do when you listen to a speaker. Therefore, try to incorporate spoken language into your preparation.

If you are an average speaker, you speak about 150 words per minute. That makes 4,500 words per half hour, or 9,000 words per hour. When speaking, we usually recap, rephrase, put in examples, pause for comments, *etc.* So, if you try to write the speech word by word, you should plan to say about 100 words per minute, *i.e.*, 3,000 words per half hour, and about 6,000 for a full hour. These benchmarks will enable you to fit the length of the presentation to the time you are allowed — if you are not experienced enough yet to know your own speed —or they will tell you how much time you need to deliver your presentation in full.

If you have never stood in front of a business audience before, it can be a help to write everything down word-for-word. But remember only to use the word-for-word manuscript to help you outline your presentation. No later than after talking through the presentation the first time, you should be able to write notes on the basis of the key words you have. Never use the word-for-word manuscript in the actual presentation.

If you are more used to preparing and giving presentations, you should write up the content in a brief form, with bulletpoints, *etc.* after the outline above and, on basis of that, develop your notes. As you get more and more experienced, you will learn to make more preparation shortcuts, including writing down key words directly instead of sentences.

Step 7 – Create the Presentation Conclusion
When you end your presentation, you should emphasize that the sum of your points and arguments is more that the parts, you should change your style to make everyone aware that you are going to finish, and you should sharpen your main point, the purpose of the presentation. Your talk should end on a high note, bearing in mind that *it* will be remembered by your audience. Possible approaches are:

A summary ending
The intention is to round off the talk in a decisive manner:

I will finish by summing up the advantages that must come from this course of action. First, the management is for it. Secondly, the employers are sympathetic. Thirdly, it means that everyone will benefit in the long run. And finally ....

A "call to action" ending
To conclude on a reasoned note:

I hope that you will go away from here and talk about and think about what I have said. But talking and thinking are not enough. Will you sign our petition appealing for this annoying traffic to be stopped at once? Will you write to your local mayor tonight? Will you march with us to parliament? Will you do this in the name of humanity?

A "presentation of alternatives" ending

To conclude on a reasoned note:

Well, we must either seek the advice of this business expert and act on his advice, or we must muddle along with the unhappy results I have indicated. The choice is yours, gentlemen ....

An apt quotation ending

To end the speech on a thoughtful note:

I would conclude with the moving words of that great and good man, Albert Schweitzer: "Life is not a cup to be drained, it is a measure to be filled."

An open ending

To provoke discussion after the speech:

Our patrons are loyal, but unless we modernize our cinemas, we cannot hope to attract new customers, and we desperately need new customers. The outlay is not light, I will admit. But we must find the money. Gentlemen, there is but one question we must ask: Can we afford not to afford this money?

Whichever type of conclusion you use, start off by reminding your listeners what the subject, message, purpose, *etc.* of your presentation was. This means that you will have told them the topic in the introduction, in the main body, and again in the conclusion, following the golden rule of presentation:

> **You tell them what you are going to tell them, you tell them,**
> **and then you tell them what you have just told them.**

This is a nearly infallible way of getting the message home. Advertising research also concludes that three exposures to a message is the threshold for a correct understanding of the message. You may be sick of repeating what you have worked on, said, and practiced so many times already. Your audience is not.

Form

Step 8 – Create Notes and Visual Aids

Speak, don't read. Notes are primarily key words on paper, written mainly for your own sake. They are not everything, word for word; they are just the key points and the transitions from the opening to the close. Most professional presenters find it useful to write down the first sentences they are supposed to say word for word so they can get going even if they have a temporary black-out when going on stage. Likewise, they write the last sentence or two so as to be able to draw everything to a successful close, without leaving the audience hanging, not knowing whether to expect more or not. Along with key words, most professionals include when and where they are going to show which visual. They also write an index number on each notecard so they will always know where they are, no matter what happens.

Most presenters find small cue-cards useful. Do not use normal A4 paper, if for no other reason that the pages are noisy when you unfold them or shift them around.[71] Only if it is possible to hide them from sight can A4 pages be used. However, for information presentations, when presenting loads of information which is hard to remember otherwise, A4 paper has its uses. Most persuasive presenters find it useful to use cue-cards which are about 1/4 of a A4 page and made out of thin cardboard.

Visuals are visuals, not sentences or notes on an overhead. Visuals are graphical elements that show an illustration, a picture, a graph, a drawing, or a diagram. They should illustrate major points in your presentation, not substitute for your words. If there is a chance that you will be misunderstood or if you are dealing with something which is not easy to understand — technical matters, complex solutions, detail-focused arguments, graphic or visual problems, *etc.* — then you should definitely use visuals. Even if you are speaking one-to-one, visuals can effectively support understanding of your major points.

Always use visuals, but do not go overboard. Keep your visuals as simple as possible and to a minimum. Do not get yourself into a situation where you spend all your time handling the visuals, and do not bombard the audience with them either. The rule of thumb is not to use more than 10 visuals in a 30 minute presentation, that is, one for every three minutes of presentation.

As you are trying to "sell" something, you should prepare a paper copy of your business idea, including all your major points and visuals. But be careful not to hand out too much. If you haven't met the investor before, only bring a short description of your business idea, not the full business plan. If you are meeting him/her for a second or third time, then bring the full plan. But, no matter what, make sure that you get the investor/client to sign a confidentiality agreement, which legally prevents him/her from taking similar actions or sharing insights from your business plan with someone else. Do not hand out copies of your presentation in advance. People will start looking through it while you speak, losing their concentration and preempting what you are going to say. Reserve copies until the end of your presentation.

Do use *graphical* visuals. Images convey meaning on a much superior level, while words you can just say in your presentation. Showing text on the screen with a voice saying the same thing creates unnecessary verbal emphasis and duplication, while good visuals present the same concepts in a new way, improving viewer comprehension. Compare among visuals:

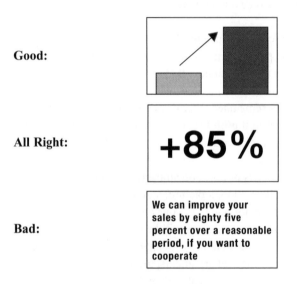

Good:

All Right: +85%

Bad: We can improve your sales by eighty five percent over a reasonable period, if you want to cooperate

When presenting data or statistics, be creative. Data and statistics are normally considered cold facts and are very persuasive because they are almost unquestionable. They can be very flexible and easy to present visually, much more than you might have thought, and you can be very "creative" without anyone's noticing. Make graphs whenever possible, rather than matrices of numbers. Enhance a curve by adjusting the scale of the axis' so you get the most significance possible, to push your point to the viewer.

Use illustrations rather than text and numbers. When doing the visuals, ask yourself:

- Have you written your notes on slides? (Visuals are for pictures, not key words)

- Are there too many?

- Are they too crowded or too small to be seen?

- Are the colors and the backgrounds consistent?

- Are you writing in multiple directions? (Keep to horizontal lines.)

- When you are presenting a complex diagram or picture, you can choose to use a series of pictures, or one where the complexity is built up by adding information. Are you using the right method for the particular idea you are presenting?

Step 9 – Fashion the Presentation Delivery

Delivery and language are about form, not content: how you deliver your presentation, how you tell your business idea to the audience, how you act, how you fight nervousness, how you phrase, how you choose words.

You can deliver your presentation or speech in several different ways: you can read aloud from a manuscript, you can learn everything by heart and recite it, you can improvise without any prior preparation, or you can extemporize. All forms of delivery can be effective, but extemporizing usually gives significantly better results.

Extemporizing means delivering a well-prepared, rehearsed, but not word-by-word-memorized presentation. It has the advantage of coming across as somewhat improvised while not exposing you to the peril of getting lost in the middle of your presentation, a hazard of fully improvised speeches. It also ensures that you will not come across as a robot reading aloud, no matter how many times you deliver the presentation. It will have a spontaneous, dynamic touch, it will involve the listeners, and it will allow for adaptation to a particular audience.

Most people face the prospect of having to make a presentation with some trepidation. It would be most unnatural if that were not the case. Even professional actors suffer from first night nerves. But pros ensure the quality of their performance, despite the nerves or butterflies in their stomachs, by two simple techniques:

1. They prepare well

2. They rehearse

The key to making effective presentations lies in preparation and rehearsal. If sufficient work and effort are put in, chances are that the "performance" will be much more than all right. It will push the right button and give you success.

Authority, energy, audience contact and summaries are the four basic components of an effective and professional speaking style in business presentations.

To increase your **authority,** look and sound as if you mean what you say, you know what you are talking about, and you are the right person to be giving the presentation. If this is missing, your audience will question your credibility.

To seem **energetic**, look and sound as if you are involved in what you say, you care about what you say, and you really think it is important for the listeners to hear what you have to say. If this is missing, your audience will tune you out.

To secure **audience contact**, look and sound as if you recognize each member of your audience, as if you are sensitive to their reactions to what you say, and as if your audience is involved in your proposition. If this is missing, you audience will wonder why they are present.

When **summing up**, convey that you are dynamic, that you are moving on. Help organize what you have said in the minds of the audience in a few last lines. If summaries are not there, what you have said will disappear fast, and the understanding and persuasive effort of your message will be lost.

The eyes have it. Talk to people, not at them. Look at the people to whom you are talking. This means looking at them with interest to see how they are reacting to what you say, thus indicating that what you are saying is truly intended for them. Your eyes act as an additional vehicle for your words. Avoid mechanical sweeps of the room. In a small group, everyone should get the impression that you are speaking to him or her personally. Avoid looking out of the window, staring at the floor, talking to the ceiling or the screen, flipchart or chalkboard. Groups of people have a tendency to intimidate. Therefore, it's important to think of your audience as a group of individuals.

As you are talking, pick out one person in the group and talk to that person. Finish one complete thought or phrase before shifting your eyes to another person and repeat the process. Concentrating on one person at a time reduces the faceless audience to just one face. It's also an effective way to impress that person. Remember that a listener is basically selfish – he/she is interested in what you have to say and how he/she feels about what you say. Establishing eye contact rivets your listener's attention to you. Not only will the listener pay more attention to you, but you can also pick up nonverbal feedback. Be attentive to signs that say, "I do not get this" or "This is great stuff," and talk accordingly. Eye contact is essential because audiences can be like sheep: when the shepherd does not look at them for a while, they stray. If they have strayed too long, they are most likely lost.

Do not do distracting things. Most people are stressed when making presentations. This can result in unconscious mannerisms which can be distracting — rocking on your feet or playing with keys, pencils, and other small objects, for example. Some people also do this when they get over-enthusiastic and need to let excess energy out. Remember's your grandmother's advice: stand straight, don't slouch. Do not lean over things or bend yourself in strange angles, touch your hair or swing it back every 30 seconds, or scratch your beard or chin more than once or twice. These quirks will shift the focus of the audience off what you saying and onto your strange mannerism(s).

Pause. Make good use of pauses; they act as punctuation for spoken words. Do not feel compelled to "talk on." A well-timed silence can be golden sometimes. You can use a pause for effect, to dramatize a point, to emphasize an important fact, to indicate that you feel a particular point is significant, to indicate that you have finished with one topic and are ready to move on to the next, or to collect your thoughts when you have lost their train. This last works as a slight cover-up but does not give a negative effect.

We have all heard people who use "you know," "uh" and "um." Usually these words are inserted because the speaker is afraid to pause. Pausing is natural — it gives you a chance to think about what you are going to say next, and it gives the listener an opportunity to think about what you have just said. Use pauses judiciously, however. A pause in the wrong place could panic or worry your audience and create problems. Can you spot the difference?

Bad: *Good morning, I have some very bad news ..... (pause)*

Good: *Good morning, I have some very bad news regarding today's lunch.*
         It will be served 10 minutes later than previously scheduled .....
         (pause)

A few seconds of silence calculated to hold your audience to your thoughts can be the most effective part of a speech.[72]

Facts are sacred and must not be tampered with, but statistics are usually flexible to suit your point. Concrete examples emphasize facts and make those facts stick in the mind. The closer the examples are to the experience of the audience, the more surely your points will find their targets.

Contrary to a common opinion, facts do not always speak for themselves. They need a good person to speak for them. Facts do not have to be colorless or less interesting than fiction. You must adroitly develop the story of each fact, giving it a good beginning, a lively motif, substance, excitement, strong close-to-home examples and a language suitable for your hearers.

Use active verbs, for example, "we reached our budget target." Do not use the passive form, "our budget target was reached." It is weak language. The former indicates that "we" did something, while the latter diverts attention away from us and directs it to the budget target. (It almost makes it look as if the budget was reached in spite of us rather than because of us.)

Use decisive language. Consider the following two statements:

Bad: *I think we have an idea which we predict will have a positive effect*
        on your sales. By accepting our idea, you will most likely increase
        your profits.

Good: *We have an idea we are confident will have a positive effect on your*
        sales. By accepting our idea, you will increase your profits.

If your immediate response was "What?" to the first statement, you have recognized how ineffectual the delivery was. Which of the two statements would you rather hear? Then talk that way, please.

Use adjectives with care. They are like perfume — a little makes it sweet to experience, a lot makes it unbearable to be in the room. Adjectives qualify what you are saying, they emphasize your subjective attitudes, and a good business person wants to come across as objective, not subjective. Therefore, be careful not to sound like the supersales person who calls you up and seriously tries to sell you his stuff as the greatest gift to mankind since toilet paper.

Use simple, active language and simple constructions. Stay away from jargon, unless the subject is specialized and the listeners are so familiar with the terms that their use aids understanding. Do not try to impress with the breadth of your vocabulary. Use simple, civil words that get the meaning across in the clearest, most effective manner. Experienced older people will be annoyed or intimidated by unfamiliar academic words rather than impressed by them. Do not separate yourself from your audience with your choice of words; try to get closer instead by using appropriate language.

You also have to **be likable**. One way of doing this is by projecting confidence. Some powerful business figures go out of their way to appear humble but, when they succeed too well, they fail to sell their ideas to their listeners. By all means, be confident and sincere. Let the listener know you know what you are talking about and never, ever lie. Come across as honest. Do not set yourself up to something you are not; instead, underplay you role and position. Speak to people directly. People like you when, after you've finished, they can walk away feeling as though you've spoken to them personally. Talking to your audience on an individual basis also means saying and using the "you" approach. This will not only make your presentation more personal but also increase your closeness with the audience.

A sure bet is to smile. A smile hold all the potential for you to be liked by the audience. But a smile is not just any smile; a good one involves both your mouth and eyes. People who smile only with their mouths convey false smiles, like sales people or tour operators who are ordered to be nice to all customers and have their smiles painted on. Your eyes tell whether your smile is sincere.

Enthusiasm is contagious. Therefore, it has to be an integrated part of your presentation. If the listener knows you believe what you say, he will believe it too. Talk sincerely, and do not let inhibitions hold you back from being excited about your topic.

Don't overkill. Many speakers find it more important to prove themselves experts on their given topics than simply to inform and persuade listeners in accord with the goals of their presentations. So avoid overkill. If you have 25 years of experience in your field, fine, but your listener does not need your 25 years of knowledge. When the President of USA speaks for 50 minutes, a television commentator condenses the speech into a ten minute synopsis; the commentator tells you what you need to know. Do the same for your listener. When you have made a point, move on.

Everyone loves a funny presenter as much as everyone hates an embarrassing joke. If you want to make sure that your humor works, it too has to be planned — unless you are among the less than 1% of all business presenters who are truly, spontaneously funny. A good joke or funny comment can come from anywhere, even yourself. If you read or hear something which makes you laugh, grab a pen and write it down for later use. When you think you have the right material for a joke, follow these steps to make it a success:

1. Learn it by heart, word for word, and practice by saying it out aloud.

2. Enjoy the joke yourself.[73] Then it becomes truly yours, and you can tell it with vitality and confidence.

3. Surprise your audience with it. Do not hint or warn them in advance.

4. Pause just before the punchline and then wait for the response (laugh).

5. Keep your joke short.

Researching for funny comments or jokes is quite easy, as there are a lot of books to help you out. One good source is, of course, books of jokes. Other sources of good material are books of provocative and memorable quotations, on funny language and twisted words and on famous speaking errors. Here are a few samples to help get you started:

The last time I gave a speech, it was to the sales force of a car company. After the meeting, a very enthusiastic sales rep came up to me and said that he thought I had given them a "Rolls Royce" of a speech. I was flattered, ... until a little later it dawned on me: the two main characteristics of a Rolls Royce are that you can hardly hear it and it lasts forever.

Working hard does pay certain dividends. When I was working for a company making briefcases, we had a fellow in our office who took a briefcase full of work home every night. He became rich. But one day we found out he was stealing briefcases.

These are not my own figures I'm quoting. They're the figures of someone who knows what he is talking about.

Now is the time to grab the bull by his horns, but please, do not wake him up. It might hurt.

I tried to be a chicken farmer once, but it did not work ...... I planted them too deep.

When being funny, try not to do it wrong. How do you know what is wrong? For starters, when people do not laugh. When you embarrass other people. When you use ethnic or religious jokes. When you swear or use profane language. The easiest way to make sure that you are not doing it wrong is to test it beforehand. Use your colleagues, family or friends as guinea pigs.

Always avoid off-color jokes. Some might find them funny, but others are bound to be offended. Can you afford that? No, since you do not know the ethics of all members of your audience or where they usually draw the line.

Being ironic can also be very entertaining, but be sure that your audience understands that you are ironic. The use of irony, either as a joke or for emphasis, is not universal: people from Great Britain and Denmark mostly find it natural, Americans and Germans usually do not. If in doubt, avoid irony.

In general, if you are speaking in a country or region other than your own, it's a very good idea to have a local, or a person with deep local experience, coach you before your presentation as to local mores and do's and don'ts.

Quality enhancement

Step 10 - Rehearsal
Now it is time to deliver the speech, but do rehearse beforehand. Presentation wizards and actors practice many times to get everything right. The more times you rehearse, the less mind power you use and the more you can focus on your actual delivery and the audience's response. If the outline and content are absolutely fixed in your mind, you can focus on improving your acting ... oh, sorry, your delivery.

Usually it will be necessary to make cuts and changes — in your speech, in your notes, and in your visuals. Practice aloud, to an audience if possible, and/or use a tape/video recorder. The best thing to do is to use your colleagues or someone else who knows what you are talking about. The next best option is to do your rehearsal in front of a videocamera. If you can combine the two, you have the best of the best.

The first thing you should check is timing. A good presenter uses a watch or timer during the presentation, and the trick is to glance at it so the audience does not detect your doing so. A big clock on the back wall is ideal, a watch next to your slides or notes is good, but a watch on your arm will give you away. You can also have someone in the back signal you when you have only five minutes left, so you know you have to bring everything to a close.

Step 11 – Quality Control
Next, evaluate the rehearsal itself. When evaluating your performance based on the rehearsal, break it down into two categories: **Content** (looking at what you presented, the content based on your notes and visual aids) and **form** (looking at your delivery, how you acted and conducted yourself). The evaluation can be used to make both aspects of your presentation better. Let us look at each of the two separately:

You evaluate the **content** to know what to modify, based on your specific weaknesses and strengths and what the test audience or your own review contributed in terms of feedback. Ask yourself questions like these:

1. How did I measure understanding? Did the test-audience help me under stand this? How can I build audience involvement to greater effect next time?

2. What went well and why? How can I capitalize on what I know now?

3. What went badly or wrong and why? How can I prevent this next time?

4. Did I meet my objectives?

5. Did the audience understand my arguments and main points?

6. Did I emphasize the points requiring high levels of understanding?

7. Did I anticipate the questions from the audience?

8. What methods were used? How well did they work?

9. Did I stick to the proposed outline of the content? A suitable introduction and a closure?

10. What else might I have done? What should I do differently next time?

After looking at the content, look at the **form** of your delivery. You can make a list of questions analogous to those above and score yourself: did I speak loudly enough?, slowly enough?, vary the pace?, the pitch of my voice? Did I emphasize the right points?, express myself naturally?, simply? Did I avoid clichés and jargon? Did I eliminate waffle? Was I looking at my audience?, using my hands properly? Have I got any habits that distract the audience? Can I relax more? Have I rehearsed enough, or do I need another go or two?

The questions and responses are a very effective way to evaluate where you have problems. They show your strengths, but those are irrelevant for the moment. Forget them, and use your effort to correct your most important weaknesses.

When you have rehearsed, review what you will do. You can even consider your actual presentation a rehearsal and the actual audience a test audience. If possible, get feed-back from someone in the audience to learn more from the experience. But be careful not to compromise yourself: try to use some-one on your side or, even better, a friend in the audience.

Re-examine your notes and visual aids and build in what you have learned, both in terms of content and delivery form. Keep this in mind:

Aim to be remembered for what you said, not how you performed.

Step 12 –The Question and Answer Session
There are five formal steps to answering questions professionally with a large audience:

1. Listen and look
Always listen very carefully to the question and look at the person asking. When he/she is done, give a little nod with your head so he/she knows you have understood it. (If not, ask clarifying questions.)

2. Repeat or rephrase
Then look at the audience. Repeat the question (into the mike) to be sure everyone heard it.

If the question is quite long, rephrase it and make it shorter. If it is aggres-sive/negative/hostile, make it positive. (This may bring forth the irrelevance or stupidity of the question.) When rephrasing, be careful not to change the meaning.

Some do not ask a question but tell a story instead. Make the tale into a question by rephrasing it. This will sometimes bring forth some interestingly strange questions; boost your credibility by answering them with a straight face.

3. Answer
After repeating the question, turn your face back to the person asking, and give the answer. If you do not have an answer, do not fabricate one. Simply state that you do not know the answer but will get the information to him, or refer to another with the competence to answer the question.

When starting the answer, look at the person asking, so he/she knows you are talking to him/her and responding personally but, while you are underway, start to shift your focus from the person asking back to the audience in general. With this trick, you can avoid a second, third or fourth question from the same person, which often tends to be rather irrelevant. This will not be considered rude because you have given the questioner what he/she needed: initial attention and an answer. If he/she really has an additional important question, you can be sure that he/she will ask it without your help.

4. Ask for more questions
Or screen the audience, moving your head from left to right and from front to back, looking as though you expect more questions.

5. Repeat the summary
When no more spontaneous questions arise, after waiting max. 5 -10 seconds in silence and after having screened the whole audience again, start to repeat your summary as wrap-up of the presentation. Never, ever end your talk on the last question. **Always repeat your summary and action step before you leave the stage,** regardless of how many times you have already said it. It will be the message the listener retains when leaving the room, and that's the essence of effective communication.

Handling of hostile questions
Usually there are two kinds of difficult questions — hostile questions and logical objections — which create the biggest problems for a presenter. Sometimes you will come across a hostile question that is less a question than an emotional value judgment.

The worst thing you can do is to start an argument. Keep your cool if you are upset. Do not get your defenses up. Do not make the issue into a personal crusade. Separate it from the person, if possible. Try not to take the hostility personally so you loose your temper. Then you will not be able to give objective answers, and you could loose your credibility in a twinkle of an eye. If you are really upset, then shut up, pause, and take a sip of your water. This will give you time to regain your composure. Often someone else will come to your rescue in the meantime. If not, try to remember the guidelines above, that is, rephrase the question positively and answer it with an answer not outlined by the question.

If you can get away with it, the best way to get around a hostile question is actually to use a little humor in a story and, by so doing, avoid answering directly. This way of responding may not answer anything, but it will put a little smile on people's faces, making them happy. Many hostile questions are not really questions that the audience believes need a direct answer.

Often hostile questions are not hostile towards you but reflect negative dynamics in the audience. Again, passing over them lightly is the best solution.

Answering critical logical questions
Sometimes you will face someone who objects to what you say and confidently presents reasonable arguments as to why your idea should not be adopted. For you to become more familiar with these types of logical counter-arguments, let us outline some of the more common ones. Normally the defense and attack strategy is used, where the one commenting first defends his own opinion against your arguments and then attacks your arguments.

Rebutting point by point
Taking up single parts of an argument and attacking the weak ones until the whole thing falls apart.

Simply denying it
"It's not true." Only effective against you if the one offering the denial has a much superior image and influence and is much more believable than you.

Disagreeing
Taking the opposite position and trying to argue for it better than you can against it.

Rejecting the authority
If you quote an expert, someone may come up with a reason why he/she is not an expert on the issue discussed.

Creating a dilemma

Someone makes up a situation where there are two equally undesirable outcomes to your idea or issue — like the choice between AIDS and cancer.

Excluding possibilities one by one

Setting up a few possibilities, where the first ones are in favor of you ...

Has the money gone to travel expenses, or tips, or has he stolen it?

... he then rebuts them one by one until he reach the last one, which is in favor of his own position:

There are no receipts for the money in the travel expense report, and there are no add-ons written by hand to show tips paid. Thus the money has to be in his own pocket.

Making it absurd

Taking the objector's point of view and expanding it until it seems absurd. For example, when he/she argues for bigger overall profits by giving a single special client a one-time discount, you counter by explaining that if the company gives one such discount, it will have to give all its clients similar discounts, resulting in overall major profit-cuts and possible bankruptcy for the company.

High-lighting your internal contradictions

Taking two of your own statements and showing that they are opposite sides or opposite arguments on the same issue.

Attacking the form of argumentation

The most important and difficult form of logical objection is someone's criticizing your way of arguing, your use of logic. One means of attacking your form of argumentation can, for example, be to claim that you are trying to persuade the audience by only using psychological appeals — not acceptable in the business environment.

Consider this counter-argument:

We run a big and very diverse restaurant operation here, and preparation of salads takes up less than 5% of our time and turnover. As we have big problems with making sauces, which all our dishes have, it would be totally unprofessional to put more time or energy into the virtually non-existent possibility of improving our salads. Therefore, our priority should definitely not be using more time and energy to improve salads, as you recommend, but rather solving the sauce problem. That would increase the quality and profit much more than focusing on salads.

This kind of logical objection is maybe the most tricky, because it calmly and objectively questions the whole basis of your idea. Therefore, these objections are the ones you have to make absolutely sure you respond to in the best possible way.

If you already have worked with the same or a similar objection during your preparation, you will know how to answer it with a sound rebuttal, and you are on safe ground. That is why your preparatory work on possible objections is so very important for the success of your presentation. If you have not thought of the objection before, then you may think you're in trouble, but you are not. The first thing you could and should do is to isolate the objection and try to make it a smaller problem, not directly related to the success or failure of your idea:

I understand that sauces are a special problem — but so are the salads. For one thing, almost all female guests in your restaurants notice the difference between a good and a bad salad. And your female customers probably makes up a minimum 40% of your guests and therefore of your profit. So perhaps you should consider solving both problems simultaneously and not ignore one of them.

In this way, you minimize the value of the objection by separating the issue into two problems — one being the sauce and one the salad. Rephrasing your best argument behind the relevance of your idea — that women, 40% of all guests, especially notice salad quality — gives you time to generate an intelligent answer. This is only a way to minimize your losses, however. What you must look for is a constructive answer to win the person over.

A trick to do just that is to use this kind of a dynamic argumentation technique, where you overcome the objection in a smooth logical way, much as a professional salesperson would:

First show **empathy:**   *I understand why you might feel that way;*

then make a **direct analogy:**   *many of our clients, like McDonald's, have often felt that way in the beginning.*

Explain the **benefit**:   *But after a week, they found that ....*

then make your **testimonial:** *this product actually saved McDonald's 40% on their salad costs and increased the quality index by 20% during the first year. Wouldn't you like to do the same?*

Finally, when you simply cannot believably answer that one-in-a-million question that throws your whole idea overboard, give way and be cheerful about the opportunity to learn something more. There could indeed be something which kills your idea that you or your colleagues have not realized.[74] You and your company would lose much more if your audience did as you wanted them to do, suffering the consequences later. Then you would be out of that business. Bad news and experiences travel about ten times faster and longer than good ones. Worse yet, you could be sued for damages. But before you let go and accept the defeat of your idea, be sure that the objection is essential to the whole thing, valid, and trustworthy. 99.99% of objections are not — the statistics are on your side.

There are gender diffferences in how men and women generally handle criticism in the form of questions. Men usually take the offensive, try to come up with a lot of new good reasons why it is not a problem, and meet reason with reason, developing their thinking as they go. Women in general take time to consider the criticism and ask themselves again if their idea or argument is bad, so their first response is either reflective or defensive.

So, if you are a man, work on learning to evaluate the soundness of the questions asked before you "shoot from the hip." If you are a woman, work on learning to be less intimidated by questions, go more on the offensive, and create "reasons why" fast instead of retreating to a defensive position.

Separating the issue from the person is essential. Do not get into a personal disagreement in front of everyone — just don't! If you disagree about something, disagree about an issue. Also, remember that questions are not asked to be shot down like sitting ducks. Turn them around so they can be used constructively to build your case even more strongly. Show respect for the one asking; be kind and tactful.

Step 13 – The On-site Preparation
On-site on-time preparation deals with what you should check just before and once you are at the presentation site. Before you address your audience, take a long look at yourself in the mirror. Search for distracting elements: missing buttons, spots on your tie, loud clothing, *etc*. Your listener will focus on the pens in your pocket or the huge diamond ring on your finger instead of your content. Inspect the venue if possible. Test the mike, acoustics, seating

arrangements, visual aids (TV, video, slide projector, *etc.*) and the like. Introduce yourself to the audio-visual staff and ask questions: are there extra plugs available?, are they the kind you need?, extension lead?, necessary spare/repair kit? Check lightning and other factors which may disturb your presentation, *e.g.*, roadwork, fire drill, *etc.* Make sure you meet the Administrative Assistant who can help you if you need something.

Remember not to stand between the audience and your screen or chart, so place your visuals and/or notes at an appropriate place. If you really need to use a pointer, use it simply to point directly and then put it away so you do not start playing with it and distract your audience. Ask yourself: if all your aids failed, could you cope anyway? Now it is time to perform, to persuade. You are as prepared as you ever will be. Good luck, go get the money!

...And Next...

Congratulations! You got the money — not as much as you wanted and not on the terms you thought would be your very last offer — but you got the money. Next, you have a company to run. Running a company is outside the scope of this book, so we shall leave you soon. But, before we go, we shall discuss some issues in setting up your company, including hiring and the various planning processes which you will have to get used to.

Chapter 5
After the Funding

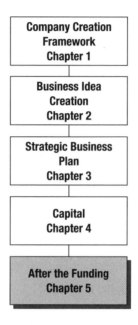

The funding effort is over (for now) – whew! We shall wrap up our coverage of company creation by reviewing some areas of importance at this point: hiring people, the formal organization of the company, and the planning process. Finally, in the last section of this chapter we shall return to the discussion we had in the Introduction about what changed in the "new" economy. As we said, the Web has brought fundamental changes in connectivity, reach and access. These changes translate into some very specific opportunities and challenges in the areas of customer acquisition, customer retention, and customer valuation – the last topics we shall cover.

5.1
People

Completing your management team is an important part of building the business when funding becomes available. The first step, which you included in the Strategic Business Plan, is to determine what functions you need to fill when, and the second step is to identify how you are going to fill them.

The Recruiting Process

The recruiting process runs through a number of steps.

- Determining which functions you need filled and the order in which you need them filled

- Outlining the profiles of the particular positions

- Identifying the manner in which the positions will be filled

- Selecting personnel for interviews and performing the final selection

- Hiring or contracting with the individual(s) selected.

The Company Overview section of the Strategic Business Plan outlined your management team as well as a plan for filling its empty slots. Use this description to identify the areas where you need to hire to round out your management team, for example:

- Sales and Marketing

- Operations

- Legal

- Financial and Administration

- Product Management.

Concentrate initially on the management level; one of the responsibilities of the managers you bring in will be to hire their own teams.

Once you have identified the areas where you need resources, you should identify which of these areas you consider core competencies for the company and thus want to staff permanently. Other areas you may wish to outsource and/or hire staff for on a short-term basis.[75] Still other areas you may decide to outsource in the early phases, bringing the expertise in house when the company has grown.

Once you have the functions identified, you need to create job profiles for them. Be aware that all functional areas have their own ways of stating requirements for positions, so you will want to get help from somebody with experience in the particular fields. Creating job profiles is important both for the permanent positions and for the ones that you would like to outsource or use temporary personnel for. In the one case it will help the applicant and/or recruiter directly; in the other it will help the agency providing the staff.

Sources of Candidates

When you have the profiles for the jobs, you need to find candidates to interview. There are a number of ways to go about it:

Networking	Friends, family, coworkers, *etc.*, in other words your network. This is a good way to find people, particularly since you probably know the biases of the recommenders.
Headhunting	Outsourcing the recruitment to a professional recruitment agency. This is quite expensive and requires a good relationship with the recruiter as well as very accurate job profiles.
The Web and other sources	There are many job sites on the Web where one can find resumes. It is easy to create a large pool of candidates. Additional sources are newspapers and journals.
Field research	Participation in conferences and professional meetings can result in finding candidates and can also help spread the news that you are looking to fill specific positions.
Advertising	Traditional advertising in dailies and magazines, and posting jobs on job sites on the Web. The former can be quite expensive but

can be targeted through choice of the specific medium. The latter is free or relatively low cost.

Personnel agencies   Temporary agencies or outside consulting organizations can provide temporary employees, in some cases on a temporary to permanent basis.

The selection process takes place, of course, through interviews.

To Manage or to Lead

Every issue of a business magazine brings new articles on how to manage people, or Human Resources — to use a popular, somewhat neutered, phrase. There is always a theory *du jour.* Although this topic is way too large to cover in one section, we shall try to put it in perspective.

First, an almost truism: management theories do not exist in a vacuum. They have to be looked at in combination with the economic times of their presentation as well as with the overall state of the societies in which they are supposed to be valid. To put this in current – early 2002 – perspective, we have seen at least three major schools of theory within the last three to four years: the one of the "Dotcomedy" of 1999 and 2000, the one following the meltdown of the dot.com era, and the one currently developing. The last combines an attempt at responding to the root causes of the events of September 11th, 2001 with the current anti-globalization backlash.[76]

Three Samples

Let us look at three samples of management theories relating to personnel:

Jan Carlzon – President and CEO of Scandinavian Airlines Group from 1981 through 1993 – wrote a book in 1985 called *Riv pyramidarna!*, the title of which translates literally to "Tear down the pyramids"[77] — the organizational pyramids, that is. He was hired into a "turnaround" situation in SAS and was very successful. His message, although not unique, was early and well-presented; it emphasizes what we now would call CRM through information and delegation of authority with resulting decentralization of decision making and improved customer satisfaction: *"...a person without information is incapable of accepting responsibility. A person with information cannot help but accept responsibility...."*

A recent issue of *Harvard Business Review* has an article titled "Leading in Times of Trauma"[78] that reports on research performed jointly by the University of Michigan Business School and the University of British Columbia into organizational response to traumatic events. The article proposes four dimensions of measuring organizational ability to respond with compassion: scope – the breadth of possible response, scale – the volume or resources, speed of response, and specialization – the degree of customization possible, all to *"...nourish the very humanity that can make people – and organizations – great."*

The same issue of *Harvard Business Review* also has an article titled "A New Game Plan for C Players"[79] dealing with managing the pool of managerial talent in a corporation. The "player" term comes from the sports metaphors commonly used in American business; the A, B, and C terms from the American grading system in which A is best, B is acceptable, and C is mediocre. The article advises:

To build a strong talent pool, senior executives must regularly remove low performers from leadership positions.... To make this happen, companies need to apply an iron hand in a velvet glove.... Executives then need to decide on a simple rating system to delineate performance levels[80]*... [and] Companies need to establish a disciplined process that will* **make**[81] *managers confront this difficult talent-management issue head-on.*

— a somewhat mechanistic, one-dimensional perspective on personnel management.

So: delegate, nourish, or make them do what they don't want to do?

Where is, or is there a, reality?
First of all, reality is relative to the societies in which the company does business; what works in the U.S. would likely not work in, for example, France. Secondly, discipline processes **making** managers or employees do this or that probably only work in totalitarian societies or where employment is otherwise difficult.

Reality is, in most cases, closer to the first example above. Creating a clear connection between activities at work and the bottom line on the balance sheet will result in the workforce's making correct choices. The deeper issue may be that this causal connection is not always either realized or quantified by management. For example, it is "self evident" at the executive level that reducing the call center response time from, say, twenty seconds to the third ring is desirable, but it may not be easy to quantify.

Which management style will work for you and your company, only you — and your employees — can decide. We provide a few thoughts on "transparent management" below for you to consider.

Thoughts on Transparent Management[82]

"Transparent management" means that corporate information, plans and results are made available to employees at all levels, to involve them more closely in the operation of the company and to motivate them through increased understanding of how their actions reflect on the corporate bottom line.

Transparent management assumes that a company already uses some form of strategic planning, budgeting and financial management; otherwise there is nothing to share. It typically has three major components: planning participation, education and empowerment, and a reward structure.

Planning Participation

Planning participation means getting employees involved in the corporate planning process, both strategic and operational, leading to a greater sense of participation and involvement on their part. Management aids in this by breaking the planning objectives into strategies, strategic activities and measurable goals that can be monitored by the employees and management.

For this to be successful, it is important that the critical business objectives are in fact well-defined for the company. If they are not, more than transparent management is at stake; the whole company is at risk.

Some outcomes of planning participation for the employees are …

- Improved understanding of the company's mission and strategy as well as its competences;

- Improved understanding of the goals set for the company and of the metrics that will show when the goals are reached;

- Improved understanding of the market, including the company's possibilities and limitations related to it.

Transparent management is also about educating employees about the financial side of operating the company, in other words, giving them a basic understanding of the financials and of the causal connections between business actions and financial results. The company should have simple and comprehensible financials that everyone is able to understand and relate to. (Note that we are talking about managerial financials here, not the GAAP financials required for regulatory filings. Much more can and should be presented, and presented in different ways, in the financials used for management purposes than in those shown in regulatory filings.)

Financial reporting within a company is an essential element of transparent management. The following conditions must be met to give employees constructive business-critical numbers to navigate by:

- The reporting must be understandable to recipients.

- The reporting must be adaptable for individual recipients.

- The reporting must show past, current and future figures.

- The reporting must be available on time.

It is vital that the company's financials are presented to suit individual recipients so an employee actually looking at the figures will know how to use them in his/her work. The complete financials and budgets are only used by the top management of the company, *e.g.*, CEOs, COOs and CFOs.

Many companies are still far from transparent when it comes to financials. They are usually set aside for top management and directors only – quite inappropriately! The aim is to make the company's financials as evident and transparent as possible in order to motivate employees. And long-run motivation is what you want!

Education
Major employee participation in the planning and monitoring of corporate performance will likely require education and training, both in business and finance. Interestingly enough, while educating the workforce is now thought important, it is still common to find companies that do not take the time to ensure that all their employees know the basics of corporate finance.

This training need not be very formal; in-house staff can do it informally. Yet imagine what the effect on your company or future company would be if you had a complete team of people pulling together – from the employees at the bottom of the hierarchy to the top. It might very well be a completely reborn company, a company with employees committed to the company's operation and future and willing to make a spirited effort.

Transparent management is also about developing employees capable of making independent decisions. Empowering employees is an education process, not something one implements from one day to the next. It starts with information and adds participation and executive commitment, leading to sharing of everyday responsibilities, including meeting of operational goals and target figures. Employees then become accustomed to and accept responsibility for them.

Reward Structure

A shared reward structure goes hand in hand with the other components of transparent management. If you expect your employees to take actions like an owner and educate them to be able to do so, it makes sense that they share directly in your success.

A reward structure within a company can take many forms, including cash bonuses, stock options, and non-monetary rewards, and many different reward systems can be in place simultaneously.[83] It is important that the reward system(s) should fit the company culture and society. The best reward is not always money. You will find that employees from different backgrounds differ in their opinions of what constitutes a reward. For example, stock options are considered near worthless is some societies.

Nonetheless, stock options and company stock purchase plans have been quite successful as a reward system in some countries. United Parcel Service, the large American package delivery company, created wealthy truck drivers as a result of its IPO, drivers who had bought stock earlier through a company stock purchase plan. Microsoft also created a large number of dollar millionaires through its stock options plan. However, equity, whether issued as shares or in the form of options, is a shared risk instrument — as the people in Silicon Valley who had stock or options in many of the dot.coms found out. If you create a stock program as a reward system in your company, make sure that everybody understands the details.

It is important that the employees themselves — or at least some of them — are involved in creating bonus programs to ensure that everyone is satisfied with the results. The key issue is that the bonus program should be directly connected to the company's business objectives and goals. The following basic rules are therefore essential for a successful program:

1. The employees or their representatives must participate in designing the bonus program.

2. The employees must understand the program and the factors that affect it, *e.g.*, the company's strategic plan, the outside economy, *etc.*

3. The bonus program must be connected to the company's objectives and goals.

4. The bonus program must be directly related to the company's earnings and performance, whether or not the company is moving in the right direction.

5. The employees must appreciate the bonus program for it to act as an incentive to work harder. In any other case, it is useless.

6. An individual bonus program should be designed for each of the company's different groups of employees.

7. The bonus programs must be updated when necessary.

There are, of course, many different types of bonus programs; what type you choose depends on the company in question and the current situation.

Our final remark on bonus programs is that they should not be seen as salary raises, but rather as a motivation to increase the individual employee's performance. It is also important that the potential size of a bonus is such that it has the desired effect, *i.e.*, large enough to make a difference.

Finally, allow us to stress once again that transparent management is about making employees feel like owners/partners of the company so they will, in turn, feel a greater sense of responsibility towards the company and perform better. This is achieved by involving them in the strategy of the company and by ensuring that they have clear, comprehensible operational goals so that they can make a connection between those goals and the company's strategic objectives and goals.

So...

What do you do tomorrow? Jan Carlzon[84] tells how, when he got his first
executive job, he started to announce decisions as "I want...," "I wish...," or
"I believe..." because he "believed that everybody expected me to know better and to make all the decisions." Finally, one of his friends in the organization took pity on him and told him that, "... he had been named CEO because
of who he was and not because of how he – Jan Carlzon — thought he ought
to behave as a CEO." Perhaps the best thing you can do tomorrow is to be
yourself and do what you have been doing. You must be doing something
right — you have successfully started a company.

5.2
Company Creation

The different ways a company can be organized — and the implications for
the Management and Board of Directors in terms of liability, for the ways of
accounting for profits and loss, and for the tax consequences thereof — vary
widely between countries. So, get legal counsel before you make any long-
term decisions.

We shall discuss the generalities of corporate structure below, after repeating
the caveats: get legal counsel and use the organization and accounting that
best fits your long-range plans.

The characteristics used to select the appropriate business vehicle are usually
the liability issues, the tax consequences, the required capitalization and, of
course, the kind of business you intend to conduct. If you look for an appropriate vehicle within which to conduct business in the U.S.A.,[85] for example,
you will likely look at the following:

- Sole Proprietorship

- General Partnership

- Limited Liability Company

- S-Corporation, and

- Corporation

Liability
While the participants in a sole proprietorship or a general partnership typically have unlimited liability,[86] the members or shareholders in a limited liability company, S-corporation or a regular corporation are typically not liable for the debts of the entity – other than losing their equity.

Taxation
Corporate profits are typically taxed twice, once in the corporation and a second time as income to the shareholder, while the other entities pass income and loss through to the participants.

Capitalization
Sole proprietorships, general partnerships, and limited liability companies are typically capitalized through contributions by the proprietor, the partners, or members while S corporations and regular corporations are capitalized through selling of shares, the success of such sales being determined by the perceived quality of the investment and the overall state of the market.

Formalities
General partnerships typically have a partnership agreement, and limited liability companies have an operating agreement. S corporations and regular corporations have articles of organization and incorporation, respectively.

If one does a similar investigation in Denmark,[87] the vehicles for conducting business will include, using the Danish names:

- Enkeltmandsfirma

- Interessentselskab

- Kommanditselskab

- Aktieselskab

- Anpartsselskab

- Selskab med begrænset ansvar

Though the distinctions are similar, there are rules as to the minimum capitalization for different types of companies. The Anpartsselskab requires approximately US$15,000 – DKK 125,000 — as minimum capitalization, while the Aktieselskab requires approximately US$60,000 – DKK 500,000, both at current exchange rates.

The last area to cover in this general overview is the relationship between a public company's officers, board of directors and shareholders. The shareholders own the company and determine its path by electing the board of directors and by voting on the resolutions brought before them by the board and the management at the annual shareholders' meeting. The relative powers of shareholders, the board, and the officers of the company vary from company to company and, even more, from country to country, but this is the theory.

Shareholders will typically not be involved in the day-to-day, or even quarter-to-quarter, running of the company, unless a given shareholder is your VC or happens to have such a large stake in the company that he/she has a seat on the board. It is the board of directors that will be involved in the running of the company, jointly with the management, between shareholders meetings. As with management, the board has responsibilities, fiscal and legal, towards the shareholders and can be prosecuted if it does not discharge these appropriately.[88]

This discussion was meant to be general and to give you an overview. As mentioned above, the rules vary a lot between countries. Don't make any choices until you have talked to counsel!

5.3
Operational Plans

When we covered the development of the Strategic Business Plan in Chapter 3, we spent some time on how to develop Objectives, Strategies, Strategic Activities, and Strategic Goals from the Mission Statement – see section 3.7. We used the strategic breakdown method – SBD – and mentioned that the same method should be used to take planning further, into Operational Activities and Goals.

Planning never stops in an organization. Operational Plans are plans of action that make the strategic business plan implementable by describing what needs to be done (**activities**), when individual actions should be initiated (**time),** and who in the organization will be doing what (**responsibility**). So you could say that an operational plan is an allocation of the strategic activities and goals on people, place and time (who, where, when and how). Just like strategic business plans, operational plans continue to evolve over time.

The responsible manager usually constructs an operational plan for his/her area of the company. It is the manager's job to make the strategic activities and goals operational, binding the strategic business plan to the operational plan by using the information in the strategic plan, by soliciting feedback or updates from the executives who developed and maintain the strategic plan, and by drawing on his/her own knowledge of the state and direction of the market as it relates to his/her area. In many start-ups, the area managers may have been involved in the creation of the strategic plan themselves, making the connection from strategy to operation more direct.

The actual planning is done on both tactical and operational levels. The executives point out the guidelines, *e.g.*, actions, time and responsibilities, after which those responsible make out the detailed plans and convert them into actionable projects. Different companies have different planning horizons, and different areas within a company may have different planning periods. A typical plan will have monthly plans for some quarters, followed by quarterly and then yearly plans, for example, monthly for next quarter, followed by three quarterly plans, followed by two yearly ones.

Tactical Planning is thus based on far more short-term activities and goals, compared to strategically defined activities and goals, and is therefore of a more concrete and detailed nature than strategic planning. Tactical planning occurs within the framework of the strategic business plan and stays within the latter's boundaries. It deals with areas such as the following:

- Marketing

- Sales

- Finance

- Operations, *e.g.*, Production and Customer Service

- R&D (Research and Development).

Operational Planning is still more detailed and short-term. It stays within the guidelines of the tactical plans and is directly connected to what work is actually carried out, the projects. Operational planning deals with plans within areas such as the following:

- Marketing campaigns

- Sales visits and management of major accounts

- Management of receivables and debts/debtors

- Material purchases

- Training classes

- Production scheduling

Execution of operational plans falls outside the scope of the book, but we cannot resist one comment: unless the responsible person(s) turns the plan into actionable projects with plans and budgets, you are asking for trouble down the line when the time comes to answer questions such as "where are we with such and such" and "is such and such effort successful." There is a lot of space for feeling, instinct, and gut reaction in business but, when it comes to executing a plan, a PERT chart is better!

Let us take a look at an example of one operational plan – an operational marketing plan. We have chosen to focus on the marketing area since it is an area you would typically want to emphasize early in the post-funding stage.

The Operational Marketing Plan

The marketing plan is the operational tool that describes the company's marketing activities, laying out both activities and goals for a given period.

The purpose of the marketing plan is to define how many and which resources to apply to individual marketing activities and when to execute. It is thus a detail- and action-oriented plan — supplementing the general marketing objectives and the marketing strategy — in which all actual activities are described. The marketing plan usually ranges only one year into the future, with the degree of detail less in the later quarters.

The marketing plan has many purposes, including the following:

- It is used as an operational tool for implementing the company's strategy, thus achieving the set marketing objectives.

- It is used for structuring the implementation process.

- It is used to monitor the implementation of the company's marketing strategy.

- It defines who will be participating in the plan and the responsibilities and tasks.

- It defines and specifies how to allocate resources, thus assuring their more structured and efficient use.

- It gives a better overview of marketing problems as well as opportunities and threats.

- It structures the timing of the marketing activities.

The company should, of course, have a separate marketing plan for each individual strategy, *e.g.*, for each strategic business unit (SBU), individual product or brand, product line and specific market.

Though there is no absolute template for the contents of a marketing plan, it usually contains the company's marketing objectives and sales targets, product and market background, marketing opportunity analyses, marketing strategies, sales forecasts and expected results, marketing activities, action plans, performance measurements, resources, financials and risks and challenges.

The figure shows a possible Table of Contents for an operational marketing plan.

0. EXECUTIVE SUMMARY	a. Summary of the marketing plan
1. MARKETING OBJECTIVES AND SALES TARGETS	a. Overall marketing objectives b. Overall sales targets
2. PRODUCT AND MARKET BACKGROUND	a. Description of product range b. Market overview
3. MARKETING OPPORTUNITY ANALYSIS	a. The marketing environment b. The competition c. Markets and buyer behavior/needs d. Strengths, weaknesses, opportunities and threats
4. MARKETING STRATEGIES (TARGET MARKET)	a. Segmentation b. Targeting c. Positioning
5. MARKETING GOALS	a. Specification of marketing goals
6. SALES FORECAST AND EXPECTED RESULTS	a. Sales forecast b. Expected results

7. MARKETING PROGRAMS FOR IMPLEMENTATION	a. Marketing mix.
	    I. Product/Brand
	    II. Channels
	    III. Pricing
	    IV. Customer communication and interaction
	b. Tasks and responsibilities

8. ACTION PLAN	a. Detailed action plan for marketing activities
9. MEASURING PERFORMANCE	a. Marketing evaluation methods b. Marketing metrics
10. RESOURCES	a. Necessary marketing resources
11. FINANCIALS	a. Marketing costs. b. Return on investment for implementing the marketing plan
12. RISKS AND CHALLENGES	a. Risks concerning the marketing plan b. Challenges of the marketing plan
13. CONCLUSION	a. Conclusion of the marketing plan

Figure 5.1   Sample TOC for an Operational Marketing Plan

Market analyses from the applicable marketing research – possibly from the Strategic Plan or other ongoing efforts — are usually included as an appendix in order to validate and document the marketing plan. All other relevant material used in connection with the development of the plan should be included as well.

5.4
Customers

As we stated in the introduction, the e-Revolution brought some fundamental changes to business — changes in connectivity, access, and reach. These changes imply a new view of what business must do when selling, when just informing, and when managing the relationship with customers.

The two most important factors for securing the success of a company are the effectiveness of the sales and of the customer relationship efforts. The nature and quantity of relationships have a direct impact on the long-term value of the sales effort, whereas selling has a more direct short-term effect on turn-over. Sales and customer relationships have to go hand in hand from the start; both are a prerequisite for economic success.

So far, nothing new. What is new is that the Web and its accompanying technologies can be leveraged for a better bottom line. The entrepreneur in the new economy – you — should be able to leverage the new Web technologies better and more effectively for generating sales and good customer relationships. The tools with which to do this are effective selling through all channels, including the Web, and building profitable relationships with customers using all channels, again including the Web. This amounts, if you will, to building a quantitative economic relationship with a customer – sales — and a qualitative non-economical relationship – Customer Relationship Management, CRM.

Web turnover

The main objective behind business use of the Internet is to sell more — whether products or services. Current studies in Northern Europe and, in particular, one in Denmark[89] of 1,215 companies indicate that about 65% of all companies have chosen "selling products" as their main e-Business objective, and 50% of the existing companies have Websites with the capacity to sell/buy products. Selling products and services through a site on the Internet is a core component of new economy business.

But there is a big difference in how successful these efforts are, how big a share of company turnover comes from selling products on-line. The latest study in Denmark documents – see figure 5.2 — that over 30% of companies selling products on-line do not have any turnover at all. They have built Websites to sell products in vain and seem to be doing something really wrong. Furthermore, an additional 45% have a turnover of between 1-5%, an insignificant amount. At the other end of the scale, there are a few companies that earn more than 50% of their turnover through Websites and about 5% that have a virtual turnover share of more than 20%. This documents a significant polarization between a small group of companies that are successfully selling on-line and a much larger group of companies that have insignificant or marginal sales through the Internet.

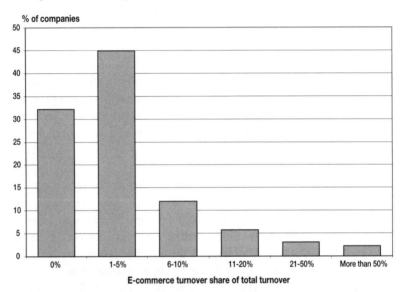

Figure 5.2   **Website sales distributions, Denmark, 2001[90]**

Web Commerce

When analyzing the Web presence of companies, one can identify some different types:

1. Information commerce. The first group of companies does not actually sell anything through their Websites, nor do they desire to. They provide potential buyers with information about products and how to buy them, typically by providing telephone numbers to company sales departments where potential buyers can talk to sales people in order to buy, through providing catalogs with order forms, or simply through providing e-mail or snail-mail addresses where potential buyers can contact the companies. There might be brand merchandise shops on such sites, but that is not the principal reason for their existence.

Typical examples of this are pharmaceutical companies like Nycomed – www.nycomed.com, Novo Nordisk – www.novonordisk.com, - and B2C

Websites for, *e.g.*, larger fast-moving consumer goods producers like Mars – www.mars.com, Coca-Cola – www.cocacola.com, and Unilever – www.unilever.com.

Results: this kind of Web site is basically an advertising/brand building strategy where the results are measured in increased knowledge/awareness, image/preference or buying intentions. A company with such a site would not have a measure of sales from the site — there will be none or very little — but they might – should – have measurements of brand awareness building.

2. Reservation commerce. The second group of companies using the Web to sell products is companies that make it possible for potential buyers to reserve a product or service. Typical companies in this group are hotels, airline/travel agents, and other T & E sites that receive reservations and then follow up with a phone call, e-mail or mail — or may only save the reservation records. Certain of these sites require non-refundable payments via the site for certain product categories; in such cases this model is closer to the STP commerce model below.

Examples: any hotel or ticket chain, for example, Hilton – www.hilton.com, or www.billetnet.dk.

Results: turnover is not directly measurable from the Website, but the percentage of reservations made through the Web vs. the total number of reservations and the conversion rate from reservations to actual purchases will be available.

3. Order commerce. The third group of companies makes it possible for potential buyers to order products or services, but the payment method is off-line: either a traditional snail-mailed invoice forwarded with the bank account number, a request for a check payment, a Giro/postal payment or some other type of secondary payment method. The types of companies in this category are many; they include many smaller retail outlets and manufacturing/production based companies.

Example: retail transactions at Kort og Matrikel Styrelsen – the Danish Mapping Agency – www.kms.dk.

Results: turnover can be measured based on Web activity.

4. Payment commerce. The fourth group is companies that clear payments on-line through direct on-line money transfers but do not process orders automatically nor deliver products on-line. These companies have traditional back end/logistics systems, and fulfillment of orders takes place manually. That means that, when an order and confirmation of payment are received, the order process starts with a manual action. The payment typically happens through the use of credit or debit cards such as Dankort, Visa or Master Card.

Examples: typical payment companies are the larger retailers and some shopping portals.

Results are directly measurable in cash-flow.

5. STP commerce. Straight Through Order Processing (STP) within a given company is commerce/procurement where a manually-given order is automatically cleared and processed by a system, but the actual product or service delivery is physical, using trucks, the mail, *etc*. The STP commerce systems are typically newer ERP (Enterprise Resource Planning), *e.g.*, SAP, or supply chain management systems integrated seamlessly with Website trading or shopping units. The procurement process takes place automatically with minimal human involvement, and the order will automatically issue an invoice or clear with a Web payment.

Examples: STP commerce companies are typically larger industrial companies trading with professional partners (B2B), larger and more professional retail outlets, *e.g.*, www.amazon.com, and advanced TV stations selling airtime, *e.g.*, TV2 in Denmark.

Results are directly measurable in cash flow, and the value/savings of process automation through non-human involvement is large.

6. Automated STP commerce. When a company deals automatically with a business partner or customer, the technological system at the customer's end automatically generates and transfers an order that is then received and handled automatically by the seller/vendor. Typical inter-company automated STP commerce systems are "just-in-time" inventory systems.

Results are directly measurable both for the company and its partner. Major effects of inter-company automated STP commerce are decreases of investment in goods in stock and savings from more effective logistics planning.

7. Full circle commerce. Full circle commerce is done by companies that receive an order, process it, and deliver the product or service on-line. These are typically companies selling services like larger Internet banks or companies selling electronic products which can be distributed via the Internet like videos, software, electronic books, films, pictures, drawings, and advertising.

Examples: video-on-near-demand from Viasat – www.viasat.dk — or Canal+ — www.canalplus.dk — and payment-based information archives like the *Financial Times* archive.

Results: turnover is directly measurable.

These different types of commerce on the Web not only represent solutions of different sophistication and cost, but also solutions that satisfy different needs of companies. If your business model does not include major sales on the Web, either because your product is not suited for Web sales — such as pre-scription drugs or six packs of Coca-Cola — or because you, for whatever reason, do not intend to do major business on the Web, a Web presence without major commerce capabilities will fit.

If, on the other hand, you are a new economy player and believe the Web to be close to the center of your selling strategy, you will want to be at least at the payment level, if not STP or full circle.

Success is not just getting the highest turnover through a Web site. Success is measured on the basis of total value contribution or economic value (ROI, EVA, turnover – cost) and not just on virtual turnover. The costs of establish-ing, implementing and updating such a system, as well as training employees to be able to handle it, might outweigh the turnover and revenues. Also, the number of customers who are able and willing to participate in STP or full circle commerce might be so restricted – *e.g.*, 0-50% of customers — that this in itself might cripple the potential value and make it necessary to operate a full scale off-line selling system to secure turnover.

However, 95% of the companies in the study mentioned above do not know the value or ROI of their e-Commerce or Website investments. This indicates that most of them have major problems in evaluating whether or not their strategy is a success or failure. If companies do not know the ROI of their Web efforts, they have a serious management problem.

Selection of a Web presence must take place after due analysis of the business and must be monitored over time.

Virtual Buying System Analysis

The starting point of Web commerce optimization is to understand how customers buy products and how a given company handles the buying process. A new methodology, "The Virtual Buying System Analysis," is a model for documenting this. Its goals are to understand how customers act and how a company works on converting window shoppers into customers.

The benefit of understanding virtual buying behavior and its effect on a company's Web presence comes in identifying how a company should improve the way it conducts business on the Web, thus impacting customer behavior in order to improve value generation.

This analysis of the buying system is a quantitative measure of how good a company is at converting its potential customer base to revenue/ROI, combined with a normative analysis of the conversion barriers — what customers think and feel and the reasons why they drop off during the buying process. We use a 12-step model, where the remaining customer population at each step is measured as a fraction of the previous step, called the conversion ratio:

1. **Customer population:** the total number of target group customers

2. **Awareness:** how many customers actually know – or expect — it is possible to buy the products on-line

3. **Preference:** how many customers would like, consider and prefer to buy the products on-line

4. **Buying intention:** customers with the actual buying intention/willingness to buy the products from the company Website in the near future/next time

5. **www knowledge:** customers finding or knowing the relevant Website address (URL)

6. **Front-page:** customers who get to the front/home page of the Website

7. **Content:** customers who find the relevant product/service they are looking for on the site

8. **Buying decision:** customers who decide to buy a specific product/service (typically by adding the product to the "shopping basket")

9. Ordering: customers who fill out the order form and input the requested information

10. Paying: customers who pay on-line for the product/services

11. Turnover: the amount of money received from customers

12. Revenue/ROI: the marginal contribution (for companies having other off-line selling systems) or the ROI (typically for pure plays or separate profit centers) of the Web commerce system.

The first four steps relate to the marketing communication efforts, whereas the steps from Buying intention to Revenue are directly related to the specific Website and company behind it. The phases from Buying intention to Revenue (steps 4-12) look like this for a real company that wishes to remain anonymous:

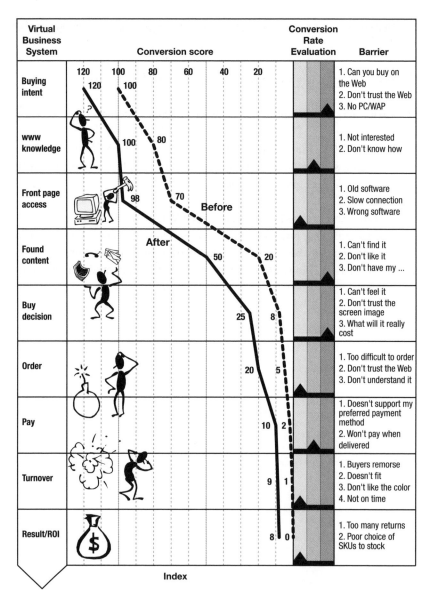

Figure 5.3 The Virtual Buying System[91]

The example shows that in the "Before" case, out of one hundred customers with buying intent two – yes, two – actually buy, with one actually creating revenue for the company (one returns the merchandise). After a minor optimization through improvements to the site, the company increased the number of customers with buying intention to 120, increased the front-page access to 98, and the ability of the users to find the relevant products to 50. The overall results were an increase of customers, contributing to the turnover by 800% (from 1 to 9), and a healthy ROI.

As part of the virtual buying system analysis, interviews with customers and analyses thereof tell us why they drop off at the different stages of the buying process. These reasons reveal more precisely what is at the core of the problems. It might be that a potential customer for a cotton shirt finds the right product on the site but, because he/she cannot easily see if the product is available in the right color and size, he/she drops off and exits the site.

The analysis methodology is actually a group of different analyses which use customer data, surveys, and Computer Aided Telephone Interviews (CATI) to document the first five steps, both in terms of quantity and in terms of drivers and barriers (reasons why or why not). We use access- based up-time robots and browser tests to measure front-page access (step 6). For the on-site analysis, we use log file analysis and exit surveys to document the customers' use of the Website (steps 6-10), and for larger sites we do in-lab customer behavior-based usability studies. And, finally, for the turnover and ROI (steps 11-12), we do a financial analysis on the basis of accounting system data.

Identifying barriers
The four key steps which are in focus when making the first rough assessment of a company's Internet selling are the conversion rates from Customer population to Buying intention (steps 1-4), from Buying intention to Turnover (steps 4-11), and from Turnover to Revenue (steps 11-12).

In the Virtual Buying System example above, out of the total customer group of 1,000, the company has only 100 customers who intend to buy from the company's Website. Then the number of customers drops off progressively until, at the end, the company only gets turnover from one customer, and the turnover from that customer alone gives the company a negative ROI for the period in question. It is also possible to estimate and measure the monetary value of the virtual buying intentions, so both volume of customers and monetary value can be tracked throughout the virtual buying process, not just from Ordering (step 9).

It is evident that the company in the example above — a large and well-known international company — has two major issues facing its use of the Web. First of all, only 10% of all target customers intend to buy their products on-line — the conversion rate from step 1 to step 4 – and, secondly, only 1% of customers with a virtual buying intention actually contribute to the turnover of the company – the conversion rate from step 4 to step 11. These low conversion rates indicate two general, major problems.

The first problem is, in essence, a customer communication issue. Out of the total customer group, only 70% know or expect it is possible to buy the products on-line and, furthermore, a significant number of customers do not prefer to buy the products on-line. The reasons behind this are identified in the analysis: lack of knowledge — because customers have not seen or been told of the on-line buying opportunity – and, more importantly, the difficulty they perceive in finding and buying these particular products on a Website.

The second problem — the low customer buying intention to turnover conversion rate — has different reasons. By far the largest one is that over 50% of the customers visiting the site to buy a product/service do not find the relevant product/service. The key reason is that the product does not show up when its presumed name is input in the search function on the first page, making it seem as though the company does not offer the desired product for sale.

There might be a third major problem, but the analysis does not contain enough data to substantiate it. Of the two customers actually paying for the products, only one counts as turnover. The fact that the other customer asks for his/her money back seems to indicate a problem with transportation or damaged goods.

Getting to "After"
When the problems have been clearly identified, it is a simple process to start designing action plans to correct the problems, such as a communication campaign to raise awareness of the possibility of buying the product on-line and a campaign to show people how easy and effortless it really is, as well as a change in the portfolio of products up for sale at the site.

But before actions are taken, you need to estimate what it will cost to fix the individual problems and how much marginal improvement in the conversion rate will result from each such fix. It is possible to calculate the monetary value of each improvement based on the virtual buying system measurement of conversion rates. It then becomes possible to do a cost/benefit analysis and calculate a ROI for each improvement initiative. The result should be a prioritized list of which initiatives to implement first.

Since improvements in the buying system conversion rates have a direct relationship with one another, a multiplier effect should appear when two or more improvements are implemented together. This means that triple-digit improvements are realistic for many sites. A large international clothes retailer has just gone through an e-Commerce optimization process; the company's new e-Commerce site, launched in August 2001, improved their turnover by 600% as of January 2002.

Commerce optimization

Most new economy entrepreneurs intend to conduct commerce on the Web, so their challenge is how to improve or optimize value for their companies. We propose the following framework for helping Web sites improve value creation, going through these steps:

Ask: does Web commerce fit with the business strategy and business objectives? Start by determining if Web commerce has a key strategic value for the company or not. If not, then optimization efforts might be bad investments in terms of ROI.

Do a Virtual Buying System analysis. A company that has identified on-line selling as an important strategic sales tool and wants to optimize its Website for maximum value should do an analysis of its virtual buying systems and find all the relevant "hard data" on how well/badly it is performing. It should measure the volume and value of conversions from the target customers' buying intentions to the economic value (turnover and/or ROI) and identify the key virtual buying drivers and key drop-off barriers.

Prioritize improvement initiatives. The next step is to consider what problems are most important to fix, based on their potentials for the highest ROI in the shortest time with the lowest risk. List the opportunities for improvement in a prioritized list with the most important at the top, and estimate the potential revenue and cost for each improvement. For some companies it will be necessary to improve the system by changing it to another, more advanced type of system. For such investments, calculations of strategic value and net present value (NPV) must be included.

Implement improvements. Implement the improvements in order, as common sense and funding permit.

Establish a Result Management system. Last but not least, the results of the improvements must be measured. Set up a system to monitor the value-added results based on the earlier Virtual Buying System Analysis in order to gauge the ongoing improvement process.

Calculating the value of a customer

What is one customer worth to a company? This is a crucial question, allowing a company to project revenues and profits based on the number of customers. As with most questions in corporate accounting, however, there is more than one answer, and most answers begin with "that depends."

The answer we are interested in here is the one that will allow you, the business owner, to calculate how much revenue and profit you will get out of one new customer and how much revenue and profit you should be able to forecast from your current customer base. So what we are interested in is the lifetime value of one customer.

Note that this is different from the value of a customer that is sometimes used in discussions about communications companies such as cable TV companies, ISPs, and mobile phone companies. That value is calculated by taking the current market value of the company and dividing by the total number of customers. The result is certainly related to lifetime customer value but includes the expected value of all marketing efforts in the company, *etc.* as well, and is not very useful for management purposes, other than possibly for M&A activity.

To calculate what a new customer will be worth to you let us first define the following parameters:[92]

- The amount a customer buys per year. For simplicity we shall assume it is the same every year. Let's call it A_p.

- The gross profit margin of the company – M.

- The probability that a customer is retained – *i.e.*, buys more product, renews the subscription, *etc.* — the next year. Again, for simplicity, we shall assume it is the same year after year. Let's call it P_r.

- The discount rate – cost of money and inflation rate – which allows us to calculate present value. Let us call it C_m.

Assuming the customer is a customer forever, the closed form solution for the present value of the Customer Contribution is:

$$\text{Customer Contribution} = A_p * M*(1 + C_m)/(1 + C_m - P_r)\text{[93]}$$

So, if a customer buys $1 worth of products each year, the gross margin is 50%, the cost of money is 10%, and 90% of customers are retained from year to year, the contribution of this customer is

$$\text{Customer Contribution} = 1*50\%*(1 + 10\%)/(1 + 10\% - 90\%)$$

or

$$\$2.75$$

This means, simplistically, that if you spent $2.75 to get this customer, you would be cash neutral under these assumptions.

What is wrong with this picture? Nothing, if it is used to create relative values for planning, but if one were trying to use it for financial purposes, there would be – even accepting using the same values per year – two major issues:

- A customer relationship is unlikely to be forever, and

- A customer will bring other customers with him/her.

One has to be careful not to double-count customers when one counts referrals, but there is a strong argument that states that if a customer is referred, the company has been spared the cost of getting the customer – the cost of the marketing campaign, cold call or whatever – and that that increases the value of the referring customer by at least the average acquisition cost of customers.

Another formula for Costumer Contribution, using the same variables as above with the addition of referrals, then becomes:

$$\text{Customer Contribution} = (A_p*M+R_c*C_a)*(1 + C_m)/(1 + C_m - P_r)$$

where

- R_c is the number of referrals per year from this customer, and

- C_a is the acquisition cost of one customer.

So, with the same values as above, if each customer on average refers one customer per year and the acquisition cost of a customer – the hard way – is $1.50,[94] the lifetime Customer Contribution becomes:

Customer Contribution = (1*50% + 1*1.5)*(1 + 10%)/(1 + 10% - 90%)

or

$$\$11.00$$

You can see a substantial difference, well worth taking into account, if market studies bear out the assumption. The following table shows the accumulated contribution with the same values as above for the first few years.

Year	Without Referral	With Referral
1	$0.50	$2.00
2	$0.91	$3.64
3	$1.24	$4.98
4	$1.52	$6.07
5	$1.74	$6.97
6	$1.93	$7.70

You should create your own model based on the industry in which you operate and other assumptions that you have created through your own market research. The above calculations are only meant to get you started. Expect to create appropriate spreadsheets that will help you in this effort and watch out for signs of numerology, *i.e.*, make sure the numbers make sense.

The Customer Contribution is a calculation of the economic benefits of relationships — the longer the customer stays, the more money you make. One should always look at the aggregated economic opportunity and remember that selling to a new customer is much more expensive than selling to an existing customer. Current – and former – customers are great targets. When you get new customers, work on maximizing the value of the relationships by either retaining the customers longer, getting them to be ambassadors for your business, and/or growing the contribution margin from the customers (higher sales, higher number of referrals, or lower costs).

Customer relations are key. Whichever way you compete, be it on brand, on service, or on lowest cost, building and maintaining good relationships are essential.

The customer relationship re-defined

In order to understand how good, profitable relations are built, it is important to understand what a relationship is and how the Web can support it. Though all of us apparently try to create good relationships, few of us reflect on what that actually means. Relationships, whether in business or in our private lives, benefit from insight and work.

Box 1. Lunatronic   www.t-doc.dk

Getinge Lunatronic is an example of a relationship-building company that uses a customer service-oriented CRM system, a Siebel system implemented by Aston Group, to increase the customer service level.

Getinge Lunatronic is a leading niche company, part of the Getinge Group, which is a leading global provider of equipment and systems to customers within health care, extended care and pharmaceutical industries/laboratories.

The only product of Getinge Lunatronic is the T-DOC system. T-DOC is a computerized system for documentation and traceability of the sterilization processes within hospitals in Europe, the U.S. and Australia. With the T-DOC system hospitals can document the full process of, for example, a reusable instrument, answering how it was washed, sterilized, by whom it was handled, and on what patient it was used. Getinge markets T-DOC through 80 subsidiaries and 100 distributors throughout the world.

Good references are a key to selling T-DOC, which means that the ongoing relationship is crucial. The relationship is built through focus on services: the installation, ongoing focus on the changing needs of the customer, customization of the product, orchestration of annual user-group meetings, *etc*.

One of the key aspects of supporting customers is a unique worldwide remote support system, which is run and administered by the Siebel system. Getinge Lunatronic can take over a customer's screen on-line, enabling them to solve 95% of all problems in less than 15 minutes.

The Siebel system has been implemented more or less out of the box, minimizing the cost of IT consulting and correction services.

Customer Relationship Management has, unfortunately, meant "customer information management" more often than strategic help in building interpersonal and/or corporate relationships.

There are four facets to a customer relationship:

1. Knowledge. A relationship depends on how well we know our customers and they know us, often based on a broad range of information. Knowledge of customers includes information about the nature of the customer's business and needs, priorities, decision processes, buying habits, buying history, use of other suppliers, and so on. The better the knowledge, the better the understanding of the customer and the stronger the foundation on which to help and advise the customer. Since a relationship is a two-way street, knowledge also includes the customer's familiarity with you. Typically important knowledge is information about your business, capabilities, key differentiating points, work methods, and the softer areas like your private lives, children, interests, values, *etc*.

2. Communication and interaction. Secondly, a relationship is defined by the quality and quantity of the interactions and communications that take place. These include the amounts/frequency of time spent together with the customer — in meetings, dinners, on the phone, via e-Mails, *etc*. The higher the frequency of communication and interaction, the better the relationship is likely to be.

3. Acknowledged mutual benefit and need – Instrumentality. The third facet is the acknowledged benefits and needs of the two parties, that is, the level of dependency or relative value of the relationship for the two parties. The higher the perceived benefit, the higher the dependency on the supplier/product. Usually the customer has the upper hand in a relationship but, the more the customer is dependent on the product – for the price, quality, delivery time, advice and help, *etc*. — the more balanced the relationship will be. For consumer goods, the relationship is between the customer and the product/brand, with service seldom a relevant factor. The instrumentality is thus with the consumption and use of the product and the symbolic values of the brand. For industrial products like ships or ERP systems, where service and advice are pivotal, the instrumentality is more in the direct and personal relationship with the people delivering the ship or ERP system. That is why it is harder in general for a customer to change consultant or adviser than to change between soft drink or pasta brands. In the network society, an effective tool to enhance relationships is to increase the benefit and need through partnerships, alliances, *etc*. where the two parties have a stake in each other, joint ownership, joint development or test teams, joint business development projects, *etc*.

4. Flow. The fourth facet is the psychological bond, chemistry, kindred spirits or "flow" between the parties. The better the flow, the tighter the mental bond with the customer. Flow is represented in relationships where 1+1 seem to become 5 when people interact.

It is obvious that the Internet and digital system's role for customer relationships mainly has to do with knowledge, communication and interaction. The Internet can play a significant role in securing a high level of customer knowledge and an intelligent use of information by the relevant people in the organization. Analyzing captured data – data mining — can often bring about new, relevant knowledge. For Internet-enabled entrepreneurs, it is essential that all the information about both potential and existing customers is documented, structured and available to the company sales team and to the people who service the customers. Modern CRM systems implement this.

Secondly, the Web can be used as a communication and interaction vehicle (e-mail, SMS, and Website communication). What is perhaps more interesting is that some companies have found out that if a supply chain system, *e.g.*, an ordering and storage system, is integrated with the customers, then the instrumentality of the supplier is increased. This is the case, for example, for suppliers who operate vendor-based inventory systems. Borealis, which sells plastic raw materials, operates the inventory/storage system for some of their most important customers. The advantage for their customers is that the vendor guarantees the supply on the customers' premises and can cut the investment in raw material inventory. For Borealis, the advantage is that once this system is installed, it will be a pain for a customer to change supplier, thus increasing the instrumentality of Borealis *vis-à-vis* the company's key customers. Virtually the same thing occurs with EDI systems, which have given some companies a temporary competitive advantage through the instrumentality level of the systems used. The message is clear: the more integrated a company's system is with its customers, the better the relationship.

The Web can increase knowledge, and communication and interaction, and also raise the instrumentality of a vendor. But how does one create flow on the Web? Not very clear, but it certainly has to do with fitting the gestalt of the Website to the target group, something like the apparent intent of the B&O Website, www.bang-olufsen.com.

Box 2. Modulex www.modulex.com

Modulex is an example of a international B2B company using one central
CRM system to save time for the dealers/sales representatives and to
improve customer service levels. The system is Siebel-supplied and implemented by the Aston Group.

Modulex's main business area is architectural sign systems. Based upon 40
years of experience Modulex's key competencies today are information
management and brand communication. Founded in 1963 by LEGO, the
company has supplied sign-based information and communication solutions for many types of organizations and places — hospitals, courts,
schools, institutions, and public administration buildings. Typical customers are organizations like Dell, Zürich Financial Services, Virgin, Daimler
Chrysler, and the Danish Departments of the Environment, Transport and
the Regions.

For a smaller international company with a de-centralized sales organization and dealerships, one of the main advantages lies in having a single
system in which all dealers and sales representatives can find all the relevant customer information they need. Secondly, the company can manage
the customers and sales process more effectively, leading to saved resources
and better customer service. An example of better customer service is
faster delivery of a wanted system through the use of a Web-enabled
configuration module. The sales representative designs, presents, and
alters the relevant signage directly with the individual customer. Because
the module is linked through the CRM system to the production system,
the data and production specifications are directly transferred to the latter
system. It is also possible to service a customer faster and better when the
customer wants supplementary signs. The last advantage for Modulex is
scalability — the ability to upgrade and enhance the system to include
marketing management, customer satisfaction analysis and management,
communication campaigns, and integration to other systems, *e.g.*, an ERP
system.

...And Next

This is it. We have taken you from the vague notion of an idea for a business to the point where you have a company to run, with operational plans to write and a board of directors – and possibly VCs – to keep happy. We wish you luck and hope you will remember to enjoy it while you can; these may very well be the "good old days." We would like to leave you with one last thought, however. The best business strategy is simple: "give your customer what you said you would, at the time you promised, and at the price you quoted."

Appendix: Facilitation Support for Business Development

This section contains the text of a set of slides that we have used as support in facilitated sessions to develop a business idea from just an idea to the point where the raw material for the Strategic Business Plan is available or well-identified. The sessions — facilitated sessions are brainstorming sessions with a leader who ensures that the group stays within appropriate distance of "the box" and that all the issues get covered — take up to a week of meetings, all rather intense.

The slides are reproduced here to give you a framework within which to develop a large part of the information that you will need in order to start your business. This framework is purposely presented in a different form than in Chapter 3. Read that first and then work through this to start off with two different perspectives. You need not go through all of this, but you should be able to relate actively to all the questions/statements below after the sessions. Most topics — not all — should apply regardless of whether your company is Web-oriented or not.

Here are a few ideas and suggestions if you decide to go through this process:[95]

- Get a facilitator to help you. The role of the facilitator is to guide the discussion, not in a controlling sense — the idea is, after all, to be open and "think outside the box" — but in the sense of guiding the discussion back when it gets totally off track.

- The facilitator can either be an outside consultant or someone you know, but it is important that the person not be one of the principals in the business, since he/she is supposed to guide, not lead, i.e., should make sure the participants talk, but not filter what they say or argue.

- Choose a room with a lot of whiteboards or blackboards or get as many easels with easel pads as you can and position them around the room. Also get some tape that you can use to tape the sheets from the easel pads to the walls — be careful to check that the tape comes off without marring the walls! One end result of a day's session will be lots of ideas on sheets — or filled boards — which will be transcribed into notes.

- Get a scribe to copy down the above notes during the sessions. This can be the facilitator if necessary, but it is better to have a separate person do the job. The scribe must be able to analyze and organize on the fly. A good administrative assistant can do it with a little training.

- Get a commitment from all the principals in the business to participate and **do not hold sessions unless everybody is there.** Murphy's law dictates that you will cover the missing person's area when he/she is not there.

- Schedule the sessions as close together as you can to get everything covered while it is fresh. No cell phones, no interruptions other than appropriate breaks, and let everybody talk. If you have some people who talk more than others, let the facilitator know so he/she can work with or around this.

- Argument and emotion are good, as long as they stay focused on the business. A session is not successful unless you have worked through at least two "I totally disagree's."

- Good luck and have fun.

Business Plan Recap

Business Fundamentals

- Who are you, or, who do you want to be?

- What is the unique product or service that your company provides or will provide?

- What is the market?

- What is the size of the market?

- What strategic milestones have you set for your company?

The Market

- Who are your customers?

- Identify and describe each customer segment

- Does demographic information exist?

- Size the customer segments

- Identify price elasticity for each customer segment

- Transaction level, monthly, household, lifetime profitability

Who Are Your Customers?

- Some customer types:

    - "Normal" customers

    - Others:

        - Buyers of demographic data, both personal, clicking, and buying history

        - Buyers of advertising space

        - Buyers of other placement services

        - Buyers of contents that you have created

User Scenarios: How Are They Going to Buy?

- Create browsing/purchasing scenarios for each segment of customers

- Describe the browsing/purchasing experience

- Identify the value proposition for each customer segment

- New customer acquisition vs. revenue expansion within current customer base (cross-selling, upselling)

- Who are your competitors? How do you hold on to your customers?

How Well Do You Know Your Customers?

- Who are they really, and who says?

- How do they shop?

- How much do they shop?

- What will make them buy?

- What will make them stay, and

- What will make them come back?

Customer Retention Opportunities
Community

- Is there a community opportunity? What is it?

    - User chat and "ask an expert"

    - Discussion boards/Messaging

    - Interaction with customers

    - Membership clubs

- What can you gain from it?

Personalization

- Identify the personalization opportunities

    - Rules-based filtering, *e.g.*, user profile

    - Collaborative filtering, *e.g.*, group behavior

    - Learning agent technology, *e.g.*, click stream analysis

- CRM opportunities

Ways of Selling: What Fits?
- Straight sale

- Escrow sale

- RFP/RFQ

- Auction

- Reverse auction

- Limited marketplace

- Vertical marketplaces

- Portals

- Other

Ways of Showing and Pricing
- Don't expect to show the same thing to two buyers; you must have a *dynamic* catalog for reasons of:

    - Personalization, or

    - Commercial agreements

- Nobody pays retail; you will have many prices, aka "discrete pricing"

Financial Issues

- How will you make money?

- What is the size of the opportunity?

- Present the revenue and cost model

The Business Context

The Competitive Landscape

- SWOT Analysis — strengths, weaknesses, opportunities and threats

- Who are your competitors?

- What are their competitive advantages?

- What are your competitive advantages?

- Identify companies with comparable business models in other business areas

- Why are they successful?

You, Your Brand, and Yourself

- Who are you?

- Who do you want your customers to think you are?

- How do you intend to maintain that identity?

- "Creative usability" vs. branding

Identify Co-branding Opportunities

- Is co-branding a relevant strategy for this space?

- If so, is it a temporary or a permanent strategy?

- Are there any companies in this, or an adjacent, space with which it would be beneficial to co-brand?

Shared Spaces

- Are there companies in this, or adjacent spaces, that you can partner with?

- Is partnering a temporary or a permanent strategy?

Levels of Cooperation on the Web
- Click-through

- Distributed surround

- New frame or window

- Aggregated content

The Value Chain

Demand Side
- What are you selling – hard goods or electrons, tangibles or intangibles?

- How are you selling?

- How will you deliver?

- How will you handle customer service?

Selling and Delivery
- What part do you want to do? What gets outsourced?

- Check inventory

- Maintain catalog

- Maintain shopping cart

- Take orders

- Receive payments

- Handle customer service

- Other

Customer Service

There are many channels:

- Telephone

- Kiosk

- On-line self help (FAQ)

- On-line chat

and many touch points:

- During shopping

- During shipping

- After receipt

- As a return

Supply Side
- What parts of the business scenarios do you want to provide?

- Who are your suppliers?

- Are you aggregating from multiple suppliers?

- What are the settlement arrangements?

- Billing/collections

Who Are Your Suppliers?
- What are their capabilities?

  - Merchandise management

  - Providing content for the Web

  - Order processing support

- Payment and settlement

- Logistics support

- Other

- Who will manage the relationship?

To Outsource or Not to Outsource
- If you outsource everything, what is left?

- Make sure you can judge the quality

Follow the Money
- Settlement arrangements

- Cost per transaction

- Billing/Collection

- Returns

- Consolidation

The Development Process
What and When
- Identify major "feature/function" sets

- Identify the desired sequence for implementation

- Create the minimum feature/function set for implementation

- Identify phases

You Want What?
- Determine the business processes

- Document the business processes

- Create a feature/function document

- Make it complete and logically closed

- Require sign-off

You Want It When?
- New economy projects are time-boxed

- The attitude is not: it will take this long to get what you want

- It's: you can get this much by the date you want it

What's the "Minimum Equipment List?"
- You cannot have it all at once, so:

- Implement the "essence," or, enough to make it "fly"

- Keep it simple

- Provide a logically closed set of feature/functions

Identify Website Development Requirements
- Identify transactions

- Identify major classes, and sources, of content

- Identify content management requirements

- Identify major type(s) of sites

- Identify candidate configuration components

Content Management
- What kind of content is envisioned?

- How is it acquired, how often, and in what volume?

- How often will the content change?

- Which events result in modification of the content?

- What processing needs to take place on the acquired content?

- Where will the ongoing content management take place? Will it be done in-house or outsourced?

- What reporting do you envision to help in content management?

Aggregation of Content
- From whom do you expect to acquire the content?

- How will you identify the desired content?

- In what form will the content be acquired?

- What is the expected volume of content acquired?

- How often will you acquire content in this fashion?

- What business agreements must be in place/negotiated for acquiring aggregated content?

- What reporting must you provide to the content owner?

- What processing needs to take place on the content?

- Where will the processing take place, and will it be done in-house or out-sourced?

Candidate Web Configuration Components
- Data base

- Web server

- Application server

- Legacy interfaces

- Remote caching and replication

How Do You Build a Performing Site?
- Watch the page size

- Watch the balance between static and dynamic pages

- Separate functionality

- Scale through replication

- Keep it simple

Review Security Options
- Any special security needs

- Customer readiness

    - Is he/she willing to share credit-card information?

    - Does he/she need reassurance about your site? In what form?

- Corporate readiness

    - Is there a security policy in place?

    - Is it well-implemented? Kept up-to-date?

    - What is the cost of compromised security? Who pays?

    - Is Denial of Service (DoS) an issue?

    - Is there an Intrusion Detection facility in place?

Testing and Deployment Options
- Will the site support automated testing?

- If not, what are the manual testing requirements?

- How will the site be deployed?

- How will site performance be measured?

- Remember the need for regression testing

How Will the Site Be Deployed?
- Who will host?

- Where will the hosting take place?

- Who measures performance?

- Who gets called at 2 a.m.?

How Will Site Performance Be Measured?
- Local performance/functionality

- Local performance/volume

- Remote performance

    - Time to home page

    - Time to log on

    - Time to conduct transaction

Organizational Capability and Readiness Issues

Review Corporate Capabilities and Readiness
- Corporate experience with the new economy

- What are corporate expectations?

- Do you have "executive support?"

- Can you turn on a dime?

Review Technical Capabilities and Readiness
- Identify technical resources available within the company

- Are all candidate technologies covered?

- How do you plan to alleviate the shortcomings?

Covering All Bases
- Are you ready for automation?

- Do you have a CTO?

- If not, who will fill the role?

Review Infrastructure Capabilities and Readiness
- What is your current level of automation?

- Are your people comfortable with the level of involvement required?

- What are the projected infrastructure requirements for the site?

- How will you alleviate shortcomings?

Who Will It Take to Run a Site?
- Creative resources?

    - Content editor

    - Producer

- Technical resources?

    - Database administrator

    - Networking specialist

    - SysAdmin specialist

    - Application specialist

Review Staffing Requirements
- Develop staffing requirements for the projected volumes

- Map to existing staff

- Identify timed staff requirements

- Hire ahead of the curve — the staff needs to be there when you need them

Success Factors
Project Success Factors # 1
- Manage expectations early and often

- Manage scope

- Force ownership, retain leadership

Project Success Factors, #2
- Anticipate and be prepared

- Conduct frequent review sessions

- Sign-off on functional and technical docs

- Define roles explicitly

- Coordinate with business owners

Notes

1. *San Francisco Chronicle*: Silverlining.com, January 21, 2002

2. Authors of the seminal manual on writing style, *The Elements of Style*, originally published in 1959. Allyn and Bacon, 2000.

3. There is a Danish saying: "When the wind blows hard, some people build shelters, while some build wind mills."

4. According to Jupiter Media Metrix, 14 companies control sixty percent of all consumer online minutes, and four control over 50%! The figure is from March 2000 and lists America Online as capturing 32%, Microsoft 7.5%, Yahoo 7.2%, and Napster 3.6%. From *Internetnews*, June 5th, 2001.

5. *San Francisco Chronicle*, December 10th, 2001.

6. *Financial Times*, December 5th, 2001.

7. Some of the data collected by Vision, Sweden.

8. Cnnfn.com, November 13th, 2000.

9. *Built to Last: Successful Habits of Visionary Companies*, by James C. Collins and Jerry I. Porras. Harper Business, 1997.

10. Even though HP is going through hard times presently, the company was still voted the most respected company in the IT sector in the *Financial Times* 2001 poll. *Financial Times*, December 17th, 2001.

11. Bove-Nielsen, Jesper and Oersted, Christian, *eBusiness – Digitale Forretningsstrategier*. Børsens Forlag, Copenhagen, 1999.

12. Goldman Sachs stopped forecasting the NASDAQ index in 1998 because the sales and earnings numbers that are usually a part of forecasting market value – stock price – for companies were missing for many of the companies that were part of the index.

13. This is not an accounting textbook. Make sure you consult appropriate accounting expertise when necessary.

14. EBITDA = <u>E</u>arnings <u>b</u>efore <u>i</u>ncome <u>t</u>ax, <u>d</u>epreciation, and <u>a</u>mortization.

15. For further information on product life cycles see, for example: *Marketing Management: Analysis, Planning, Implementation, and Control*, by Philip Kotler. Prentice-Hall, 1999.

16. Gary Hamel is chairman of Strategos, an international consulting company, <u>www.strategos.com</u>.

17. "Strategy and the Internet" by Michael E. Porter. *Harvard Business Review*, March 2001.

18. "Managing the Digital Enterprise" by Michael Rappa (<u>http://digitalenterprise.org/models/models.html#anchor1802433</u>). See the reference for additional sub-classifications.

19. Donald K. Clifford, Jr., and Richard E. Cavanagh. *The Winning Performance: How America's High-Growth Midsize Companies Succeed.* New York, Bantam Books, 1985.

20. For example, "Strategy and the Internet" by Michael E. Porter, *Harvard Business Review*, March 2001.

21. One of the authors participated in a conference a while back where one speaker asked the audience, "How many of you have ordered from Amazon within the last year?" Most hands went up. He then went on to ask, "How many of you are absolutely, positively sure you got the lowest price for what you ordered?" Less than ten percent of the hands went up. That is one strong brand!

22. Source: <u>www.nasdaq.com</u>

23. Source: the 10Q

24. Source: <u>www.nasdaq.com</u>

25. Source: <u>www.i2.com</u>

26. <u>www.i2.com/web505/server_media/media/00916645-0E9B-11D5-9EE6-0008C7FA726A.pdf</u>

27. Adapted from *Value Based Marketing: Marketing Strategies for Corporate Growth and Shareholder Value* by Peter Doyle. John Wiley & Sons, 2000.

28. *Webster's Dictionary*, Web edition

29. From *A Technique for Producing Ideas*, by James Webb Young and William Bernbach. McGraw Hill, 1988.

30. "How Competitive Forces Shape Strategy," by Michael E. Porter. *Harvard Business Review*, March-April 1979.

31. Note that these two are really modifications to two of Porter's forces, modifications which were not thought of in 1979.

32. Young and Bernback, *op.cit.*.

33. Adapted from Kenichi Ohmae, who identifies three ways to create new ideas: remove bottlenecks, create new combinations, and maximize strategic degrees of freedom. *Creating the Climate for Innovation*, by Kenichi Ohmae. McKinsey & Co., 1993.

34. Inspired by *Neue Kombination Philosophy* by Austrian economist Joseph Schumpeter.

35. Kenichi Ohmae, *op. cit.*

36. An example comes to mind: back in 1999/2000 when the hardware and networking companies could not satisfy the demand from the dot.coms, Cisco pre-ordered a large amount of components from their suppliers to secure the sources for their products. This seemed a perfectly reasonable step at the time, but then the dot.coms tanked and Cisco was left with a large amount of unsold invertory which was rapidly becoming obsolete. The step seemed reasonable at the time, but the purist can object that pre-ordering supplies is not consistent with a strategic business plan that is built on rapid obsolescense.

37. Obviously this is an area where different localities will have quite different rules. Appropriate advice should be obtained to ensure that the applicable rules and regulations are being followed.

38. It is common in the dot.com world to have two boards, a formal Board of Directors which may have a high percentage of members with financial and

venture capital experience, and a Board of Advisors consisting of members with deep executive and domain expertise in the relevant business areas. The Board of Advisors has no formal power and acts purely in an advisory capacity.

39. Make sure that title equivalents are shown if you are creating a company in Denmark, say, but making English language presentations for funding; a "Director" in English is not the same as a "Direktør"!

40. The example only deals with one year. A typical market analysis would cover, say, three or five years.

41. "How Competitive Forces Shape Strategy," by Michael E. Porter. *Harvard Business Review*, March-April 1979.

42. Note that these two are really modifications to two of Porter's forces, modifications which were not thought of in 1979.

43. Product, Place, Price, Promotion. Philip Kotler, *Marketing Management.* Prentice Hall, 1999.

44. Peter F. Drucker, *Innovation and Entrepreneurship: Practice and Principles.* Harper Business, 1993.

45. Michael E. Porter, *Competitive Strategy: Techniques for Analyzing Industries and Competitors.* Free Press, 1998. Porter's three strategies are discussed further in the section on Positioning.

46. *Ibid.*

47. See *Crossing the Chasm: Marketing and Selling High-Tech Products to Mainstream Customers*, by Geoffrey A. Moore and Regis McKenna (Harper Business, 1999) for a classic description of these customer segments.

48. There is a dark side to this aspect of Web connectivity. The point here is not to focus on "us versus them," but rather to realize that slight differences in interests and wants create opportunities to fashion a specific offer.

49. For a computer company, calling its most basic manual its "Bible," may not be a wise idea abroad. Calling its salespeople "evangelists" is even worse.

50. Preparing your financial statements in accordance with the appropriate accounting standards creates a common base and is a requirement. Other formats allow much more analysis relevant for investment – and general management – decisions. Expect to do both.

51. It is somewhat unlikely you will pay taxes the first year(s) of operation since you will likely not make a profit. The treatment of taxes is another area where country-specific information is required.

52. The figures are quite artificial, used as examples only.

53. See "How Fast can Your Company Afford to Grow" by Neil C. Churchill and John W. Mullins (*Harvard Business Review*, May 2001) for an example of the use of some of these ratios, in this case to determine cash needs.

54. We are assuming for the sake of the example that all other parameters are constant, and we are not taking taxes into account.

55. In addition to a large number of other requirements, in both cases.

56. Depreciating as opposed to a same year deduction.

57. See http://americanhistory.si.edu/csr/comphist/olsen.html for an oral history interview with Ken Olsen, the founder of DEC, in which he discusses the venture capital funding.

58. Ken Olsen, *op. cit.*

59. Source: www.pwcmoneytree.com, a site created by the accounting firm PriceWaterhouseCoopers.

60. *Ibid.*

61. Source: www.vcapital.com

62. *Ibid.*

63. http://www.vcapital.com/Site+Content/CEO+Letter/Archive/CEO+Letter +040301.htm

64. Nils L. Randrup, *The Art and Science of Persuasive Business Presentations*. Handelshøjskolens Forlag, Copenhagen, 1995.

65. See Lloyd F. Bitzer's "The Rhetorical Situation," in *Philosophy and Rhetoric*, vol. 1, no. 1, 1968, pp. 1-14.

66. Principles in accordance with neuro-linguistic programming.

67. Nils L. Randrup, *op. cit.*

68. See, for example, W.D. Jacobson, *Power and Interpersonal Relations*. Belmont, CA, Wadsworth Publishing, 1972.

69. Adapted from a similar demonstration by Thorbjörn Holmqvist in *Presentationsteknik.* 1989.

70. For a further understanding of rhetoric, argumentation and reasoning see, for example, *An Introduction to Reasoning* by Toulmin, Rieke and Janik. London, Macmillan, 1984.

71. The American equivalent is size 8.5 x 11 inch paper, slightly wider and shorter than A4.

72. Americans need to understand that inflected but nonverbal sounds, such as "uh-huh" or "un-oh," will sound odd to nonnative speakers of English whose languages have no equivalents.

73. If telling jokes in public is truly not your personal style, then do not do so.

74. An appropriately thorough analysis of your information gathering and analysis practices would also be in order after the presentation.

75. The rules vary widely in different countries as to how you can hire, and specifically fire, personnel. Be careful that you are aware of what you can and cannot do.

76. One interesting way to gauge the current status of people management from the perspective of a class of prospective employees is to read the yearly stories in the business press of where the year's crop of MBA students from top schools desire to go.

77. Published in English as *Moments of Truth*. HarperCollins, 1989.

78. "Leading in Times of Trauma" by Dutton *et al. Harvard Business Review*, January 2002.

79. "A New Game Plan for C Players" by Axelrod *et al.* *Harvard Business Review*, January 2002

80. The performance review technique at Enron was colloquially called "rank and yank." *New York Times*, "As Enron Purged Its Ranks, ...," February 4th, 2002.

81. Emphasis added in original article.

82. See, for example, *The Open Book Management Experience*, by John Case (Nicholas Brealey, 1998) for similar ideas.

83. Routine raises are excluded from this discussion.

84. Carlzon, *op. cit.*

85. See, for example, http://www.bizfilings.com

86. Remember the "Names" in the insurance syndicates in Lloyds's of London. That was, and is, unlimited liability.

87. See, for example, http://www.dansel.dk or http://www.eogs.dk/

88. There is an interesting case unravelling in the U.S. currently. The Enron Corporation, a Houston based energy company, went into Chapter 11 – a certain kind of bankruptcy – with many recriminations flying between the outside auditors, the corporate executives, the board, and most everybody else. It is far too early to say what the permanent fallout, if any, will be, but it is highly likely that this case will result in permanent changes to rules and regulations governing corporate behavior in the U.S.

89. Source: AIM Nielsen, Future Lab Business Consulting, *Børsens Nyhedsmagasin*, April 2001 – www.futurelab.dk

90. *Ibid.*

91. Source: Nils Randrup – Aston Group

92. The model we are building here will use some simplifying assumptions, for example, that the amount a customer purchases is the same year after year. Whether this is true will depend on the business. We use the assumptions to allow us to derive a simple closed form solution. The general case is some-

what more involved and will most likely not have a closed form solution. In that case creating a spread sheet for a year by year analysis will work best.

93. The solution to $F(x) = a + xa + x^2a + ...$ is $F(x) = a/(1-x)$ when x is less than 1.

94. One way of looking at this value would be to say that this company expects a customer to start to make a contribution after four years when counting only the actual sales to the customer. The ratio used should be consistent with the standards of the particular market.

95. Books have been written about how to do successful facilitation. Don't take it too seriously; it is meant to be intense, exhausting, and fun. The end result will be worth it.

About the Authors

Nils Randrup, nils.annika@post.tele.dk

Nils Randrup is an External Professor at Copenhagen Business School, where he teaches M.B.A. classes in e-Business, Communication, Marketing and International Business. He is also Director of E-Consulting in the Aston Group.

Nils holds an M.B.A. degree from the J.L. Kellogg School of Management, Northwestern University/Copenhagen Business School, and post-graduate diplomas in International Advertising (IAA) and in International Business Management (INSEAD). He is the author of several working papers, text-books and articles.

Nils built and leads the e-Business Consulting practice at the Aston Group's Management Consulting Business Line – one of Scandinavia's leading management consultancies – and was the founder of J. Walter Thompson Nordic's Interactive E-Business agency. Nils has developed groundbreaking strategies and solutions for e-Business, interactive digital TV, interactive "advertainment," brand building, media planning, and network cooperation/synergies.

Prior to Aston, Nils was Director/Partner of Future Lab Business Consulting (an international-oriented strategic management consultancy affiliated to Grey Global Group) and worked in marketing and management at Coca-Cola Co., Unilever, MediaCom, and Leo Burnett. As a consultant, Nils has worked with a long list of companies, including Kellogg's, Nestlé, Kraft/Phillip Morris, McDonald's, Nycomed, Siemens, Procter & Gamble, Shell, Ameritech/Tele Danmark, Duni, and Rolex.

Torben Moller, tmoller@pacbell.net
Torben Moller is a consultant in Berkeley, California, advising companies on business processes, business strategy, enterprise automation, and change management.

He holds a Cand. Scient. degree from the University of Copenhagen, Denmark, and a Ph.D. in Computer Science from the University of California, Berkeley.

Since graduating, he has worked for over twenty-five years at the intersection of business, technology, and people, designing and implementing high-impact solutions in many industries, including technology, manufacturing, finance and brokerage, healthcare, and communications. His clients have ranged from Fortune 500 companies to start-ups.

Dan Hoeyer, dan@hoeyer.net

Dan Hoeyer is Executive Partner and Co-Founder of the AVT Global Business Network and the AVT Institute of Executive Education, providing leading-edge educational programs for European executives in cooperation with worldwide partners, including the University of California, Berkeley - Haas School of Business.

Dan has a commercial degree, specializing in marketing, from Copenhagen Business College and an M.B.A. from Rushmore University, specializing in strategy and entrepreneurship. He has also studied at the Danish Direct Marketing School, Oxford University, and the University of California, Berkeley - Haas School of Business.

Dan has worked with e-Businesses at the strategic- and operational level since the commercial beginning of the Internet. He was co-founder and CEO of the Web agency A2Z-NET, later sold to the Aston Group, one of the largest new economy consultancies in Scandinavia. Following the sale of A2Z-NET, Dan became Director of the Digital Communication Division at Aston Group. As an e-Business consultant, Dan has worked with companies like Citroën, EURO RSCG, J. Walter Thompson, Leo Burnett, Enterprise IG, Nestlé, Microsoft, Castrol, and Kraft Foods International. Prior to A2Z-NET Dan started operations for Avis Rent-a-Car in northern Poland and also worked in real estate.